POISONED BY LIES AND HYPOCRISY

Venue of the Continental Army's first major defeat in the early morning, New Year's Day, January 1, 1776. The defenders' view looking up the Sault-au-Matelot.

Detail from a painting by James Pattison Cockburn, 1830 (Library and Archives Canada, C-040044).

POISONED
by
LIES
and
HYPOCRISY

AMERICA'S FIRST
ATTEMPT TO
BRING LIBERTY
TO CANADA,
1775-1776

GAVIN K. WATT

DUNDURN
TORONTO

Project editor: Shannon Whibbs
Copy-editor: Laurie Miller
Design: Courtney Horner
Printer: Webcom

Library and Archives Canada Cataloguing in Publication

Watt, Gavin K., author
          Poisoned by lies and hypocrisy : America's first attempt
to bring liberty to Canada, 1775–1776 / Gavin K. Watt.

Includes bibliographical references and index.
Issued in print and electronic formats.
ISBN 978-1-4597-1762-6

          1. United States--History--Revolution, 1775-1783--Campaigns.
2. United States--History--Revolution, 1775-1783--Influence. 3. United
States--History--Revolution, 1775-1783--Participation, Canadian.
4. Canada--History--1775-1783. I. Title.

E230.W28 2014   973.3'3   C2013-907405-8
                                                 C2013-907406-6

1   2   3   4   5   18   17   16   15   14

Conseil des Arts   Canada Council
du Canada   for the Arts

Canada

ONTARIO ARTS COUNCIL
CONSEIL DES ARTS DE L'ONTARIO

We acknowledge the support of the **Canada Council for the Arts** and the **Ontario Arts Council** for our publishing program. We also acknowledge the financial support of the **Government of Canada** through the **Canada Book Fund** and **Livres Canada Books**, and the **Government of Ontario** through the **Ontario Book Publishing Tax Credit** and the **Ontario Media Development Corporation.**

Visit us at
Dundurn.com
@dundurnpress
Facebook.com/dundurnpress
Pinterest.com/Dundurnpress

Dundurn	Gazelle Book Services Limited	Dundurn
3 Church Street, Suite 500	White Cross Mills	2250 Military Road
Toronto, Ontario, Canada	High Town, Lancaster, England	Tonawanda, NY
M5E 1M2	LA1 4XS	U.S.A. 14150

CONTENTS

ACKNOWLEDGEMENTS

I am again indebted to the selfless assistance of my re-enacting friend Todd Braisted, a Fellow of the renowned Company of Military Historians and the foremost authority concerning the American loyalists. Todd shared several archival findings that added considerable depth to this tale of the early war.

The ever-generous Dr. John A. Houlding, of *Fit for Service* fame, contributed many details of Regular officers' careers, some of whom later served in the Provincials.

I am deeply grateful to the superb *Dictionary of Canadian Biography* for many in-depth studies of contemporary personalities.

My friend Mario Lemoine kindly supplied me with photographs of the *Quebec Gazette*, which provided a great many details of the invasion years.

The Royal Highland Emigrants played a critical role in the defence of Canada and their historian, Kim Stacy, was of great help in describing their efforts.

My portrayal of the rebels' regime in Montreal was greatly enhanced by Elinor Kyte Senior's study, "Montreal in the Loyalist Decade 1775–1785." Consulting her work reminded me how limited I am in my study of Canadian history without a thorough knowledge of the French language.

Paul L. Stevens's doctoral thesis, "His Majesty's 'Savage' Allies," was a key resource to understanding the Natives' reactions to the rebel invasion and the actions taken in the far west.

I am beholden to Christopher Armstrong, who applied his wonderful skills to design the book's cover and to enhance many images and maps, and to John W. Moore for his photograph of "moi," the ancient faux-warrior.

Gavin Watt
King City, Ontario
2013

INTRODUCTION

My use of the term "Canadian" to refer to the anglophone citizens of Quebec is anachronistic, as that descriptive did not come into common use until the time of the War of 1812. Nonetheless, it is the clearest method of delineating Quebeckers who had come from Britain, Europe, and the lower colonies and were resident in the province before the American rebellion.

When I employ the word "Canadien," I am referring exclusively to franco-Canadians. When I use the term "Canadian," I am referring either to anglo-Canadians or to both.

Also, I confess to mixing French and English spellings, in particular place names such as Quebec City, Montreal and Fort St. John's, which appear solely in English, and others, such as Trois-Rivières, which appear only in French. I often employ hyphens in the Quebecois manner, but not always — thus, Île-aux-Noix. Am I at times inconsistent? Yes, I am afraid so, but that is one of the delights of living in a bilingual country.

THE "INTOLERABLE" QUEBEC ACT

Joy, and Gratitude, and Fidelity to the King

CARLETON RETURNS TO QUEBEC

After a four-year absence in Britain, Guy Carleton resumed the governorship of Quebec Province on September 18, 1774. During the time away he had helped to pilot the Quebec Act through Parliament. Now, on his second day back in office, he opened a dispatch from his military superior, Lieutenant-General Thomas Gage, the commander-in-chief (C-in-C) for North America, and read orders to dispatch the 10th and 52nd Regiments to Boston to assist in clamping a lid on the intense discontent that had begun to boil after the June 1 closure of the port. Disturbingly, those two regiments constituted one half of Carleton's infantry for the defence of the settled portions of Quebec.

While in England he would have heard a great deal about American reactions to Parliament's attempts to raise revenue, yet he could not possibly have realized the depth of unrest in the old British colonies. Nor could he have anticipated Quebeckers' reactions when Gage complicated the situation by enquiring "whether a Body of Canadians and Indians might be collected, and confided in, for the Service in this Country."

Both Gage and Carleton had strong personal memories of the competence and valour of the Canadien militia during the French regime. The practice of compulsory service established in Quebec had effectively militarized the general male population. Although Canadien numbers were small compared to the manpower of the British colonies, the *habitants* had become accustomed and hardened to mandatory martial duties and were able to play merry hell with British colonial expansion. In the late 1750s, however, France was threatened around the world by British encroachment into its more valuable colonial zones, such as the Caribbean, and found it necessary to withdraw active support for Quebec. Consequently, in 1760 the colony was literally swamped by British armies and fleets, and ultimately succumbed.

Five years later the occupiers abolished obligatory service, although they retained the officers of the militia (the old regime's principal agents in each locality) as justices of the peace to serve in what were known as the militia courts. A captain of militia was generally the most responsible and respected citizen in the community. Legally he received his powers from above, but practically he derived his authority from below. The new magistrates' first duties were to administer the oath of allegiance and disarm the populace, although firelocks for hunting were obtainable through application. The militia captains quickly became the eyes and ears of the new regime and maintained the special relationship with the citizenry they had previously enjoyed.[1]

These appointments met with opposition from the anglo population, who objected to military officers holding judicial office and Catholics serving on juries. These agitators had been settling in Quebec since 1760 and were manoeuvring to keep Canadiens away from political power, while at the same time attempting to inflame them against the British administration, a process that was assisted by the southern colonies' opposition to custom duties and other interferences imposed by the home government. Rebellious thoughts simmered in Quebec.[2]

GUY CARLETON

Irish-born Guy Carleton, at fifty-one, was one of the British Army's most senior generals. At seventeen, he had entered the army as an ensign in the 25th Foot. Three years later he was a lieutenant and in 1751 he joined the 1st Guards as a lieutenant with the army rank of captain. In 1757 he became the aide-de-camp to the Duke of Cumberland, a most prestigious role. Just over a year later he was captain-lieutenant in the Guards with the rank of lieutenant-colonel in the army. The following year he was appointed to the 72nd Regiment as lieutenant-colonel. In the process Carleton had become a protegé of James Wolfe, who sought his assistance for the 1758 attack on Louisbourg; however, Carleton had been openly critical of Hanoverian troops, and King George II blocked the appointment. Despite this setback, after much importuning by his powerful friends, Carleton was able to join Wolfe as quartermaster-general and engineer for the attack on Quebec and was appointed a colonel in America. During the Plains of Abraham action, he commanded a composite battalion of Grenadiers and received a head wound while pursuing the French.[3] Over the next four years, he served in two more campaigns — first off the northwest coast of France, and then as quartermaster-general for the assault on Cuba, where he was

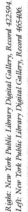  

Right: New York Public Library Digital Gallery, Record 422594.
Left: New York Public Library Digital Gallery, Record 465406.

Left: Captain-General Guy Carleton, Governor of Canada.
Right: Lieutenant-General Thomas Gage, Commander-in-Chief America.

seriously wounded during the siege of Havana. He was now a colonel in the army and transferred from the 72nd to the 93rd Regiment in 1764. In 1766 he was appointed a brigadier in America and, although he had no prior civil experience, the lieutenant governor and administrator of Quebec. Such was the advantage of having influential friends and allies.[4]

Carleton was a restrained, aloof, forbidding man who always stood on his dignity. His portrait reveals a heavy jaw, prominent nose, and wooden features, which hid a treacherous temper. He was not one to accept criticism with grace, nor one to reconsider his decisions, even in the face of contradictory evidence. Yet he was an intelligent, astute, and honest individual who, upon arrival in Quebec, quickly absorbed the political situation. When his predecessor, James Murray, failed to return to Canada after an investigation into his administration, Carleton was appointed captain-general and governor-in-chief of the colony in 1768.

QUEBEC SOCIETY

Although Quebec's pragmatic clergy was fully aware of Britain's anti-Roman Catholic laws, they had offered prayers for the British royal family during services as early as 1762, much to the approval of the military administration. Four years later a Vatican cardinal recommended, "We must give credit to the English for their goodwill with respect to religion; and for their part, priests and bishop must, in this particular, sincerely forget that they are French." In March that year, after much searching negotiation, Murray supported the consecration of a new bishop for Quebec, which ensured the continuation of the Catholic faith.[5] The clergy responded by petitioning for a new form of the oath of allegiance to the King to which the province's Roman Catholics could subscribe with a free conscience.

When Carleton succeeded James Murray as governor, he recommended the raising of one or two Provincial regiments of Canadiens to the home government, noting that there were fifty-one officers of various ranks available among the gentry — the noblesse — ten of whom had been French Regular captains. He intended to give these men commissions in the new colonial regiments and, ideally, a few would be accepted into the British Army. It was Murray who had observed in 1759 that maintaining Quebec as an entity, rather than subsuming its identity, was "a guarantee for the good behaviour of its neighbouring colonies,"[6] and what better tool than embodied regiments? However, Carleton was reminded that these concepts were impossible to implement as, under British law, Roman Catholics were not permitted to hold office — and, besides, Canadiens were French!

With the active support of former governor Murray, Carleton and Lieutenant Governor Hector Cramahé[7] guided the passage of the Quebec Act through the British Parliament in the summer of 1774. This legislation restored many of the province's traditions by officially accepting the French language, providing roles for Canadiens in a governing council, and reestablishing French Civil Law. The Roman Catholic Church was fully accepted within the province, which one historian viewed a benchmark "in the history of religious liberty." To secure the far western fur trade territories the province's borders were expanded dramatically, even beyond the scope of the old colony.

Although the unrest of the lower colonies was to an extent mirrored in Quebec, the bulk of Canadiens primarily focused on provincial affairs. The closure of the port of Boston in 1770 and the transfer of two British Regular regiments from the small Canadian garrison were causes for curiosity and speculation, and there was concern about Parliament's various acts to raise revenue, yet Carleton had great confidence that franco-Quebeckers would be delighted with the act's measures. He also was well aware that elements of the anglo population would be angered over their lost opportunities for dominance. As he wrote to

Gage, the Canadiens "have testified to me the strongest marks of Joy, and Gratitude, and Fidelity to the King" and, "should matters come to Extremities," a "Body of Canadians and Indians might be collected, and confided in, for Service in this Country."

Quebec's Natives

As to the Natives, he advised, "The Savages of this Province, I hear, are in very good humour, a Canadian Battalion would be a great Motive, and go far to influence them," although he tempered his remarks by adding, "but you know what sort of People they are."[8] His dismissive postscript reflected the prevailing British opinion that Natives were fickle. Nonetheless, it could not be ignored that these same Natives had readily, and effectively, co-operated with the French armed forces and Canadien militia in *petite guerre* operations that were the scourge of the lower colonies and the western territories.

Lieutenant Governor Cramahé had insightfully written to Lord Dartmouth, the senior secretary for the American colonies, that "the Indians sensibly feel their loss of consequence since the conquest, and would not be displeased to see the Renewal of a contention, which would restore them to their former Importance."[9] Yet he and Carleton were unaware of certain undercurrents.

It was true that the Canada Indians continued to be aggravated by New Englanders and New Yorkers encroaching on their hunting territories, and, only a dozen years before, they had been in open warfare against them, but other factors had come into play. In midyear two Protestant missionaries from New England visited the communities of St. Francis (Odanak) and Kahnawake and explained the reasons for the colonists' dissatisfaction with Britain. Their words fell on receptive ears, as many of the village headmen were descended from white captives who were deeply attached to their roots. When these missionaries returned home they took four young men to be educated at Dartmouth College. The youngsters were related to Chief Joseph-Louis Gill of St. Francis, who himself was the offspring of acculturated white parents.

Josiah Dunham, 1789 (Wikimedia Commons).

Dartmouth College, Hanover, New Hampshire: "for the Education and Instruction of Youth of the Indian Tribes in this Land."

There was another important factor that affected the Natives. During the French regime, the Indians had known that they were a recognized component of humanity, in great part because of their conversion to Christianity; although the traditionalist Nations to the west also enjoyed a good relationship with their trading partners. Native customs and practices were accepted by the French, not just tolerated. In contrast, with few exceptions, the British were disinterested in Native souls and feared and deplored the Native lifestyle and customs. To them, Indians were a necessary evil to be dealt with, honourably or otherwise, and ideally, dominated. Such ethnic differences in attitude were obvious to the observant Native mind.[10]

CANADIENS

As to the Canadiens, by the time of the implementation of the Quebec Act the following May, Carleton found it necessary to advise Gage that he was "considerably less sanguine about the prospects of raising a military force among the local population." He reported that the gentry would be willing to serve, but the general populace — the habitants — had "in a manner emancipated themselves" and would need time and "discreet management" to persuade them to return "to their ancient habits of obedience and discipline." Unacknowledged, and unwisely ignored, was the flood of persuasive, rebellious propaganda that continuously flowed north to germinate in various strata of Quebec society.[11]

Once Britons spent time in Quebec, many concluded that Canadiens were lazy. They were observed to have little interest in commerce and were content with their easy existence on the farms, or ranging the woods. Nonetheless, visitors had to concede that the habitants were energetic, vivacious and, rather threateningly, devoid of that engrained sense of social place common to Britain's lower orders. From the Canadien point of view, the British regime brought an interesting benefit. They no longer faced the aggravating requirement to attend unpaid labour corvées and, when work was done, they were paid in coin.[12]

After the two Regular regiments had sailed for Boston, a number of British-born citizens of Quebec City requested that the governor embody the local militia. Two battalions had been organized by the end of July, one anglo- and the other franco-Canadian, and a former French Regular officer, Charles-Louis Tarieu de Lanaudière, was appointed Carleton's aide-de-camp.[13]

UNREST IN NEW HAMPSHIRE

The February 16, 1775, issue of the *Quebec Gazette* printed a proclamation by New Hampshire's royal governor decrying outrages committed by rebellious persons who had overwhelmed the tiny Regular garrison of Fort William and Mary and seized supplies of gunpowder, cannon, and stands of arms in mid-December. Loyal magistrates, military officers, and citizens were called upon to bring the offenders to justice.[14]

NEW ENGLAND AGENTS

By March 1775 a committee of Boston activists had become so concerned about attitudes in Quebec that they sent John Brown,[15] an intrepid and energetic Berkshire County lawyer, to investigate. Brown was escorted by two guides from the New Hampshire Grants; one fellow was a previous captive of the Kahnawakes, and the other was well acquainted with the Abenakis. Brown was directed to contact sympathizers in the anglo community to persuade them to organize a system of communications between lower Quebec and Massachusetts and to convince them to elect delegates to attend the Continental Congress.

Upon arrival, he sent his two guides to Kahnawake to deliver a letter of friendship and to assess whether the village harboured any warlike intentions toward the colonies. He met with several Canadiens to ensure them that the colonists had pacific intentions and were only interested in preventing them from being reduced to slavery by the King's ministers. Then, in the next breath, he threatened that if any Canadiens took up arms to assist the British troops they would be in danger of having their properties confiscated by the rebels. So, the carrot-and-stick method was immediately employed in the cause of "liberty."

When Brown returned to Boston he reported that the Kahnawakes, the leading Nation among Quebec's seven, were "a very simple, politick people, and say that if they are obliged to, for their own safety, to take up arms on either side, that they shall take part on the side of their bretheren, the English of New-England."[16] He added that some Canadians were considering opening communications with Massachusetts, but there had been no interest in sending delegates to Congress.

The Kahnawakes' position was reinforced by a visit by James Dean, another Dartmouth College missionary. Dean was a perfect ambassador, as he had been raised at Oquaga in Six Nations' Indian Territory and spoke several Iroquoian dialects. He took up residence in Montreal from late March to mid-June, making frequent trips to Kahnawake and one to St. Francis. In addition to the Abenaki students at the college, a youth from Kahnawake had been recently admitted and Dean brightened the school's chain of friendship with the villages by explaining the roots of the disagreements with Britain and the colonies' struggles for "liberty and freedom." He returned to Dartmouth quite convinced that the Canada Indians would "take no part in the quarrel." Although these visits boded ill for Carleton's plans of defence the governor's intelligence was poor and, by early May, he continued to believe that the Seven Nations would wholeheartedly support the British cause.

The adventurous John Brown returned to Montreal in April and met again with many sympathizers, but they could not be persuaded to send delegates to Congress. Yet his visit was not wasted, as he was able to return with detailed descriptions of the weak defences at Fort St. John's, Crown Point, and Ticonderoga, and the welcome information that the habitants were not hostile to the rebels' aspirations.

LOYALISM IN NEW YORK PROVINCE

Inimical to the Liberties of America

In Alexander Flick's seminal study about loyalism in New York, he observes that two parties quickly emerged in America as a result of the controversies with Britain. These parties were not defined by one being in favour of Parliament's acts and the other opposed to them, for both were firmly in opposition. Rather, they were separated by how to proceed with their opposition, either by militancy, or by negotiation.[1]

JOHN PETERS, LOYALIST

John Peters hailed from Moortown in Gloucester County, New York, on the west side of the Connecticut River. In the 1760s he had been a successful farmer and mill owner in New Hampshire, and a militia captain, and the deputy surveyor of the King's Woods. In 1770 he moved across the river into New York where he acquired large tracts of land, built a house, a barn, and saw and grist mills. New York's royal governor, William Tryon, appointed Peters a militia lieutenant-colonel, justice of the peace, probate judge, county registrar, court clerk, and judge of the Court of Common Pleas.

Peters's uncle Samuel was an Anglican clergyman, representing the religious faith that taught that loyalty to the King and obedience to his laws were duties.[2] So John Peters's religious beliefs, coupled with his thorough entrenchment in the province's system of governance and defence, determined his role in the coming conflict.

His life began to unravel in 1774 when the "spirit of discord and rebellion" became rife. As a senior county politician he was asked to attend the first Continental Congress in Philadelphia, to be held on September 5. He agreed, but when his party of friends and family were passing through Connecticut, they were confronted by a mob of Liberty Boys, whom Peters saw as "the bankrupts, dissenting teachers and smugglers" who were intent on rebellion. After "suffering much ill language" he was released, although his uncle, the Reverend Samuel, continued to be held and received further abuse. John went on to Philadelphia to see exactly what was afoot.

Assuming Peters's political outlook matched that of other loyalists, he would have expected the law to be upheld, but at the Congress he became "convinced that nothing short of independence would satisfy them," which was perhaps hindsight on his part, as other reports of the first Congress indicate that independence was very low on the agenda.[3] He refused to take an oath of secrecy regarding the proceedings and knowledge of his lack of co-operation must have preceded him, for on his way home he was pilloried by mobs at Weatherfield, Hartford, and Springfield. He did not reach Moortown until April, where he was seized by his neighbours and threatened with execution as an enemy of Congress. He was taken before a district Committee of Correspondence headed by Deacon Jacob Bayley, who later proved an active arch-enemy of the Crown. The committeemen put Peters in jail while a search of his papers was conducted for evidence of alleged correspondence with Governor Carleton; however, when no proof could be found, he was released. Soon after he was again seized and ordered to sign a covenant to "oppose the King and British army with my life and property," but he refused. After giving bonds for his good behaviour, he was released only to be embroiled again when news arrived, with typical rebellious exaggeration, that "the

British troops had marched out of Boston and were murdering the inhabitants, both young and old." The committee demanded that he give orders to his militia regiment to be ready to march at an hour's notice, to which he complied, earning himself a few days of favour. But Peters's ordeal had just begun.[4]

YET ANOTHER INTOLERABLE ACT

While Carleton was thoroughly pleased with the passage of the Quebec Act, Massachusetts was enraged. The Bay Province viewed the legislation as yet another of Britain's "intolerable acts," for it confined the lower colonies' boundaries to the continent's eastern margins and made several astonishing accommodations to the Catholic Canadiens. Some historians believe the Quebec Act contributed more than any other measure to precipitate rebellion.

Certainly, it prompted the meeting of the first Continental Congress, at which Paul Revere represented Suffolk County, Massachusetts. He presented the county's resolutions as proposed on September 9, which included the statements:

> The late Act of Parliament for establishing the Roman Catholic religion and the French laws in that extensive country now called Canada is dangerous in an extreme degree to the Protestant religion and to the civil rights and liberties of all America; and therefore, as men and Protestant Christians, we are indispensably obliged to take all proper measures to protect our safety.[5]

John Peters's account of the Congress made no mention of this resolution, but his mind was probably filled with many other issues more important to him personally.

In anticipation of papist-motivated military actions, Quebec's ancient neighbour and principal colonial foe had been the first to sound the alarm over the reinstatement of French institutions. When Congress met it adopted Suffolk County's resolution without a single dissenting vote. Several days later, Congress condemned the Quebec Act for creating "an arbitrary government ... and discouraging the settlement of British subjects in that wide extended country: thus by the influence of civil principles and ancient prejudices ... [it would] dispose the inhabitants to act with hostility against the free Protestant colonies whenever a wicked minister [should] choose to direct them."

Many New Yorkers were similarly concerned. A Seven Years' War veteran and migrant from Massachusetts, and two of his prominent associates, offered to raise a regiment of Minutemen to defend their county against "regulars, Roman Catholics, and the savages at the northward."[6]

QUEBEC INDIAN DEPARTMENT

It was not only the passage of the Quebec Act that gave Carleton great satisfaction, as he had finally achieved control of Indian affairs in his province. In the process he had successfully blunted outside interference from the New York–based Six Nations' Indian Department, which, he was convinced, had favoured the lower colonies' fur-trading interests to the detriment of Quebec.[7] As head of his new department the governor would have preferred to name the French regime's colonel of Indians, Luc de La Corne, also known as Chapt de La Corne, or La Corne Saint-Luc; Carleton knew, however, that the home government distrusted the old Canadien partisan, who had been so prominently successful against British and colonial forces in the Seven Years' War. As a surrogate, he chose La Corne's son-in-law, John Campbell, a former British Regular officer of proven valour, who had settled in Quebec after marrying Saint-Luc's daughter, Marie-Anne. Of necessity Campbell would defer to his father-in-law on delicate issues, for, although fluent in French, he spoke none of the Native dialects and Saint-Luc had mastered several.[8]

Anonymous, 1750-1761 (© McCord Museum M22334-P1).

Colonel Luc de Chapt de La Corne Saint-Luc, famous Canadien partisan.

Campbell's appointment flew in the face of conventional wisdom, which held that successful Indian affairs' management required practitioners with an intimate knowledge of Native psychology and customs and the ability to discuss issues in the Natives' own tongue. The Six Nations' department's deputy superintendent, Daniel Claus, offered these opinions:

> The persons therefore who are to have the care and superintendency of their affairs under government and would carry on business with them by persuasion and influence, ought to be possessed of an even temper, great patience and good nature, being well acquainted with their customs manners and language, persons of authority and consequence, of merit and character in publick life, and, according to the Indian phrase, have been great and successful Warriors in their time.[9]

And, Claus concluded, "Without some of the above requirements, no one can be of much service to the Crown in Indian matters." No matter how valorous and militarily capable Campbell was, his performance would be hampered by a lack of knowledge, which did not seem to concern Carleton one whit.

In far-off Britain the Crown's American Secretary, Lord Dartmouth, recognized that this appointment would prove contentious and instructed Campbell to comply with all orders and instructions from Sir William Johnson, the superintendent-general of Northern Indians, who ran "an autonomous branch of the imperial government"[10] headquartered at Johnstown in New York's Mohawk Valley. Johnson's mandate included the care of the Seven Nations of Canada, and his son-in-law, Claus, was his deputy in that jurisdiction. Under this new situation, how were Campbell and Claus supposed to relate? To whom would Claus's two Quebec-based interpreters report? Who would pay their salaries?[11] Answers were not forthcoming.

Fort Niagara was in the Iroquois Confederacy's tribal lands at the mouth of the Niagara River and in reasonably close range of the department's Mohawk Valley headquarters. The way-station post at Oswegatchie on the south shore of the St. Lawrence River in New York was even nearer, so that the management of the Confederacy, its affiliates, and allied Mississaugas was relatively uncomplicated by the new department in Quebec, especially as Lieutenant-Colonel John Caldwell, commanding officer of the 8th King's and commandant at Niagara, proved surprisingly adept at Native diplomacy.[12] Although, in the near future, Caldwell's reporting route changed from Gage to Carleton, and the lines blurred.

To further complicate matters, the Quebec Act set the province's southwestern boundary at the Mississippi River in an attempt to provide the far western territories with a form of civil government. In the process, a score of Native Nations critical to the health of the fur trade were added to the province's responsibilities, as well as several Canadien trading and farming settlements from the old regime. This altered the arrangement of 1768, which had given Quebec responsibility for supervising the trade north of the Great Lakes at Michilimackinac, while New York controlled the trade at Fort Niagara and Detroit, and Pennsylvania controlled the Ohio and Illinois country. Now responsibility for the far west fell upon Quebec's government, which had no control over opportunistic traders from the bordering British colonies, or, for that matter, over Spanish traders from St. Louis.

The newly acquired twenty-odd Nations, formerly allied with the French through trade and missionary zeal, were being overseen by a tangle of officials, primary of which was Sir William's deputy superintendent, the mixed-blood Pennsylvanian Alexander McKee.[13] He lived at Fort Pitt and had a Shawnee wife and children living at one of the tribe's villages. As the numerous Shawnee were a significant Nation among the Ohio Indians, McKee enjoyed substantial influence, but his locus of operations lay in the midst of a violent conflict fomented by land-greedy Virginians; his attentions were soon overwhelmed.

As well, McKee was located at quite a distance from the Lakes' and western Nations who traded and held councils at Detroit and Michilimackinac — the latter being the fur-trading centre of the far west. At those posts, Native diplomacy rested in the hands of two highly competent Regular captains of the 8th (King's) Regiment, Richard Lernoult and Arent DePeyster.[14] They had been taking distant advice from Sir William and reporting to Gage in Boston, but now that their posts fell within the expanded jurisdiction of Quebec, a new relationship would have to be developed. Notably, no detailed instructions had been received from the home government delineating departmental interrelationships.[15]

The military had no presence among the Wabash Confederacy (Miamis, Macoutens, Kickapoos, Weas, and Piankashaws) in modern Indiana and their only departmental representative was a trader named Alexis Maisonville, one of the few Canadiens employed by Sir William.

Influence over all the Natives was based on the flow of trade goods, on which they had become extremely dependent when they abandoned many of their ancient craft skills. By opening the traders' taps, a post officer could keep the Natives happy and in good humour, and he could express his displeasure by shutting them. Needless to say, neither measure could be pursued to excess.

GUY JOHNSON REPLACES SIR WILLIAM

Sir William Johnson died at his Mohawk Valley home in July 1774 while conducting a Six Nations' council. He had been fully aware of his failing health for some time and had sensibly made succession plans, so the transition of his duties to his proficient son-in-law, Guy Johnson, went smoothly. Nonetheless, the news of the loss of the much-revered superintendent reverberated across the northern colonies.

Guy was still adjusting to his father-in-law's absence that October when Daniel Claus, his deputy and brother-in-law, returned from a tour of his Canadian responsibilities with the troubling news that the colonial unrest was well known among the Canada Indians. Of more personal import, he advised that John Campbell had been appointed as the agent for a new Quebec Province Indian Department. Significantly, although Governor Carleton had returned to Quebec while Claus was in the province, they had not met. From earlier experiences, Claus knew that Carleton was hostile, but it is unknown whether the deputy was denied an interview, or had waited for a summons that failed to come. How Campbell's new appointment would impact Johnson's administration was an open question; consequently, Johnson wrote to General Gage in Boston to seek clarification.

Unknown to Johnson and Claus, Carleton's instructions from the home government placed all decisions for governance and employment of the enlarged province's Native population in his hands. As a result the breadth of influence formerly enjoyed by Sir William was considerably truncated and the lines of communications between whites and Natives thoroughly obscured. To what depth emerged only later.

Left: Detail from oil painting by Benjamin West, 1776 (National Gallery of Art, Washington, D.C.). Right: Unknown artist, circa 1770 (Library and Archives Canada, C-083514).

Left: Colonel Guy Johnson, Superintendent of Northern Indians. Right: Lieutenant-colonel Daniel Claus, Deputy Superintendent, Seven Nations of Canada.

Adding to Johnson's pressures, Lord Dunmore, the royal governor of Virginia, had chosen to wage a unilateral war against the Shawnees and Mingoes in the Ohio country for control of the Kentucky Territory. As part of Dunmore's strategy, the Virginians — known to western Natives as the Big Knives — had occupied Fort Pitt, much to the astonishment and consternation of Pennsylvanians, who viewed the post as lying in their jurisdiction. Although the Six Nations were deeply resented for their cavalier surrender of massive sections of Shawnee hunting grounds during the Fort Stanwix Treaty negotiations of 1763, the Shawnees sought their assistance in the fight against the Big Knives. Conversely, the other colonies were distraught over Dunmore's rashness and relied upon Johnson's Indian Department to dissuade any other tribes from widening the conflict, which became the primary goal of the department's officers.

In November 1774 Johnson held a treaty council at his Guy Park home, during which the plight of the Shawnees and Mingoes was examined and the Six Nations were persuaded not to interfere. These negotiations were a bright spot in Johnson's career, but his success was marred by an open discussion between the delegates of the fractious relations between the colonies and Britain, which required him to exert all his powers of persuasion to deflect their concerns.

The political unrest that was so widespread throughout Britain's colonies had yet to affect the Upper Posts of Niagara, Detroit, and Michilimackinac. No committees had been formed by the civilian populations and the traders were more interested in generating profits than in agitation. At Detroit, the intentions of Lord Dunmore's[16] Virginia troops generated far more concern among the Natives than squabbling in far-off Boston. Gage had instructed his officers to advise the Native leadership that the behaviour of land-hungry Virginia was thoroughly disapproved of by the King, which was duly obeyed, although it must have mystified them why the Crown was unable to prevent it.

Pressure on John Peters

At Moortown the tribulations of the loyalist John Peters continued. His rebellious neighbours again searched his house "for letters of secret correspondence with General Carleton, with whom in fact I never had correspondence." They stole all his papers, insulted him, and forced him to sign over some of his land deeds. He was ordered to stay within the town limits and threatened with death if he transgressed their orders. "The mob again and again visited me, and ate and drank, and finally plundered me of most of my moveable effects." To add to his grief, his father sided against him and urged on the mob by claiming that his son's uncle, the Reverend Samuel Peters, had "taught him bad principles."

Political Chicanery

On October 21 John Jay, a former New York City committeeman and provincial delegate to the Continental Congress, wrote an "Address to the People of Great Britain" on behalf of that body to protest many issues and, in particular, the Quebec Act. He noted that Congress was astonished "that a British Parliament should ever consent to establish in the country a religion that has deluged your island in blood and spread impiety, bigotry, persecution, murder, and rebellion throughout every part of the world."[17] Jay's letter was followed on October 21 by Congress's memoir to all the colonies representing the act as a gross injustice to British citizens.

Ironically, and duplicitously, these actions were immediately followed by the writing of a "Letter Addressed to the Inhabitants of the Province of Quebec," in which an attempt was made to woo the Canadiens into joining the cause against Britain. Thus, the people whose religion, customs, and very existence were held in such fear, loathing, and contempt by Congress were now being approached with the persuasive and subtle hand of friendship and entreaty. The points made were clever and aimed to confuse, if not convince, the mass of people who traditionally had been disinterested in, or understood little, about politics and governance. Although the majority of Canadiens were illiterate, Congress did not repeat the mistake of Carleton's administration, and their letter was immediately translated and printed by two expatriot Frenchmen and, through the auspices of Massachusetts, distributed to anglo sympathizers in Quebec, who cast it broadly among the Canadien populace, in particular the literate.

François Cazeau, a successful French-born fur merchant, took a primary role in circulating the letter throughout Montreal district and by mid-November it was in the far reaches of the province. In contrast, a French translation of the Quebec Act did not appear until December 8, which meant the majority of Canadiens had no direct knowledge of its provisions before then, and a great many had already been influenced by Congress's appeals.

The fact that Congress's letter gained the tiniest bit of sway among Canadiens is remarkable, as the fanaticism of Protestant New England was notorious. How could entreaties of friendship and tolerance by their known enemies be believed for even a blink?

LE CANADIEN PATRIOTE

Following the distribution of the Quebec Act's translation, a fellow with the nom de plume "Le Canadien Patriote" wrote a circular letter refuting Congress's assertions and had it disseminated throughout the province. The letter emphasized that the act "not only allows you the free exercise of the Roman Catholic religion but ... lays open to you all the employments and places of trust in the province. This is the thing that shocks these Englishmen [the colonists] and makes them declare in the public newspapers that the said act of Parliament is a detestable and abominable act authorizing a bloody religion, which spreads around it, wherever it is propagated, impiety, murder and rebellion." Making the cheese more binding, excerpts of some of the rebels' newspaper articles were circulated, as was a comparison of the expressions in the "Address to the Inhabitants of Great Britain" to that of the address to the Canadians; however, it was primarily anglo-Canadians who were apprised of these counterattacks, while the mass of the franco-populace continued to be bombarded by the rebel campaign.[18]

NEWS OF UNREST IN NEW YORK PROVINCE

An article appeared in the April 20, 1775, issue of the *Quebec Gazette* dated New York City, March 27. Armed rioters in Cumberland County, New York, had challenged the royal sheriff and magistrates to prevent the sitting of the court, and gunfire broke out with casualties being sustained by both sides. Although the court was able to sit the next day, more rioters arrived from nearby Bennington in Vermont and from across the river in New Hampshire, swelling their number to almost five hundred. This prompted the magistrates to adjourn, but the rioters seized them and the sheriff, the court clerk, and their supporters, and sent out parties to collect other suspected loyalists. All of these persons were then sent to a jail in Hampshire County, Massachusetts. Other magistrates in Cumberland County were warned not to conduct their business, other than two who would be allowed to try criminal cases only.[19]

AN OUTRAGE IN MONTREAL

On May 1, 1775, the day of the implementation of the Quebec Act, a shocking event occurred in Montreal. A bust of King George III was found painted black with a rosary of potatoes and a wooden cross draped around its neck and lettered with the phrase, *"Voilà le Pape du Canada et le Sot Anglois,"* which roughly translates as, "Behold the Canadian Pope and the English Fool." The insult caused quite a tumult among the loyal citizens. The military assumed that disgruntled anglo-merchants were the culprits and Roman Catholics were outraged that the sanctity of the Pope had been violated. A guard of Regulars patrolled the streets amidst a stew of unrest.

Picoté de Belestre, a prominent Canadien, loudly exclaimed that the perpetrator should be hanged and David Franks, the youngest member of a Jewish family who supplied the local British garrisons, replied that no one should be hanged for such a piffling offence. De Belestre pulled young Franks's nose and he retaliated by knocking the Canadien to the ground. The next day the indignant de Belestre swore a warrant against Franks, who was jailed without bail. A second fight broke out between another prominent Canadien who stated that the Jews had disfigured the King's statue. Levy Solomons, a prominent merchant, retaliated by throwing that fellow to the ground. Solomons was jailed, but this time bail was allowed. When no evidence could be found against the Jewish community, the pair was released. Unsettlingly, a two-hundred-dollar reward for information about the perpetrators remained unclaimed.

This bit of nastiness was followed by the proclamation of the new Council for the Affairs of the Province of Quebec. Of seventeen councillors, seven were Catholic Canadiens, which should have given great satisfaction to his majesty's "new subjects"; however, Carleton had made the grave error of ignoring the professional and business classes and the captains of militia. Instead, he had chosen solely from among the noblesse and seigneurs, which gave both townies and country folk much displeasure.[20]

NEW YORK POLITICS

In open defiance of royal authority, the first meeting of the Albany County Committee of Correspondence was held on January 24, 1775, in the city at the home of innkeeper Richard Cartwright Sr. Over the next few months a great deal of attention was given to the formal organization of this body and to addressing the appointment of suitable representatives to the first Continental Congress in Philadelphia. On April 12 the Albany committee received a complaint from its opposite number in Berkshire County, Massachusetts, about the citizens in the New York communities of Kinderhook and Kings districts. The Albany committeemen agreed that those people were behaving in a disaffected manner, but offered no remedy to redress the issue, only their assurances that they personally would firmly adhere to the "Association of Congress." Two weeks later, the committee received a message from Pittsfield Township, Massachusetts, advising that the King's troops had commenced hostilities against that province and requesting their aid. Again, the committeemen weaseled, stating they were only a subcommittee and would leave the issue to a later day when "the Sense of the County" could be taken.

Then, on May 3, the war came home to roost in New York Province. The committee was visited by two Boston gentlemen who advised, in the strictest secrecy, that the Massachusetts Provincial Council had information that the British-occupied fort of Ticonderoga, located in New York's Charlotte County immediately north of Albany County, was "furnished with several Peices of Brass Cannon or Ordnance and many fine Stand of Arms, a Quantity of Gun Powder and other Military Stores." They stated that the fortress was about to be surprise-attacked and all its "Warlike Stores" taken, and, as this was a "Post of Great Importance" that the King's troops from Canada would likely occupy and refortify, it was hoped that Albany County would support the scheme and supply flour to the expedition.

Once again the committee wobbled, telling the gentlemen that, because of demands made daily from New England, the county was "very scant of Powder &c in this City & County, the whole Country in these Parts but illy provided with Arms and Warlike Stores especially the Poorer Sort [of citizens], and the City is in a very Defenceless situation, not a Peice of Artillery in it." They said nothing about flour.

Of particular note, the covert loyalist Joseph Anderson, of the Rensselaerwyck subcommittee, was absent from this meeting, and the news of the coming assault on Ticonderoga remained secret.

———

Indeed, Albany County's lack of preparedness was of great concern, as the Six Nations' Confederacy's most eastern village of Fort Hunter was only twenty miles from the city of Albany itself. The Confederacy, particularly the Mohawks of Fort Hunter and nearby Canajoharie, had been firmly attached to Sir William Johnson, the King's Superintendent of Northern Indian Affairs. As mentioned above, Sir William had recently died and been replaced by his nephew and son-in-law, Guy Johnson, and the committee was deeply concerned about just when, where, and how Guy was going to jump. Rumours were rife that the Six Nations were "unfriendly to the Colonies," and a three-man deputation was sent to interview Johnson. He assured them that there was no truth to the rumours, but that he had "it from good Authority that the Canadians were to come down upon the back of the Colonies." This contention was sheer nonsense, but Johnson was a thorough King's man and putting his rebellious, upstart neighbours on edge was a sensible ploy — and alarmed the committee was. A subcommittee was struck to apply to Colonel Dirck Ten Broeck, who was likely a former Crown appointee, for two hundred stands of arms and to arrange for them to be made fit for service. Not only was there the threat of an invasion from Canada, but the possible rising of black slaves and freemen was, as ever, a concern, and the committeemen recommended the setting of "a Strict and Strong Watch well Armed and under proper Discipline." On May 4 the officers were chosen for the city's five militia companies; how these varied from the Crown's former appointments is unknown.

On May 10 the Albany County Committee met at city hall with representatives from all eighteen of the county's district subcommittees. Two names stand out — in Cambridge district, Simeon Covell, who would join Burgoyne in 1777; and, once again, Joseph Anderson for Rensselaerwyck Manor. When the committee sat the next day, another letter was received requesting supplies for the parties going against Ticonderoga. Again the issue was sloughed off, this time in favour of a decision from the Provincial Council which was to meet on the twenty-second. Posterity has not recorded whether the two covert loyalists attempted to warn the garrison; however, the next day, an electrifying letter was delivered by the ubiquitous John Brown of Pittsfield from Ethan Allen, the notorious New Hampshire Grants' bandit. Ticonderoga had fallen! An immediate dispatch was sent to the New York City Committee, which body was as pusillanimous as their Albany brethren. They replied on the thirteenth that the "Powers invested in them and us, are too limitted to permit either Body to take an Active step in the Matters proposed" and referred the issue to the Provincial or Continental Congress.

On May 18, the Albany Committee took a very firm step toward controlling the Tory minority and arming the city's militia.

Resolved 1st. That any Person in this City or County, who has Arms, Ammunition, or other Articles necessary for our Defence, to dispose of; or shall import any of those Articles for Sale, and shall not within ten Days after the publication of these Resolutions, or in ten days after the Importation of such Arms, Ammunition &c. aforesaid inform the Chairman, or deputy Chairman of this Committee, of the Quantity and Quality of the same; he shall be held up to the Publick as an Enemy to this Country.

Resolved 2nd. That any person in this City, or County who shall, during the unhappy Contest with our Parent State, dispose of any Arms[,] Ammunition, or other Articles aforesaid to any Person, knowing or having reason to believe such Person to be inimical to the Liberties of America; or shall put those Articles in the Hands of any Such Person, or any other Person knowing, or having reason to believe that they are to be Used against those Liberties; he shall be held up as an Enemy to this Country.[21]

OPEN CONFLICT ERUPTS

A mixture of ignorance, fear, credulity, perverseness & Prejudice

REBEL ACTIONS ON LAKE CHAMPLAIN

The shocking news of open conflict in Massachusetts arrived at Carleton's Quebec City headquarters on May 19 in a dispatch from Gage. Of particular significance to Quebec, the C-in-C acknowledged his isolation from the interior and transferred military command of the northwestern upper posts to Carleton. In hopes of diverting the rebels' attention from the Boston area, he requested that Carleton send a body of troops and Canadians south to Crown Point;[1] however, the very next day that appeal became moot, when the governor was visited by Moses Hazen, a renowned Massachusetts-born Seven Years' War captain of American rangers and half-pay lieutenant of the 44th Regiment, who owned seigneuries at Sabrevois and Bleury near St. John's.[2] Hazen advised that Benedict Arnold of Connecticut had landed a large armed party at Fort St. John's on the Richelieu River on May 13, captured the twelve-man garrison, and sailed away in the King's sloop *George* with several smaller craft loaded with stores. Arnold, who was acquainted with Hazen, had informed him that the rebels were in possession of the legendary fortress of Ticonderoga and the supply depot at Crown Point on Lake Champlain.

Arnold was no stranger in Quebec, having made several commercial visits as a horse buyer. During the Seven Years' War he had served in the New York Provincials and recently had raised a company of Connecticut militia when the situation in Boston was coming to a boil. Upon hearing the news of the fighting at Lexington, he called out his company and marched to the Cambridge siege lines to offer his services. He was a man of action and not one to take a back seat. Champing at the bit, he proposed the attack on Ticonderoga as a method of obtaining much-needed artillery and powder. The Massachusetts Committee was taken with the idea, not only because of the possibility of obtaining crucial supplies, but because possession of Ticonderoga would seal off a traditional invasion route from Canada. Arnold was commissioned a colonel and immediately set off for Ticonderoga, leaving his subordinates behind to recruit his allotment of four hundred troops.[3]

Yet, when Arnold arrived at Ticonderoga, he was disappointed to find the outlaw Ethan Allen and his Green Mountain Boys from the New Hampshire Grants poised to steal his thunder by launching an assault on the fortress. With little grace, Arnold allowed Allen to take the lead; however, he chose not to be outdone a second time, and after Ticonderoga and Crown Point fell to the Boys, it was Arnold who led the first attack on Fort St. John's.

Soon after Arnold's party left St. John's, a second wave of rebel opportunists landed – Ethan Allen and a contingent of his Green Mountain Boys. Hazen also witnessed this event and rode to Montreal to bring the news of the incursions to the garrison commander, Lieutenant-Colonel Dudley Templer, 26th Regiment. Templer ordered his major, Charles Preston,[4] to march a 140-man reinforcement to the relief of the Richelieu post.

Montreal was abuzz with the news, and a disaffected merchant, Joseph Bindon, saw an opportunity to assist the rebel cause. He boldly crossed the St. Lawrence in the same craft as the soldiers, and, after obtaining a horse at Longueuil rode to St. John's to give Allen a warning of the approaching Regulars. Allen then gave Bindon a letter addressed to several sympathetic Montreal merchants with requests for arms and spirits, and the merchant set off to return. En route, he fell in with Preston's advancing Regulars north of St. John's and the major urged him to return to St. John's so that he could eventually carry intelligence of their success or lack of same to Colonel Templer. Bindon again proved nervy and slippery and said he had an important letter to deliver to Montreal. Preston permitted him to leave and the troops marched on, only to discover that Allen's men, who had thought better of opposing such a large number of Regulars, were reembarking. An exchange of musketry occurred during which several raiders were wounded and one taken prisoner before the Green Mountain Boys pulled out of range.

When Bindon arrived in Montreal with news of the gunfire at St. John's, there was panic among the citizenry who expected Allen to appear at any moment. Colonel Templer had the alarm sounded

Montreal from the St. Lawrence River.

Detail of an engraving after Thomas Patten, circa 1762 (Library and Archives Canada, C-002433).

and urged the citizens to gather at the Recollect chapel to decide on a method of defence. Everyone was inspired to take up arms, but in the midst of this discussion a messenger arrived from Major Preston with the advice that Allen's men had retreated and, in some manner, implicating Bindon with treachery.

When the troops returned from St. John's, they seized the merchant and led him to the pillory; however, some of their officers interfered and freed the culprit. The next day, several merchants had the effrontery to complain of the insult offered to Bindon and he was allowed to return to his business.[5]

Hazen travelled to Quebec City to inform the governor. Disaster at St. John's had been avoided, but the point had been made — the province was vulnerable to attack[6] and, clearly, Carleton could not afford to comply with Gage's request for a troop movement to Crown Point.

SKENESBOROUGH

Along with the bloodless surprise seizures of Ticonderoga and Crown Point, Allen's Green Mountain Boys looted loyalist properties in the settlements around the two posts.[7] At the bottom of South Bay one of their parties occupied the extensive estate of Colonel Philip Skene, a retired British Regular officer who openly favoured the Crown and the British connection. As such, he was a particular anathema to the Grants' men.

Skene had seen much service during the Seven Years' War. He had been with the 27th Regiment in the disastrous attack on the French works at Ticonderoga in 1758 and, the following year, had acted as General Jeffery Amherst's brigade-major when that fortress was taken. This experience was followed by a posting to Crown Point. This exposure to beautiful Lake Champlain roused his entrepreneurial spirit and, with Amherst's blessing, he purchased land at the mouth of Wood Creek where it merged with South Bay and settled thirty families there at his own expense. He then went with his regiment on the West Indies expedition against Martinique and Havana in 1762 and, after the latter's capture, served as the city's brigade and town major. When the campaign ended, he exchanged into the 10th Regiment in order to remain in North America, but when he visited his infant wilderness settlement he found that most of his settlers had become discouraged without his guiding hand and had gone off, leaving behind only fifteen persons.

Being of a resilient, positive nature, Skene recruited twenty-four men of means and made plans to settle a hundred families. In November 1763 the consortium petitioned for a grant of twenty-five thousand acres surrounding the mouth of Wood Creek, which was allowed, and in March 1765 the area was incorporated as the township of Skenesborough. Skene had retired from the army by 1769, and, two years later, successfully petitioned for an adjoining nine thousand acres, which became known as "Skene's little patent."

Dr. Asa Fitch, an early upper–Hudson River historian, described Skene as "a man of intelligence, wealth and enterprise, beyond any other person that was in the country for several years." The late-nineteenth-century historian Horatio Rogers wrote that Skene "sedulously devoted himself to the settlement and improvement of his township and the development of the resources of the surrounding district. He burned lime, quarried stone, and reared buildings of a character far more substantial than any other private individual in the province aspired to possess in those days. He erected and operated a forge, and built and ran saw mills. He constructed and navigated vessels on the lake north of him, and laid out and opened roads to communicate with the settlement south of him."

A clash with the Green Mountain Boys came on August 24, 1774, when New York's royal governor, William Tryon, directed Skene, Sheriff John Munro, Patrick Smith, and John McComb, all justices of the peace for Albany County, to bring to trial Robert Cochran and fourteen other armed rioters for dispossessing citizens of their lands near Argyle Township. The outcome is unclear; however, those four justices were destined to become significant loyalists, and Cochran an inveterate rebel.

———————

On May 9, 1775, Philip Skene was crossing the ocean to America with his new wife. He had two new Crown commissions — "Lieutenant Governor of Ticonderoga and Crown Point," and "Surveyor of His Majesty's Woods and Forest Bordering on Lake Champlain." On that same day the dedicated Green Mountain rioter Samuel Herrick led a thirty-man party to Skene's home and captured his aunt and two sisters and his son Andrew.[8] Having accomplished another bloodless coup, the Boys seized the colonel's sloop and several bateaux and set sail for Ticonderoga.[9]

QUEBEC'S DEFENCES

Carleton marshalled his sparse forces that had been so badly reduced by the transfer of the 10th and 52nd Regiments and, turning over the defence of Quebec City to Lieutenant Governor Cramahé, rushed to Montreal, followed by a detachment of the 7th Fusiliers and some artillery pieces. As neither John Campbell nor Daniel Claus was in the province, Carleton's advisor on Native affairs was his friend La Corne Saint-Luc, whom he had earlier appointed to the province's legislative council.

Upon arrival in the city the governor was distressed to read some intercepted letters, in particular one from Benedict Arnold to the agitator Thomas Walker, asking him to supply information "from time to time" about the number of troops in the town and their movements and whether the Indians joined them. Walker had emigrated from England to Boston and then migrated to Montreal in 1763 where he became a leading fur and wheat merchant. Perhaps his status prompted Carleton to tread lightly, as he took no action despite this evidence of possible treason.

The province's defences were sparse. The 7th and 26th Regiments were divided between St. John's, Chambly, Lachine, Montreal, and St. Francis. Carleton's third regiment, the 8th, was in the upper posts and unavailable. The governor had little choice but to raise Canadien troops, but how?

A few months after Lexington, the reverberations of open conflict had reached even the tiniest, most remote Ohio and Illinois settlements, inciting agitators to set up committees and assume political powers. Lord Dunmore's War [see Chapter 2] had receded into the background.

ATTEMPTS TO MOBILIZE CANADIENS

As a solution for the government's lack of troops the esteemed Montreal notary Simon Sanguinet recommended that the governor reinstitute the militia system of the old French regime. Carleton was inspired by the suggestion and proclaimed martial law, calling out the militia to defeat a "treasonable invasion" by speedily bringing all traitors and their abettors to justice.[10] The vicar-general of Montreal, Etienne Montgolfier, wrote a circular letter to Montreal district's parishes in support of the measure.[11] However, the governor again stumbled, repeating his earlier error, and selected the militia's officers from the upper classes. Although many of the noblesse had performed notable service during the old regime, they had served primarily as officers of Colonial Marines or Metropolitan Regulars, not the militia. Further, the governor appeared to believe that the compulsory nature of the old militia service had been feudal (that is, that the habitants had been obliged to turn out under the demands of their seigneurs) when in fact they had responded to their captains of militia.

The historian A.L. Burt observes:

Although the wealthier seigneurial families lent grace
to the society of the towns, chiefly Quebec, and
many of the noblesse had distinguished themselves
in numerous campaigns and more numerous forays,
the real leaders of the people were two classes of men
who sprang from their own midst and remained in
daily and intimate contact with them — the curés and
the captains of militia. They were the true shepherds.

Adding to the negative effects of Carleton's misjudgment, some
of his appointees gave senior ranks to their families and friends and
only junior positions to some veteran militia officers, bypassing many
others altogether. Montreal's bourgeoisie was in a tumult and, in the
outlying parishes, the habitants refused to turn out. Many claimed that
a senior British officer had promised they would be allowed to elect
their own officers. This intransigence was reinforced by the flood of
rebellious propaganda that entered the province. An anglo-Quebecker
observed, "it is certain that all Winter the people of our Colonies have
been corresponding with the Canadians and English people settled
here and I am apt to think that is the cause of the present coolness."[12]

Quebec's Chief Justice, William Hey, reported that Congress's
agents had employed every conceivable argument to prevent the
rural habitants from supporting the government, including appeals
to their prejudices and private interest, and threats of severe penalties.

They are terrified or corrupted to a degree that your
Lordship can have no idea of, & are impressed with
the strangest ideas that ever entered into the minds
of men. Sometimes they believe that they are to be
sent to Boston [as troops] and nothing can persuade
them that a few transports which are waiting for
Provisions, are not lying in wait to receive them, at
other times they are told that the People of Boston
are fighting merely to prevent the return of the [tax]

stamps which they seem to think a matter of great politeness & do not wish to see them disturbed in so good a work. Some amongst them believe they are sold to the Spaniards (whom they abominate) & that Gen. Carleton has got the money in his pocket, in short such a mixture of ignorance, fear, credulity, perverseness & Prejudice never yet I believe took possession of the human mind or made it more difficult to know what to do with them.[13]

He noted that most of the officers employed to organize them were seigneurs or their relatives, who in many cases were harsh and indiscreet in commanding their military services.

They on their parts have been and are too much Elated with the advantages they supposed they should derive from the restoration of their old Privileges & customs, & indulged themselves in a way of thinking & talking that gave every just offence, as well to their own people as to the English merchants.

Almost tauntingly, these negative reactions were full in the governor's face, and he was not one to bow to such pressures. Ignoring the problems, he issued commissions to the men nominated by his appointees, which did nothing to improve co-operation. Carleton reported to Dartmouth,

The Noblesse of this Neighbourhood were called upon to collect their Inhabitants, in order to defend themselves, the Savages of those Parts likewise had the same orders; but tho' the Gentlemen testified great zeal, neither their Entreaties or their Example could prevail upon the People; a few of the Gentry, consisting principally of the Youth, residing in this Place, and it's neighbourhood, formed a small Corps of Volunteers under the command of Mr. Samuel Mackay, and took Post at St. John's; the Indians shewed as much Backwardness as the Canadian Peasantry.

The Consternation in the Towns and Country was great and universal, every Individual seemed to feel our present impotent situation, for tho' in Danger of Internal Commotions, we are equally unprepared for Attack or Defence; Not six hundred Rank & File fit for Duty upon the whole Extent of this great River, not an armed Vessel, no Place of Strength; and ancient Provincial Force enervated and broke to Pieces; all Subordination overset, and the minds of the People poisoned by the same Hypocrisy and Lies practised with so much Success in the other Provinces, which their Emissaries and Friends here have spread abroad with great Art and Diligence; had it not been for those few Troops, three hundred Rebels might have procured all the Arms, Ammunition, and Provisions can afford, and have kept Post at St. John's with great Security. We are at present fortifying a Post there and at Oswegatchie, tho' there are other Avenues into the Province, I hope the above may be made sufficiently strong to resist any sudden Attack of this Sort; a considerable Force here might not only secure ourselves, but assist General Gage in extinguishing the Flames of Rebellion in the other Provinces more speedily, I fear he has none to spare, and it may be too late in the year to have them from Europe, however I shall see what in our present Situation is further practicable for the King's Service.

Within these few Days the Canadians and Indians seem to return a little to their sense, the Gentry and Clergy have been very useful upon this Occasion and shewn great fidelity and Warmth for His Majesty's Service, but both have lost much of their Influence over the People: I propose trying to form a Militia, and if their Minds are favourably disposed, will raise a Battalion, upon the same Plan as the other Corps in America, as to numbers and Expence, and were it established, I think, it might turn out of great public Utility; but I have many Doubts whether I shall be able to succeed.

These Measures, that formerly would have been extremely popular, require at present a great Degree of Caution and Circumspection: so much have the Minds of the People been tainted by the Cabals and Intrigues I have from time to time given Your Lordship some information of, I am as yet uncertain whether I shall find it advisable to proceed in the aforementioned undertaking; to defame their King and treat him with Insolence and Disrespect, upon all occasions to speak with the utmost Contempt of His Government, to forward Sedition and Applaud Rebellion seem to be what too many of His British American Subjects in those Parts think their undoubted Right.[14]

———————————

In addition to Mackay's small band of worthies the Montrealer Sieur François-Marie Picoté de Belestre, a veteran officer of notable and extensive experience, led a contingent of volunteers to Fort St. John's that he had drawn from as far away as Quebec City. He had twenty officers who had served under the French, sixteen militia officers from Montreal and Trois-Rivières, and ten others from rural parishes.[15]

———————————

The issuing of the militia proclamation went smoothly in Trois-Rivières and Quebec City for, unlike the commercial hub of Montreal, those centres were not as infected with ambitious anglo immigrants and the northward flow of propaganda. Throughout the months of June and July, the capital's men were organized into British and Canadien companies, although in a few outlying parishes the habitants were in as violent opposition as those near Montreal. Quebec's bishop, Monseigneur Jean-Olivier Briand, intervened by warning the rebellious that they were committing a sin by being false to their oath of allegiance to the King, but the unrest continued.[16]

John Nairne, a veteran Seven Years' War captain of Fraser's Highlanders, who had settled east of the capital at Murray Bay, had some very discouraging experiences. He was instructed to recruit men in his home district with the assistance of the militia captains and was given commissions for captains and subalterns, and ordered to compile a roll of men fit to bear arms, making note of those with prior service. His efforts were supported by Briand, who sent instructions to the district's priests urging their parishioners' compliance, yet he had little success. Most of Murray Bay's farmers were Canadiens and, although respectful, they expressed concerns about serving in the army. He was accorded the same respectful but noncommittal reception in many of the district's other communities, but in one locale even his instruction to assemble was ignored and at another he met with open hostility. Entirely frustrated, Nairne applied to Carleton in mid-August for a vacant captaincy and a few weeks later received an urgent summons to come to Quebec City. From that point on he would serve till the war's end with distinction.[17]

Mackay

The decision to defend Quebec came easily for Samuel Mackay, the seigneur of Pointe aux Roches on Lake Champlain and a land speculator on Ile Saint-Jean (now Prince Edward Island). He had been a distinguished subaltern in the Royal American Regiment and married into the Canadien gentry in 1761, settling in the province when he left the army in 1768. Mackay's bride, Marguerite-Louise Herbin, was the daughter of a renowned colonial officer of New France who had commanded at Crown Point and was a Knight of the Order of St. Louis. Samuel occupied two government posts — he was the province's Deputy Surveyor for the Royal Navy and a magistrate in the city of Montreal.

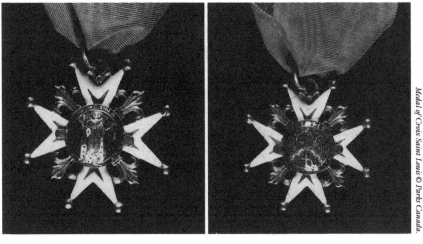

Medal of Croix Saint Louis © Parks Canada.

Croix de Saint-Louis — awarded to Knights of the Royal and Military Order of Saint Louis.

Samuel and his brother Francis (another noteworthy RAR subaltern) had enjoyed the patronage of Governor Murray's family and that of Sir William Johnson, the Indian Superintendent. In 1763 the brothers had offered to raise a corps of six hundred Canadiens to serve against Pontiac's uprising and, although the concept was not pursued, the offer was duly noted. To be sure, Samuel's past, present, and future were enmeshed with the British connection; his path was clear.[18]

When Preston returned from St. John's with news that Allen's party had retired, Mackay urged Lieutenant-Colonel Templer to garrison the fort, but the commander said he had insufficient men. Mackay then persuaded the colonel to allow him to raise a party of volunteers. It was this party that held the post until Carleton arrived in Montreal with reinforcements and sent Preston out with his large detachment.[19]

Mackay's collection of seigneurial and bourgeois volunteers included several men who would be very prominent in fighting the rebellion over the next two years, including two former French Regular officers, Réné-Amable Boucher de Boucherville and Jean-Baptiste-Melchior Hertel de Rouville,[20] and David Monin, a former

Oil painting by Gilbert Charles Stuart, 1786 (Wikimedia Commons).

Jean-Baptiste-Melchior Hertel de Rouville, prominent Canadien captain.

franco-Swiss ensign of the Royal Americans. Attempts to raise support for the volunteers at Kahnawake failed. The Natives explained that they were confused, as they had been constantly persuaded in the past "to consider the Kings English subjects as their friends & Brothers" and to forget "all former Hatred agst them."

A second blunder was committed in late May, this time with the Natives. While on patrol outside Fort St. John's, Mackay's volunteers seized a suspicious party led by a well-known political figure, the sachem Abraham Nimham of Stockbridge in Massachusetts. It was known that the rebels had employed Stockbridge headmen the year before to influence the Confederacy's Mohawks in favour of the colonists, so a search was made of Nimham's pack. Wampum belts, the traditional vehicles for calling Natives to war, for the Canada Indians were discovered, along with a persuasive letter from Ethan Allen cajolling the Kahnawakes to join with him, and several letters to Montreal's anglo sympathizers.

Nimham and his two fellow tribesmen were trussed up and left lying in a bateau overnight. The next day they were taken to Montreal, where they were summarily sentenced to be hanged as spies and traitors. The Kahnawakes were outraged and twenty headmen and warriors arrived in the city to meet with the commandant. They remonstrated that the Stockbridges had been escorted to Canada by several of their townsmen, and, in Native tradition, should be considered inviolable ambassadors. The rhetoric grew more and more heated until the commandant blurted out that he did not care the snap of a finger for all the Indians.

When tempers finally cooled, the Stockbridges were released into the hands of the Kahnawakes under threat of instant hanging if they showed their faces in Quebec again.[21]

Shortly after this ugly confrontation Carleton hired Claude-Nicholas-Guillaume de Lorimier (Chevalier[22] de Lorimier) as a lieutenant and interpreter in the Quebec Indian Department. The de Lorimiers had served with the Indians in the earlier war and his two brothers would soon join the chevalier. The eldest was François-Marie-Thomas (Sieur de Verneuil) and the youngest Jean-Claude-Chamilly. In recent times the family had been fur traders and become well-connected in Kahnawake society, yet when the chevalier went to the village he was disappointed to recruit only one fellow, whom he knew was a rascal.

Carleton was never one to be fobbed off. Ever conscious of his position and the country's peril, he threatened the Kahnawakes with dispossession of their lands and with having his redcoats turn their muskets on the village. In consequence, when the governor's troops assembled at Montreal, the Kahnawakes were so concerned for their safety that they posted sentries and lay on their arms all one night.

Under this pressure their headmen had reconsidered their position by June 2 and met with Carleton in Montreal to give him their agreement to defend him "to the utmost of their power, should he be besieged in Montreal." Satisfied for the moment, Carleton sent them home with gifts of ammunition and food. Once the senior Nation gave in, the three communities at Lake of Two Mountains agreed to assist in similar fashion.

MORE REBEL ACTIVITY

After receiving an encouraging report from James Price, a Montreal merchant, New York's Provincial Congress prepared its own address to their northern neighbour. Their message emphasized that the quarrel between the colonies and Britain was about whether citizens should be subjects or slaves. Fifty copies were printed in English and fifteen hundred in French and the lot was sent to supporters in Montreal for distribution.[23]

This contention that the British wanted to enslave their colonists had a ring of truth with the Canadiens in view of Carleton's decision to restore militia service and his choices for officers.

On June 1, the Continental Congress resolved not to undertake an expedition into Canada. Their decision was phrased to give comfort to, or perhaps to lull, Carleton and the Canadiens and was translated into French for distribution in Quebec.[24]

THREATS AND REACTIONS

On June 8, Carleton added a postscript in his report to Lord Dartmouth.

> I find the Rebels are returned, and have taken Post near to St. John's, and there have the King's Sloop and Major Skene's Schooner well armed, with several Bateaus; tho' I have not as yet been able to procure exact accounts of their Numbers or Intentions, I have Reason to believe from the imperfect Information already received, they are more in Number than upon their former Incursions.

The kettle was simmering.

That same day Carleton dispatched a party of twenty Mississaugas, who had willingly responded to one of La Corne Saint-Luc's war belts, to scour the woods between St. John's and Île-aux-Noix. It seems that the isolation of their fishing villages along the north shore of Lake Ontario kept them free of rebel influence, as their loyalty to the Crown was firm and would remain so throughout the rebellion.

The governor also approached the Kahnawakes to send warriors to assist the Regulars at St. John's, but was rebuffed. The village headmen referred to their agreement of June 2 to defend Montreal, but to do nothing more. Then several days later there came a sudden reversal of policy and the Kahnawakes agreed to post parties at St. John's. This was followed by similar commitments from the other villages; however, their posture continued to be defensive. Nonetheless, the change represented an improvement.

At Detroit, Captain Richard Lernoult received Carleton's proclamation of martial law on June 9 and had mobilized the Canadien population into several militia companies by early July. Unlike the Canadien companies in lower Quebec, these militiamen would see active service throughout the war, albeit in the far western territories.

ALBANY AND THE MOHAWKS

At a county Committee of Correspondence meeting in Albany on May 22 an interpreter delivered a message from Chief Little Abraham of the Mohawks' Fort Hunter village. A message from a prominent Mohawk headman had great weight, as the tribe was considered the most prominent in the Six Nations' Confederacy, which, in turn, had influence over all the Nations in America's northeast; however, the committee was mistrustful, for the Mohawks were also known to be under the Crown's influence. The message stated:

> Brothers. Our present situation is very disagreeable
> and alarming, what we never expected, therefore
> desire to know what is designed by the Reports that

are spread amongst us, We hear that Companies and Troops are coming from one Quarter to another to Molest us, particularly that a large Body are hourly expected from New England to apprehend and take away by Violence our Superintendant and extinguish our Council Fire, for what reasons we know not.

Brothers. We desire you would inform us if you know of any such design on Foot either by the New England People or in your Vicinity, and not deceive us in this matter for the consequences will be important and extensive[.]

Brothers. We shall support and defend our Super-intendant and not see our Council Fire extinguished, We have no inclination or purpose of interfering in the dispute between Old England and Boston, the white People may settle their own Quarrels between them-selves we shall never meddle in those Matters, or be the aggressors, if we are let alone[. W]e have for a long time lived in great Peace with one another and we wish ever to continue so, But should our Superintendant be taken from us, we dread the Consequences, the whole Confederacy would resent it, and all their Allies, and as reports now are, we should not know where to find our Enemies; the innocent might fall with the Guilty: We are so desirous of maintaining Peace, that we are unwilling the Six Nations, shou'd know the bad Reports spread amongst us & threats given out[.]

Brothers. We desire you will satisfy us as to your knowledge of the foundation of those Reports, and what your News are, and not deceive us in a matter of so much Importance[.][25]

Although Little Abraham's appeal was pacific, it held an under-current of threat, which deepened the committee's concerns. On May 23 they wrote to Superintendent Guy Johnson "about the unfriendly dispositions of the Indians, and other disturbances in Tryon County."

These "disturbances" probably referred to his fortification of his home, Guy Park, and the mounting of a rotating guard of employees, tenants, and trustworthy men from his militia regiment. It was also known that his deputy, brother-in-law, fellow militia colonel, and neighbour, Daniel Claus, had joined him in the defence.

Johnson had earlier written to "the Magistrates, Committee of Schonectady, and the Mayor and Corporation of Albany" (perhaps displaying confusion as to exactly who was steering the rebel ship of governance) in which he expressed alarm about a possible attack on his person by New Englanders, which, he said, had prompted him to fortify his house. The committee was aware that he was about to conduct an Indian council and their letter advised him to keep the Natives from interfering "in the present dispute between Great Britain and her Colonies." As part of his defensive arrangements, Johnson had interrupted movement along the King's Highway and the communication urged him to reopen the road.[26]

Johnson received no sense of reassurance from this correspondence. Besides, keeping the Natives out of the conflict was entirely against his training and inclination.

CONGRESS SENDS INSTRUCTIONS

On May 25 the Albany Committee received specific instructions dated seven days earlier from New York's representatives at the Continental Congress concerning the support required by the occupying force at Ticonderoga. First, the committee was to supply "a number of Men Competent for the purpose recommended by the Congress." Second, "a Suitable Quantity of Provisions be immediately sent thither." Third, "a number of Carpenters to construct a few Scows to be imply'd on Lake George in transporting the Cannon & Stores[,] Pitch[,] Oakum, Nails, Ropes[,] Gins[,] & Carriages (to convey the Cannon across the carrying Place) will be absolutely requisite." Fourth, "the Men … imployed in this Service [to be supplied] with Ammunition." This instruction was very specific in type and bewilderingly unspecific in quantity, which left much for the Albany Committee to consider.

The committee noted that Colonel Dirck Ten Broeck held a number of Provincial arms that were much needed throughout the county. Committeeman Leonard Gansevoort and the mayor, Abraham Cuyler,[27] were sent to examine the quantity and quality of arms. This duty may have been rather awkward for Cuyler, as he was a Crown appointee and the arms were owned by the Crown and placed in Ten Broeck's trust. The pair reported that there were about 450 muskets, most in poor condition, and a subcommittee later assessed that only 100 were repairable. An inspection of the city's magazine revealed that 250 pounds of powder was "damnified," that is, condemned. Although these findings imposed limitations, the city requested that its "Association Company" of volunteers march immediately for Ticonderoga and "prevent our Enemies from Quebec advancing into the interior Parts of this and the New England Colonies." This was a rather puny response to Congress's instructions and one might suspect that the volunteers, who had come together for the security of the city, were rather astonished.

Intercepted Mail

The committee had intercepted mail from Canada and examined it for useful intelligence. A letter from a 26th Regiment lieutenant to his wife in Ireland revealed his supposition that his unit would soon be sent "to serve against the rebellious New Englanders." An anonymous letter to a man in Boston noted that the Quebec governor had the authority to raise a Canadien regiment and send it where he pleased; which news, of course, fueled everyone's fears. A third letter was from an anglo-Canadian to a Boston merchant complaining that "The English in this Country are in a deplorable situation, being deprived of all their Liberties and Priviledges, and are afraid to speak or Act relative to public affairs," and a fourth letter bemoaned the shedding of blood between Englishmen — all told, a quite informative haul.

THE COMMITTEE TAKES ACTION

John Visscher appeared before the board and offered to raise a hundred-man company for duty at Ticonderoga, but whether he represented the city's Association Company is unknown. The districts of Claverack and Kings were approached to supply another two or three companies. They were urged to comply, as "No Time is now to be lost[,] every Hours delay is big with Danger as the Canadians are soon expected down to retake Ticonderoga." Governor Jonathan Trumbull of Connecticut Province was appealed to for a supply of powder and troops.

So, despite the earlier fumbling response, from a standing start two militia companies had marched for Ticonderoga by May 27 and another two were raising, only two days after the committee received Congress's instructions.[28]

GUY JOHNSON ABANDONS THE MOHAWK VALLEY

By June the rebels' pressure on the Indian Department and the Native visitors to Guy Park had become so disagreeable that Johnson decided to accept Daniel Claus's recommendation and remove his family and department members from the Valley. The two agents abandoned their properties and travelled westward with a retinue of 120 armed men composed of family, friends, employees, tenants, and local Mohawks, among them John and Walter Butler and Joseph Brant. After some false starts the superintendent held an Indian council at Oswego in mid-July, during which his wife died in a complicated childbirth aggravated by their sudden exile. She was one of the first fatalities of the rebellion in the Mohawk Valley. Despite this personal tragedy, and the Six Nations' decision to remain neutral, Johnson persuaded a few Confederacy warriors to accompany his party to Montreal in company with Lieutenant-Colonel Allan Maclean and a number of his recruits who had just appeared at Oswego from the Mohawk Valley. Johnson's circuitous pilgrimage would end at Montreal just prior to the rebel invasion of Canada.

William Berczy, circa 1810 (© McCord Museum M966-02-3-P2).

The famous Mohawk war captain, Joseph Brant.

A MAJOR CHARACTER EMERGES

Allan Maclean was a Scotsman with substantial military experience, first as a junior officer with the Scots brigade in Holland, then in America as a lieutenant in Frederick Haldimand's 4th Battalion, Royal Americans. He was gravely wounded in the failed attack on Ticonderoga in 1758 and, after recovery, became the captain of a New York Independent company and served at the taking of Fort Niagara in 1759. He returned to Britain, and, as lieutenant-colonel commandant successfully raised the 114th Foot, which was disbanded after the peace and almost ruined him financially. In 1772, after a long, complicated period of recovery, he was taken back on strength as a brevet lieutenant-colonel.[29]

Just days before the Crown's pyrrhic victory at Bunker Hill on June 17, 1775, Maclean arrived in Boston with the King's warrant for the raising of a regiment to be named the Royal Highland Emigrants. He was expected to recruit from Scots immigrants and "other loyal persons," so, with Gage's approval in hand, Maclean and a few of his officers left the port city and began to quietly recruit throughout the colonies. Maclean and a pair of his lieutenants infiltrated through rebel-dominated country to arrive at Sir John Johnson's fortified home in

Left: Miniature by unknown artist (Courtesy Lord Maclean of Duart and Morvern). Right: Unknown artist (Library and Archives Canada, 1976-14-50).

Left: Lieutenant-colonel Allan Maclean, Royal Highland Emigrants.
Right: Monseigneur Jean-Olivier Briand, Bishop of Montreal.

the Mohawk Valley not long after Guy Johnson had left with his Indian Department retinue. One of Maclean's captains had earlier recruited among Sir John's Scots tenantry with substantial success, but the baronet recommended that the colonel be cautious about assembling a large number of men, as it could provoke a strong rebel reaction.

As a result a rather disgruntled Maclean left Johnson Hall with his subalterns and only thirty of the four hundred men who had declared for service. As Sir John had recommended he avoid taking the Lake Champlain route to Canada where the rebels were very active, Maclean's party followed Guy Johnson's path to Oswego.

QUEBECKERS' OATH

On May 22 Bishop Briand responded to Governor Carleton's request for assistance by issuing an Episcopal mandate in which he declared that the rebels were "subjects in revolt against their lawful sovereign who is also ours." He reminded his flock of the kindness and mildness they had enjoyed under British rule and the recent favours granted them in the Quebec Act. He closed with two thoughts: "Your oath and your religion impose upon you the solemn obligation to defend your King and country to the utmost limit of your power.... There is no question of carrying war into the farther provinces; all that is asked of you is that you lend your aid to repulse the enemy and to withstand the invasion which threatens this province."[30]

PACIFIC INTENTIONS

By June 3, the New Hampshire Provincial Congress had received intelligence of Carleton's attempt to raise the Quebec militia and decided it was critical to inform Quebeckers that New England had no intention to invade Canada. When Massachusetts received a copy of New Hampshire's letter to Quebec, her politicians sent a suggestion to the Continental Congress to address another solemn declaration of their pacific intentions to their "brothers in Canada."

New York got into the act and sent a letter to the British merchants of Montreal stating there was no plan to declare independence from Britain. The Montreal merchant James Price acted as the courier to deliver New York's letter and eight hundred copies of Congress's. The colonies continued to fear an invasion from Quebec and organized two fifty-man scouts to patrol the Lake Champlain corridor and the environs of Montreal, and Massachusetts sent yet another agent to visit the St. Francis Indians.[31]

JOHNSON IN QUEBEC

Although Carleton was desperate for manpower, he did not welcome the arrival of Johnson and his supporters when they appeared in Montreal on July 17 with a number of Confederacy warriors who clearly expected to see some fighting. Understandably, the superintendent was bursting to avenge his personal losses and, making his arrival more complex, he and Claus still believed they had the right to manage the Seven Nations. Adding to Carleton's discomfort, "the affable and competent"[32] Claus held a very successful consultation at Kahnawake in the face of considerable opposition from the war captain, Louis Atayataghronghta, or Black Louis, a mixed-race black and Native who, as a child, had been taken in New York. This was followed by Johnson's major council at Lachine on July 26 when over sixteen hundred Natives assembled to hear the superintendent's words. Persuaded by Johnson's rhetoric, the Natives readily agreed with the resolutions that the superintendent claimed had already been adopted by the Six Nations and accepted a large, black war belt. Now, hundreds of warriors volunteered to act against the rebels, which must have surprised and disconcerted the governor, in view of the many fruitless attempts his agents had made earlier. Clearly, of the three factions in the villages, those in favour of the Crown emerged the strongest at this time, and those either favouring the rebels or counselling remaining aloof from the conflict were temporarily muted.

This rift in the Native villages was mirrored in the awkward relationship between the governor and the Indian Superintendent. Carleton complained to Gage about Johnson, "This Gentleman understands he has the supreme command over all the Indians & I wou'd not dispute it, though I believe we can manage those of this Province better.... As Colonel Johnson intends residing in the Province, I could wish his Rank and Command were clearly described, and how far the General Officers, and others upon the same Service may, or may not interfere with, or direct, him."[33] Such words painted a tense, untenable scenario.

Johnson cautioned the governor about the importance of keeping Natives active, noting that once they embraced hostilities they were easily discouraged if not quickly utilized; however, Carleton ignored the warning. He did not want to escalate the war by making a wholesale commitment of Indians and kept the warriors inside the boundaries of Quebec, issuing instructions not to deploy south of the forty-fifth parallel of latitude except on official scouts.

The defacing of the King's statue had taken a destructive turn when rebel sympathizers pulled it down, cut off its head, and threw it down a well. Guy Johnson's bateaux master, James Cusack, earned praise from the loyal citizenry when he fished it out.[34]

The Grants Take a Major Role

In the midst of this political upheaval New York's governance in eastern Charlotte, Gloucester, and Cumberland Counties — parts of which formed the so-called New Hampshire Grants — was surrendered to Ethan Allen's Green Mountain Boys, whose aggressive spirits had been understandably roused by their easy successes at Ticonderoga, Skenesborough, Crown Point, and Fort St. John's. New York's Provincial Congress bowed to what must have seemed inevitable and instructed Allen's party to formalize a regiment that would be accredited to the province. The request gave Allen's followers their long-sought-for recognition, and they accepted the condition.

On July 26 the various townships of the Grants met in committee and, by a substantial majority, elected Seth Warner as the new regiment's lieutenant-colonel commandant, with Samuel Safford as his major. Although both men were very prominent in the Grants and friends of his, Allen was mortified to be passed over; his own committee had recognized his propensity for intemperate behaviour.[35]

Maclean Well Received

Although the arrival of Guy Johnson posed problems for the governor, the appearance of Maclean, his officers, and thirty recruits was purely a blessing. One of his lieutenants was Patrick Daly,[36] who had been a close friend and personal physician to Sir William Johnson; another was Stephen Watts,[37] Sir John Johnson's young brother-in-law. Carleton gave Maclean free rein to recruit and soon another

Unknown artist, circa 1800 (Courtesy of Janeen Soderling).

Lieutenant Stephen Watts, Royal Highland Emigrant.

hundred men were added to his ranks — many of them veterans of the Black Watch and Fraser's Highlanders, including several experienced officers, such as John Nairne, Malcolm Fraser, and Daniel Robertson,[38] the latter a former lieutenant in the 42nd Regiment who had been serving as a major of the Montreal militia. Maclean appointed Robertson the Royal Highland Emigrants' captain-lieutenant, in the place of Sheriff John Munro, who had been unable to get away to Canada. Another valuable addition was François Dambourgès, a French immigrant, who had come to Quebec in 1763.

Brigadier Richard Prescott, colonel of the 7th Fusiliers, arrived in Montreal from Boston with Gage's advice that he would not be able to send troops or seamen to Quebec. Instead, the C-in-C again requested that Carleton make a strong diversion on Lake Champlain. As Prescott had been sent to assist Carleton, he became the governor's deputy and took command of Montreal district.[39]

DEFENCE ALONG THE RICHELIEU

In obedience to Carleton's orders, Guy Johnson sent three of his ranger officers — Captain Gilbert Tice and Lieutenants Walter

Butler and Peter Johnson — thirty Confederacy warriors and some Mississaugas[40] to Fort St. John's with a body of Canada Indians managed by Carleton's Quebec Indian Department officers. Events developed quickly. One of Tice's patrols was fired upon when it came across rebels at Pointe-au-Fer at the north end of Lake Champlain. When the other Natives heard this news they "appeared very spirited" and were ready to launch themselves against the rebels, but, once again, Johnson was ordered not to go out of the province, and the troops were held to the same restriction.

As Johnson had foretold, Natives required activity or, in their metaphorical words, "the Axe would cut them if they kept it long without using it." Ironically, entirely unknown to Johnson, Carleton was being encouraged by Gage to employ the Indians against the rebels on Lake Champlain, but the governor was unmoved. An early defection occurred when several Six Nations and Akwesasne warriors, who had waited until August 12 in hopes of some activity, took their war belt to Onondaga. They assured Johnson "they would be ready to return whenever there was a prospect of vigorous measures."[41] In an attempt to maintain a semblance of contentment, the superintendent continually rotated the men of the St. John's standing patrol.

In addition to his patrolling Indians, Carleton had a garrison at Fort St. John's under Major Preston's command composed of thirty-eight artillerists; 474 Regulars of the 26th and 7th Regiments; ninety Canadien volunteers — over half of whom were former French regime officers — and twenty of Maclean's Provincial Highlanders led by Captain-Lieutenant Robertson. There were also two companies of 7th Fusiliers at Chambly under Major Joseph Stopford.[42] Preston set his men to work to improve St. John's fortifications, but no changes were thought necessary at Chambly.

Fort St. John's needed substantial improvement if it was to withstand a determined attack. Engineering captain John Marr was appointed to oversee the efforts. Two earthen redoubts were already in place; one surrounding the barracks and the other around a substantial stone house previously occupied by Moses Hazen. Marr decided to combine the two redoubts by running a palisaded link between them and surrounding the combination with a seven-foot-deep ditch. He also installed a horizontal fraise along the outer base of the walls to discourage an infantry assault.

Lieutenant William Hunter, who commanded the brigantine *Gaspé*, was sent to St. John's to build vessels for operations on the Richelieu River and Lake Champlain and set his men to work on a schooner and a pair of row galleys.[43]

DANIEL CLAUS SIDELINED

If Johnson was disappointed with his underutilization, Claus had much more reason for concern, for his position continued to be undermined by the governor, who, despite the evidence of the New Yorker's considerable influence with the Seven Nations, was extremely cool to him. Although Carleton claimed that Campbell's appointment did not conflict with Johnson's operations, Claus saw it as a direct blow to his authority as Quebec deputy. His arrival in Montreal had confirmed his worst fears — he had no real role to play, for it was La Corne Saint-Luc's appointees who accompanied the Canada Indians to Fort St. John's, not Claus's.

A SIGNIFICANT PATROL

On August 22 a St. John's patrol of four Lake of Two Mountains Algonquins directed by the Chevalier de Lorimier discovered a bateau hidden under branches near the Riviére Lacolle. While paddling their prize north, they were challenged from the shore by someone shouting a warning that his men would open fire if the warriors did not return the boat. The Algonquins refused and threatened to return fire, which prompted the leader to taunt them about being forbidden to engage; then he ordered his men to fire. Two Algonquins were badly wounded and the patrol returned fire into the woods and retired to the fort. The next day a detachment of thirty-three Regulars, twenty-five warriors and five "volunteers" went to view the damage and discovered the notorious New Hampshire Grants' captain Remember Baker, with a ball between his eyes. The Indians removed his scalp, lopped off his fingers, and beheaded his corpse. The head was mounted on a pole on the fort's parade for several days and the fingers displayed to the impatient Natives waiting at Montreal.

Baker was possibly the first rebel officer to die at the hands of Native Americans during the conflict. He had been a key member of the Green Mountain Boys and a great thorn in the side of the New York provincial government. His chance death was a considerable coup, as a search of his corpse yielded papers that exposed subversion. Among the culprits were Louis Atayataghronghta, and the agitator Thomas Walker.[44]

Johnson augmented the St. John's patrols with ninety-one warriors and two lieutenants. Activity was feverish in and about Montreal, as the city was poorly prepared for defence. To enhance security, Johnson sent a Native guard to the King's magazines near Lachine. Shortly after, his little Native army was joined by eighty-six Kanehsatake Mohawks spoiling for a fight.

THE REBELS' NATIVE DIPLOMACY

While this confused frenzy of activity was ongoing in Quebec, the rebels decided to become active in Native diplomacy in an attempt to make up for their previous lack of direct participation. Delegates from the Seven Nations, including Louis Atayataghronghta, were entertained at Boston by General Washington; St. Francis hunting parties were feted along the upper Connecticut River; secret visits continued to be made to all the Canada villages and, most significantly, a major council was conducted by Major-General Philip Schuyler, Congress's newly appointed Northern Department Indian Superintendent, at which a handful of Six Nations' delegates proclaimed the Confederacy's neutrality with these words:

> We, the Six Nations, and our allies, which extend to Detroit, Ohio, and Caughnawaga [Kahnawake], upon our first learning the bad news that circulated along

the eastern shore of this island, assembled and resolved upon a union amongst us Indians, and to maintain peace; and we rejoice that nothing more has been asked of us.[45]

DECISION TO INVADE

Although critical, Native diplomacy was the less demanding of Schuyler's responsibilities, for on June 27 he had been appointed by the Continental Congress to command the Continental forces on and about Lakes George and Champlain. He was instructed to prevent a rumoured British invasion by taking control of the lakes, and — in order to guarantee the security of the United Colonies — to occupy St. John's, Montreal, and any other pertinent Canadian post. Ironically, Schuyler was instructed that the invasion was contingent upon it being acceptable to the Canadiens.[46]

The Continental Congress had received firm intelligence that Carleton had no more than eight hundred Regulars spread across Quebec, and that a third of them were in the upper country. Yet, despite the governor's paucity of resources, which proved he was unable to mount an invasion of the colonies, and, despite their protestations to the contrary only days earlier, the members decided to invade Canada.

Oil painting by John Trumbull (Wikimedia Commons).

Major-General Philip Schuyler, Continental Army commander.

Invaded by the King's Enemies

Carleton's strange negligence

The Halting Invasion

Schuyler's problems were legion. He had to organize a staff, assemble sufficient troops, develop their sense of cohesion and purpose, collect adequate supplies, build and collect enough vessels to mount the invasion, and somehow determine the opinions of the Canadiens. That all of this activity was well underway before the Canadiens' opinion was even sought strongly suggests the invasion would go ahead regardless, but, as it happened, making a token stab at ascertaining Quebeckers' thoughts was Schuyler's easiest chore. In contrast, the building of a competent staff and army was extremely difficult, as regional rivalries were strong and New Englanders, including the men from the Grants, were dissatisfied with Congress's choice of a patrician New Yorker as commander. When a second New Yorker, the former British Regular officer Richard Montgomery, was selected as deputy commander, unrest deepened, which was in no way helped by that province's tardy raising of its share of troops and supplies.

There could be few objections to Montgomery's qualifications for the role, as he had served on Lake Champlain under Amherst in 1759, and under Haviland the following year for the advance on

New York Public Library Digital Gallery, Record 422632.

Brigadier-General Richard
Montgomery succeeded Schuyler.

Montreal; however, he was connected by marriage to the powerful Livingston family, and they were as upper crust as the Schuylers.[1]

Schuyler's efforts were assisted substantially by Carleton's decision not to allow his troops or Natives to harass the rebels below Quebec's borders, which permitted him to build and organize his army and assemble supplies without interference.

In order to determine Canadian attitudes Schuyler sent the indefatigable John Brown to Chambly to visit the New York migrant James Livingston,[2] a relative of Montgomery's wife. After hearing Brown's news Livingston began to enlist Canadiens in the rebel cause and, when Brown returned to Schuyler in mid-August, he reported that he had been "protected by the Canadians, who I can assure you, are our friends ... they wish and long for nothing more that to see us ... penetrate their country." How odd. Brown could scarcely have seen more than a handful of habitants and he must have relied on the opinions of Livingston, an anglophone, for a summation of Canadien desires, but such questionable intelligence had precipitated actions throughout history and would do so frequently again.

Yet, the information collected by Brown about the sad state of Carleton's forces was certainly accurate. He urged, "Now it is time to carry Canada. It may be done with great ease and little cost, and I have no doubt but the Canadians would join us." He cautioned about further delays and reasoned that if a British reinforcement arrived, the Canadiens would have to take up arms against the colonies, "or be ruined." Yet, notwithstanding Brown's persuasive intelligence, Schuyler delayed to collect more men and supplies until he was called away for the Indian Council at Albany.

English-born John Platt, a mill owner and distiller from Saratoga, left his family and business interests, "and proceeded on to Fort George, at which place he remain'd for some time in taking a survey of the Rebel Army, he then proceeded over Lake George to Ticonderoga where General Montgomery than lay, and got an exact account of the whole of their Route towards Canada, from thence he proceeded to Crownpoint, and exactly traced their movements keeping Company with the Rebel Officers, and spending his money freely amongst them." Having obtained a pass from a rebel major, he hired a man and boat at Crown Point which took him to St. John's, where he met with Major Preston and gave him all the intelligence he had collected.[3]

While Schuyler was away from the army conducting the Albany Indian council, Montgomery heard from Brown that the two vessels the British were building at St. John's were nearing completion and made the decision to act. On August 28 he embarked twelve hundred men and two guns and headed for Île-aux-Noix where he intended to emplace the artillery to prevent the new ships from entering Lake Champlain. Montgomery got as far as Isle La Motte when Schuyler rejoined the army and was visited by some friendly St. Francis Abenakis.[4]

CHARACTERISTICS OF QUEBECKERS

In a dispatch of August 26 Quebec's Chief Justice, William Hey, advised Britain's lord chancellor of what he believed were the Canadiens' reasons for hesitating to support the Crown. "I am sometimes willing to think that fear, joined with extreme ignorance and a credulity hardly to be supposed of a people, have been over-matched by the subtlety and assiduity of some colony agents who were very busy here last winter. They [the Canadiens] are not at bottom an ungenerous or disobedient people."[5]

THE FIRST LANDING REPELLED

On September 5 the rebel shipping disembarked a thousand troops a mile and half below Fort St. John's. The next day they made an advance into "a close, deep swamp … in grounds marshy and covered with woods." As they started to cross a deep, muddy stream, their vanguard was met by "a surprising blast of close fire." Twenty-four Six Nations' and seventy-two Seven Nations' warriors[6] had sallied forth under the direction of Quebec Indian Department officers, the brothers the Chevalier and Verneuil de Lorimier, and two interpreters, with three officers of the Six Nations' department. No Regular troops were sent, which made the Natives suspicious that Major Preston was unwilling to risk his Europeans.

Sotsienhoouane, a principal Kahnawake chief, took command and his men hammered the Continentals as they forded the brook, caus-ing them to recoil. The Six Nations' ranger captain, Gilbert Tice, was wounded by return fire and Sotsienhoouane, armed with a spontoon and the chevalier's short sword, leapt the stream, rushed the rebels, and swiftly cut down three, but was himself killed by musket fire. Inspired by his valour the warriors charged twice, closing with the rebels in hand-to-hand combat. Typical of heavy woods actions, the fighting was confused, yet the green rebel troops held bravely. After thirty minutes the Indians retired, but their spirited resistance had been enough. The next day the landing was abandoned.

In this action the Indians lost three officers, including their popular interpreter Louis Perthius, and had five men wounded and eight killed. Several Canada Indians were of that number — Sotsienhoouane and a second Kahnawake, and men from Kanehsatake and Lorette; and, of the Confederacy's men, a Fort Hunter war captain and a Canajoharie

— a remarkable representation of Seven and Six Nations' warriors! This little skirmish delayed the rebels' next attempt by two weeks and, in part, prevented them from enjoying good weather for their attack on Quebec City, which ultimately contributed to its successful defence; but there was a downside to the event.

Aggravated and distressed by the lack of the army's support and the deaths of a chief and a favourite interpreter, the Canada Indians went home. Preston recognized the fort's vulnerability with only the remaining screen of two dozen Six Nations' warriors and rangers and sent Chevalier de Lorimier to pursue the Kahnawakes and persuade them to return. De Lorimier reported,

> I managed to catch up with them at Laprairie the same night but was not able to convince a single one to return to the fort. I had to follow them all the way back to Caughnawaga [Kahnawake] where the Council was assembled. One Huron and Thomas Welman [an influential, acculturated white captive] did the talking. They said that they had seen the American army and that it was very big; its soldiers were as numerous as the leaves of the forest, and General Montgomery had advised them to go back to their villages and stay neutral; this advice had been approved by all of the Seven Nations of Lower Canada.
>
> This same Huron and his companion told the assembled warriors that at that very moment Fort St. Jean was completely blockaded and that it was now impossible to get in or out.

De Lorimier saw this assertion as an opportunity, and, when night fell, he travelled to Fort St. John's and, by employing clever fieldcraft, infiltrated into the works and advised Preston of the council's results. He then exfiltrated the fort and returned to Kahnawake and, by boasting of his feat, proved that the Huron had deceived the council. The chevalier's tactical skills and ringing oratory persuaded the warriors and a large party returned to the fort.[7]

REINFORCEMENTS FOR ST. JOHN'S

As soon as news of the invasion arrived at Quebec City the governor set off for Montreal with several members of the governing council. Maclean was ordered to follow with his Emigrants and a body of Regulars. Quebec City's militia assumed the duties of guarding the walls and gates. Lieutenant Governor Cramahé posted a proclamation requiring all non-residents to report their arrival in the city and their business on pain of being considered rebel spies.[8]

When two Native couriers arrived in Montreal with news of the rebels' misadventure at St. John's, the commanding officer ordered the citizens and militia levies to assemble and march to the relief of the fort. Nearly all the habitants stayed home, but the city's young gentlemen and bourgeois came forward to volunteer and soon twenty more of Maclean's Emigrants were on the way with a handful of artillerymen; two Six Nations' department officers; seventy warriors; 120 franco-Canadians; and six anglos including Thomas Walker, a cousin of the notorious Thomas, under the command of Sieur Joseph-Dominique-Emmanuel Le Moyne de Longueuil, a member of one of Quebec's most prestigious military families.[9]

QUEBEC CITY STRENGTHENED

Notwithstanding Carleton's difficulties in raising men in Montreal district, the militia proclamation had been relatively well received in Trois-Rivières and Quebec City, where rebel agitation was less effective. Cramahé employed his considerable military experience and popularity to improve the capital's defence. On September 17, he reviewed the British and Canadien militia regiments. The former fielded six companies and the latter eleven, with a total strength of 994 all ranks. Each regiment had an artillery company. Two companies of British militia mounted guard that very night. Within days communications with Montreal were threatened and, as there were no naval ships available, the lieutenant governor hired and armed four small vessels to protect the navigation of the river and placed an embargo on the crews of five transports that had arrived from Boston. This measure provided a further eighty men for the defence of the city. By month's end, the city's fortifications were much improved and thirty-two guns had been mounted on the walls and tested by the militia artillery companies.

It was just as well that Cramahé had taken concerted action to offset the city's lack of a Regular force garrison, as Benedict Arnold — fresh from his Lake Champlain exploits — had persuaded Congress to allow him to lead a second invasion of Canada over an extremely difficult route up the Kennebec River from its mouth at the Atlantic Ocean, through the wilderness to the Chaudière River, and thence to Quebec City. By September 15 Arnold had set off with twelve hundred troops and instructions to communicate with Schuyler on Lake Champlain by utilizing St. Francis Abenakis who had agreed to act as couriers. Arnold had orders that, once he was in Quebec Province, his army was to pay for all supplies at full value and his troops were to be respectful of the Catholic religion.[10]

New York Public Library Digital Gallery, Record 1102486.

Colonel Benedict Arnold, dynamic expedition leader.

A Successful Sortie from Fort St. John's

General Schuyler was visited by Moses Hazen at the Continental Army's Île-aux-Noix base. Carleton had authorized Hazen to raise militia to reihforce Major Preston at St. John's, but he had vacillated, torn by concern for his properties, which lay in the path of the rebel army, versus his loyalty to the Crown. Rather than raise reinforcements for Preston, he decided to visit Schuyler to recommend against invasion, predicting there was little chance of success; however, his counsel was thwarted when James Livingston arrived from Chambly shortly afterwards and spoke very optimistically of the prospects. As a result, Hazen was viewed with suspicion and arrested.

Livingston promised assistance from sympathetic franco- and anglo-Canadians. This encouragement led to a second landing attempt, but it also failed when the troops panicked over several real and a great many imagined Indians and fled to their boats. A larger third landing was made, this time supported by a fleet of armed boats and sloops sent to confront the possible appearance of the British schooner the *Royal Savage*, the threat of which had been haunting rebel efforts previously.

Once ashore Montgomery was joined by Livingston and his associate, Jeremiah Duggan,[11] a former Quebec City barber living at Sorel. They brought a party of Canadiens, forty of whom were led by the omnipresent John Brown. Livingston advised that he, Duggan, and their Canadiens had taken two British bateaux transporting provisions and powder and had killed eleven crewmen and guards.[12] Montgomery dispatched Brown with a large detachment to cut off the fort's communications with the settlements to the north, and he succeeded in capturing a cart train of supplies and taking post in a small fieldwork that overlooked the roadways.

In retaliation Major Preston sent a company of Regulars, Mackay's volunteers, and a body of Canadiens under Picoté de Belestre and Longueuil to oust the interlopers. A sharp skirmish resulted, during which a Canadien loyalist was killed, before Brown's men were forced out of the fieldwork. In the course of the action Antoine Dupré had charged into the fortification and captured Moses Hazen, who had perhaps been released from arrest by volunteering to serve with Brown.[13]

When the fighting for the fieldwork broke out, Chevalier de Lorimier was patrolling with four Mohawks, a Kahnawake, and an Akwesasne chief. Just before he left the fort a Kahnawake friend named Kontitie had furtively approached him with the warning that he and "M. Hertel"[14] should escape while they had the chance. Peremptorily dismissing his well-meaning friend, de Lorimier set off on the reconnaissance.

With the crackle of musketry in the air, de Lorimier's patrol rushed to join the fighting, but arrived too late to assist. Just as the chevalier turned away from congratulating the Regulars and volunteers on their success, he heard his name being softly called from the underbrush, followed by whispered advice that there was a party of Natives and Canadiens coming to rescue him. He returned to his own men and together they went to find the source of the whispering, which proved to be Kontitie. Despite the likelihood of other rebels hiding nearby, the chevalier seized his friend by the throat while his men secured him. One of the Mohawks had earlier had a brother killed by the rebels and wanted to kill Kontitie in revenge, but a Regular officer intervened and urged de Lorimier to protect the man. After an exchange of some hot words and a scuffle with the aggrieved Mohawk, de Lorimier slyly freed his friend. The incident clearly illustrated the internecine nature of the conflict.[15]

As to Hazen, he was arrested and sent to Montreal, where he was closely confined. This affair must have been rather awkward for both Hazen and Mackay, as they had previously been partners in the timber business.[16]

REBEL AND ONEIDA DIPLOMACY

While Montgomery was completing the encirclement of Fort St. John's, Schuyler entrusted the impulsive Ethan Allen and John

Brown to deliver his "Declaration to the Inhabitants of Canada." When the pair arrived at the village of Chambly they were met by several militia captains and other respectable gentlemen. The manifesto was sent off to nearby parishes and Kahnawake. In answer, two Kahnawake captains came to Chambly with some wampum strings and the assurances of the Canada Indians' sincere friendship. They met with Allen and Brown in a solemn ceremony attended by a number of approving Canadiens.

This event was soon followed by the arrival of four Oneida emissaries from New York with news of the Six Nations' decision to remain neutral. The four happened to fall in with a contingent of Canada Indians on the march to reinforce Fort St. John's. They delivered their news, which prompted an acrimonious dispute to break out among the war party, and the majority of the warriors returned to Kahnawake with the Oneida agents. Soon after, a council of representatives from the various villages and Johnson's Six Nations' warriors met to hear the Oneidas speak. The emissaries presented the rebel commissioners' condolences for the Indians' recent losses and, somewhere in their message, issued a veiled threat that Schuyler would destroy Kahnawake if the Indians continued to assist the British, which caused much concern.

After receiving a report of the Oneidas' arrival, Claus, Brant, and several loyalist Indians visited Kahnawake to deliver Guy Johnson's invitation for the Oneidas to come to Montreal for a conference, but the emissaries were warned by the village's rebel faction of the risk of being abused like Nimham's Stockbridge party and declined, then hid outside the village in case Johnson made an attempt to seize them by force.

———————

John Platt, the Saratoga loyalist, somehow contrived to arrive in Montreal in the guise of a rebel prisoner and stayed in the barracks for three weeks until Carleton arrived. When granted an interview with the governor he provided intelligence of the situation below and was promised that his expenses would be paid by the government.[17]

MAJOR CAMPBELL ARRIVES

On September 10 Major John Campbell arrived in Montreal from Britain bearing his new commission as "Commandant of the Indians and Superintendent & Inspector of Indian Affairs within the Province of Quebec." The disagreements that had been simmering between Guy Johnson and the governor now boiled over. Daniel Claus was outraged; he saw Campbell as an incompetent parvenu brought in by Carleton and the devious La Corne Saint-Luc. It was clear to him that his own commission as deputy superintendent of the Canada Indians was now meaningless.

Johnson had already blotted his copybook by not visiting Kahnawake to counteract the upsurge of rebel propaganda after the killing of Remember Baker, so when he queried Carleton about Claus's displacement, he was abruptly told that New Yorkers had no authority in Canada and that he, Claus, and their rangers should go to Niagara where they could be more profitably employed and leave Canada to the Quebec Indian Department. In expectation that the two agents would lead them Carleton told Johnson that he should have a number of his men winter in and about Fort Niagara, as this would put them near their charges and safe from rebel interference. Although Johnson had the Campbell business foremost on his mind, he recognized the wisdom of Carleton's recommendations and appointed two of his department's officers to go to the Seneca villages and Claus's young nephew, who had been serving with merit in the defence of Fort St. John's, to live with the Mississaugas. His most important appointment was John Butler, whom he reluctantly promoted to deputy agent and sent to Niagara.

Johnson's mandate he had inherited from Sir William included responsibility for the Canada Indians, as they were historically dependent allies of the Confederacy. He resolved to go to Britain to obtain Lord Dartmouth's confirmation of his appointment and to argue the case about the Seven Nations. Perhaps realizing that Johnson had too much on his plate, Claus decided to accompany him to plead on his own behalf. Carleton viewed their decisions as a deliberate abandonment of their responsibilities in the face of a major crisis. Both men earned his lasting enmity, while the compliant Butler gained his patronage.

John Brown was stationed at La Prairie and Ethan Allen at Longueuil, two communities on the St. Lawrence's south shore across from Montreal and far to the north of the besieged Fort St. John's. The former urged the habitants to come to his camp with their arms to protect his men who were "menaced by people seeking our slavery." Simultaneously, Livingston and Duggan were working hard to recruit additional Canadiens. In keeping with the Sons of Liberty's intimidation methods, the rebels at times turned vicious when the Canadiens spurned their advances.

A PRIEST IS THREATENED

Two of Carleton's couriers who had been betrayed were found asleep in the priest's house at Saint-Denis. Twenty American rebels and their Canadien sympathizers surrounded the building. When the *curé* appeared he was seized by the scruff of the neck and his cassock was torn. He was ordered to hand over the couriers; if not, the house would be set on fire. When he went inside to relay the order to his guests, his curious servant showed her head at a window and was shot dead. The couriers were taken and led off to Île-aux-Noix. Historian Gustave Lanctot comments about this incident, "For the first time in their history Canadians had gone beyond disregard of ecclesiastical directives. Not only had they threatened a priest with violence, they had actually placed violent hands upon him."[18]

Carleton was very discouraged. When he had passed through Trois-Rivières en route to Montreal he told the local militia colonel,

Louis-Joseph Godefroy de Tonnancour,[19] that the only Canadien he had seen under arms for the King was the sentinel at the seigneur's door. When in Montreal, the dispirited governor failed to protect the loyal and neutral habitants and remained behind the city walls, perhaps out of depression, perhaps from caution, but all Canadians took note, and many were driven to cooperate with the rebels.[20] His troubling inaction was observed by Chief Justice Hey, who wrote that by some "strange negligence or timidity or ignorance of local government," the governor failed to use his authority to crush subversive propaganda and curb those who flouted the law, or even to put them under watch. Rather, they were left at large to continue their disruptive behaviour.[21] Carleton's feeling of helplessness was readily apparent in a letter of September 21 to Lord Dartmouth, in which he claimed that the retention of Canada would depend upon the arrival of "ten or twelve thousand men here, early next spring, completely equipped with some frigates."[22]

Alarmingly, La Corne Saint-Luc became so upset with Carleton's irresolution that he decided to meet with the rebels and asked his Kahnawake friends to make the contact. He and six of his associates met with rebel emissaries at the Native town. This lapse of faith became widely known, but when Carleton became aware of it he turned a blind eye, as he did with disaffected anglo-merchants. These were confusing times for loyal Canadians.[23]

As General Schuyler's health continued to plague him, he handed over command to Montgomery on September 16 and retired south. Montgomery was anything but confident; he was thwarted by bad weather, inadequate artillery, insufficient supplies, and the poor discipline of his troops, to the extent that he contemplated resigning.[24]

On September 19 a hard, driving rain set in along the Richelieu, pelting down on defenders and besiegers alike. Preston had a large number of guns, many sizeable, and he relied on the skills of his thirty-eight gunners to keep the rebels at bay. As an initial measure he had several buildings flattened that blocked the gunners' view of rebel activities. Then he had his long-range pieces play on Montgomery's two batteries located north and south of his redoubts. On the twenty-second and twenty-third rebel deserters came into the fort with news of a new battery position and Preston's gunners rained shells on it. In the first weeks of the siege, the Royal Artillery threw ten times more metal than their opponents.[25]

A FAILED ATTACK ON MONTREAL

The rebels' first attempt on Montreal was made on September 25. Allen and Brown planned the attack, but when Brown inexplicably failed to show at the rendezvous Allen pressed on with a mixed force of 140 American and Canadien rebels.[26] Never one for caution, he was convinced the weak garrison could not possibly withstand his determination; after all, Ticonderoga had easily succumbed to a smaller force and Montreal's defences were known to be ineffectual.

Peter Johnson, eldest son of Sir William Johnson and Mary Brant.

Unattributed oil painting (Metropolitan Toronto Library Board, John Ross Robertson collection, record number T15018).

A loyal young habitant named Desautels spotted Allen's men advancing and ran to the city with the news. Surprisingly, the citizenry was thoroughly aroused, and 120 franco-volunteers and eighty anglos mustered with a company of thirty-four Regulars and twenty of Johnson's Indians and rangers, all under the command of Major Campbell of the Indian Department.[27] The defenders marched out and fell in with Allen's men about three miles from the city gates. A sharp skirmish decided the day. Allen took flight and was run down by a painted warrior and a department officer. Legend claims that, while the officer kept the warrior at bay, Allen proffered his sword and uttered a typical blustering oath that he would never surrender to a "damned savage." Ironically, the lad who accepted Allen's surrender was a "damned savage" named Peter Johnson, Sir William's half-blood son by Mary Brant, who was awarded a Regular army commission for his decisive leadership in the defence of Montreal and the capture of the notorious outlaw.[28]

Despite the governor's refusal to send mounted volunteers to chase down the fugitives, this little success had a tremendous impact on the countryside. Humbled and humiliated in defeat, the rebel giant Ethan Allen was paraded through the streets of Montreal, sent aboard a ship in the harbour, and put in irons in the hold. Now, people from all over the region crowded into Montreal to offer their services; even some anglo-merchants were roused in favour of the Crown.

On September 28 Lady Maria Carleton, wife of the governor, and her three children sailed for England, which must have affected morale in Quebec City.[29]

On September 29 an Indian courier made his way into Fort St. John's with the electrifying news of Allen's capture, but his advice that four thousand rebel Canadiens were in arms dampened the troops' spirits. Of course, none of the garrison knew that this number was a gross exaggeration.[30]

***

After Allen's defeat Carleton received intelligence that Thomas Walker was continuing to "preach rebellion," so on October 5 a detachment of some twenty Emigrants with seven loyal Canadien militia captains and some militiamen was sent to L'Assomption to take him. Forewarned, Walker armed his servants. Between two and three in the morning his house was surrounded and a musket was fired, which was warmly answered by Walker's servants. When the Emigrant's ensign, John McDonell, and another Highlander were severely wounded by shots fired from the windows, the doors were broken down with axes. Walker took up a brace of pistols and a short rifle and joined his wife in the garret. After he defied all demands to surrender, the building was set afire and all were quickly apprehended.[31] This decisive action was generally viewed favourably and the number of militiamen under arms accordingly increased.

That the governor had been so slow to move against the anglo-agitators and rebel propagandists demonstrated his concern for British rights, but it was a grave error to have tolerated their activities for so long.

***

During Allen's attack on Montreal Johnson and Claus remained offshore in a King's vessel, which did nothing to improve Carleton's opinion of them. Mind you, the fact that neither Carleton nor garrison commander Templer had taken an active role had equally puzzled local loyalists. In Johnson's defence — despite the many reports and queries that he had dispatched to Lord Dartmouth, nothing had come back in return. He had chosen not to risk being forceful with the governor, as he was painfully aware that he lacked official confirmation of his commission as superintendent. Further, Claus' plight was extremely distressing for, no matter what justifications Carleton gave, all that Johnson could see was that his brother-in-law had been shunted aside after sixteen years of faithful service and in the process his own responsibilities had been substantially reduced. Soon after Allen's attack the ship, with Johnson's substantial party of family, employees, and Six Nations' delegates, slipped downriver to Quebec, then onward to Britain on November 11.[32]

On October 5 an article appeared in the *Quebec Gazette* that should have given all Quebeckers pause for thought; however, it gained very little traction at the time. The light would dawn later.

> These people to whom you have done no harm, come into your province to take your property with arms in their hands under a pretext of being your well-wishers, can you think, that these people who are without food and ammunition will allow you to enjoy peacefully the fruits of your labours, no; they will take your grain, your cattle and everything that you have (of which they have need) and they will pay you with notes (which they call Province Bills, or Bills of Credit); what will you do with such money? [N]othing.[33]

Senior Catholic clergymen were most proactive in their support of the Crown. When Bishop Briand heard that a parish priest who had been expounding the doctrine of obedience at mass had been shouted down by a habitant, he wrote for the offender's name and threatened, if it were not forthcoming, to pronounce an interdict on that parish and its neighbours. At Montreal Vicar-General Montgolfier declared that any persons who violated their oath of allegiance would be excluded from salvation; and be unworthy of receiving the sacraments; and, if killed in arms against the King, be refused a Christian burial.[34]

SIEGE OF FORT ST. JOHN'S

Meanwhile, the siege of Fort St. John's ground on. The rebels' many delays had allowed Preston's garrison to greatly strengthen the fort's works. What might have been a walkover a few months before had become a formidable task.

Most Natives had left the fort because of the rebels' threat to destroy Kahnawake, so Chevalier de Lorimier had only the support of the Akwesasne chief, Hotgouentagehte; the Kahnawake Tohams Tanannonsiagon; and four Confederacy Mohawks, one of whom was the Fort Hunter Castle's senior war captain, John Deserontyon, who would be a noteworthy partisan throughout the war.

With the besiegers were three significant Kahnawakes: the acculturated white captives Thomas Wellman and Philip Sanorese, and Louis Atayataghronghta. The New Hampshire colonel Timothy Bedel, a Seven Years' War veteran much respected by the Canada Indians, was Montgomery's Native liaison.

A month of dreary, damp, muddy life had passed for the fort's defenders. Preston had brought all of the garrison's women and children inside the walls, swelling the number of miserable people to thirteen hundred. Boredom was periodically relieved by the bateaux venturing onto the river to pull close to the rebel positions and deliver a close range bombardment. Even the *Royal Savage* slipped her moorings to indulge in some shelling, but her capability to manoeuvre in the close quarters of the river was limited. October 4 was noteworthy when Captain Monin and a fellow Canadien sortied out to drive in some cattle that had been grazing in local fields, which brought the garrison some welcome fresh meat and proved that the rebel cordon was either weak or very lax.

RECRUITING REBUFFED

At Quebec City loyalist spirits were raised on October 12 by the arrival of the sloop HMS *Hunter*, ten guns, but the situation in Montreal remained grim. With the governor's encouragement several prominent men in the district attempted to raise the militia at their seigneuries. La Corne Saint-Luc's young nephew went to Terrebonne to embody his habitants and was rebuffed with the argument that they had become subjects of England and were no longer Frenchmen required to perform mandatory service. The dialogue became heated and young La Corne answered his tormentors with blows, but he was roughly handled and went back to Montreal sore and empty-handed. He returned to the seigneury in the company of Captain Henry Hamilton,[35] a distinguished veteran officer who had been Carleton's brigade-major in 1767. The habitants said they would obey British officers, or even soldiers, rather than submit to their seigneur, whom they viewed as a "petit gars," an insignificant, raw youngster.[36] Hamilton was able to quiet the uproar, although the men still refused to turn out for service.

A visiting French officer attempted to raise his father's habitants at their Richelieu seigneury and was grossly insulted. When he rashly drew his sword he was disarmed and severely beaten. Hundreds of

Unattributed artist (Library and Archives Canada, C-018757).

Charles-Louis Tarieu de Lanaudière
— aide to Governor Carleton.

his father's habitants took up whatever arms came to hand and prepared to resist any force sent against them, but the governor decided
to be conciliatory. At Berthier a half-pay British officer who owned
the seigneury was similarly denied. At nearby St. Anne Carleton's
aide-de-camp, Charles-Louis de Lanaudière, recruited seventy of his
habitants, but when he marched them to Berthier a mob dispersed
his recruits and took him prisoner. He was released, but not before
they threatened to turn him over to the rebels. He joined Maclean
at Sorel, where Carleton had plans to have an entrenched camp
built, which had to be abandoned due to the locals' intransigence.[37]

THE WESTERN POSTS

In the midst of these disruptive events Captain Henry Hamilton
began his long journey to Detroit to assume the new role of district
lieutenant governor. Carleton had recognized the impossibility of
providing governance for his province's far western regions from
Quebec City and had appointed civil governors for the three important centres of Detroit, Vincennes, and Kaskaskia. The Vincennes
appointee apparently failed to take up his post, and Kaskaskia's did
not arrive until 1777; however, Hamilton was to immediately play a
significant role in the western war.

AVOIDING KILLING ENGLISHMEN

Despite the many problems, recruiting and volunteering in and
around Montreal and Sorel favoured the Crown and eleven hundred
militiamen were assembled. The rebels posted at Longueuil became
so worried about the governor's success that they had their boats
packed up for a quick retreat should the militia march, but Carleton
mysteriously failed to take the initiative. His reticence again confused
and angered many Canadiens, and rumours flew about that he was

avoiding killing Englishmen, for why else would he not march to raise the siege of Fort St. John's? Dispirited, many returned to their farms to begin plowing. The opportunity was frittered away.

Perhaps there was an underlying cause — Carleton had become embittered about the Canadiens; he referred to their "stupid baseness" and noted they shared the Natives' characteristic of being "easily dejected" and were apt to vanish at the least sign of a defeat. He worried about how he could dare to attack the rebels without a large body of Regulars.[38]

THE UGLY SIEGE

While rebel shelling produced remarkably few casualties inside Fort St. John's, it had a considerable effect on the morale of the garrison and followers. Preston noted in his journal on October 15 that the weather had become very cold and, because all the windows in the stone house were broken, a great many people stayed in the basement. Fetid air kept many others from following suit and they spent the nights on the upper floor braving the dangers and cold, or walking about outside.

The rebels had transferred heavier artillery pieces from Ticonderoga and built new batteries on the Richelieu's western shore. These not only nullified a previously easy entry for scouts and couriers, but directly threatened all of the Crown's vessels. Preston dispatched a row galley with a 24-pdr to challenge the enemy gunners, but it was driven back to its berth with some of its crew wounded. Lieutenant Hunter advised Preston that there was no possibility of the vessels staying out of range of the new batteries and recommended that they be hauled close ashore between the redoubts. He reasoned that if the rebels sunk them their stores and artillery could be saved and, when possible, the craft could be refloated. This recommendation was followed, but the *Royal Savage* was soon sunk to the depth of her gun ports before the ordnance could be removed.[39]

Fort Chambly Succumbs

On October 16 Brown, Livingston, and Duggan moved against Fort Chambly with three hundred men, including their Canadien recruits, and two 9-pdr guns that Duggan had managed to sneak past Fort St. John's in boats. The stone walls and bastions of the old French fort appeared imposing; however, it was not the fortress that was irresolute. When the rebels' solid shot penetrated the walls with their guns' first firing, the fort's commandant, Major Joseph Stopford, chose to surrender his garrison of seventy-six officers and men. By this stroke a substantial supply of guns, ammunition and provisions fell into the enemy's hands, all of which were badly needed in the siege lines at Fort St. John's. Bonus items of booty were the regimental colours of the 7th Fusiliers — the first stand taken by the Continental Army and a substantial propaganda victory.[40]

Detail from painting by Philip John Bainbrigge, 1838 (Library and Archives Canada, C-011856).

Scene of a British Army disgrace — the imposing stone fort at Chambly.

That same day at Berthierville and Verchères two senior militia officers, Louis-Joseph Godefroy de Tonnancour and Jean-Baptiste-Marie Blaise Des Bergères de Rigauville, were prevented by other Canadiens from assembling loyal militia to relieve Fort St. John's. Rigauville was so distressed he drank himself into a stupor and was taken by a party of American rebels.

The surrender of Chambly was a tonic for the failing spirits of the rebels surrounding Fort St. John's. The weary defenders were thoroughly dejected when they watched the members of Chambly's forlorn garrison boating south on the Richelieu on their way to captivity.

When the rebels erected yet another gun battery, a patrol led by Mackay and Monin sortied to determine its exact location and returned with the grim news that the opposition now numbered two thousand troops. The new battery gave the fort its worst shel-lacking of the siege and signalled the end was near.

INFUSING THE PRINCIPLES OF LIBERTY

In Quebec City, Attorney-General Francis Maseres,[41] an opponent of the Quebec Act, wrote an account of franco-Quebeckers' dissatisfaction. His observations touched directly on the governor's excessive trust in the noblesse.

> The ill effects of this new establishment have been felt almost as soon as it took place. For at that very instant the frontiers of the province were invaded by the king's enemies, and the Governour endeavoured to excite the inhabitants of it to take arms in its defence. But they were far from complying with his exhortations. For many of the parishes joined the rebels: and throughout the rest of the country

the inhabitants have, in general, refused to take arms for the government, and to defend, as they express it, a pack of rascally pensioners of the crown [the noblesse], and their damn'd French laws. For those, Sir, are the very words that they make use of. Add to this, that no persons have been employed to endeavour to raise them on this occasion but such as they hold in utter detestation.

Administration may now easily see (if they are not determined to remain in perpetual blindness and ignorance) what operates with the Canadians in this grand unhappy contest, and that it is not in the power of a Governour, a beggarly Noblesse, or their seigneurs, (whom they detest) nor in the power of their clergy with all their threats and interdictions (if you can suppose they preach the same in private, as they do in publick) to make the Canadians take up arms to shackle themselves in slavery. If we dared to apply to the Canadians for an union with us to petition the King for an amendment of the Quebeck bill, we should find the tradesmen, most of the merchants, and all the country-inhabitants, unanimous in our favour. But we are deemed, and (I do believe,) are represented by those persons who are the authors of all our misfortunes, to the Ministers of State to be worse than the Bostonian rebels, for infusing the principles of Liberty, (the birthright of every Briton), into our fellow subjects in Canada. For they must make somebody or other bear the blame of the behaviour of their faithful Canadians, as they used to call them, which has been so contrary to the false reports they had made, concerning their sentiments, to his Majesty's Ministers of State. And if the secret, wicked plots of these persons take place against us, many innocent persons must suffer on account of this defection of the Canadians, though the real causes of their behaviour, at this time, are these: First, a general cowardice; for they seem to have a horrid aversion to taking arms: secondly, a sharp remembrance of their former state of slavery; and a dreadful apprehension of returning into the same state, under their ancient laws and customs now confirmed to them; to which we must add, in the third place, that the canting Enthusiasts, who have come at different times from New England to preach Liberty and independence among them, have had more influence over their principles, (if you allow them to have any), in this unhappy contest, than all the Jesuits in France, before their expulsion from that Kingdom, could have had; and, lastly, the behaviour of their seigneurs towards them (for General Carleton would hardly employ any others to command them) increased their disobedience to government. This days post brings advice that a strong body of men was to have crossed over the river Saint Lawrence on Tuesday last, and that another body was to march up under the command of Colonel MacLeane, a very active officer: and that then both these bodies were to clear the country before them, join each other, and relieve the Fort of St. John's. This week must determine our fate, whether there be a probability to keep the country until we have a re-inforcement from England next Spring, or become subjected to the American colonists.[42]

Among the British high command in Boston there was some confusion about the purpose of Benedict Arnold's wilderness expedition and reinforcements were sent to Halifax for fear that he might turn toward Nova Scotia. When Carleton's request for assistance was received a battalion of Marines was alerted and transports were made ready by October 13, but the responsible admiral believed the navigation of the St. Lawrence would be too hazardous and stopped their movement.[43]

———————

The anglo-rebel Duggan persuaded a number of Canadien "adventurers and idlers" to dig trenches and raise breastworks around St. John's with a promise of good wages. They were kept hard at work with further promises of looting the fort when it fell. These opportunists were fully cognizant of the rebels' weaknesses and cunningly made sure not to commit any open hostilities against the Crown forces.[44]

DISASTER AT LONGUEUIL

With the failure of de Tonnancour and de Rigauville to raise militia to relieve St. John's, Carleton was finally prodded into action. He sent orders to Maclean at Quebec City to assemble all possible Emigrants, whatever Regulars he had at hand, and as many loyal militiamen as possible and march to Sorel. When he arrived there, he had a force of 120 Emigrants; sixty Regulars and, with Tonnancour's help, some four hundred Canadien militia. Captain François Chabot's armed schooner soon arrived with several bateaux filled with arms and ammunition.

Meanwhile, Carleton had called for Canadiens and Natives to join him on St. Helen's Island off Montreal. Because the rebels had persuaded the Kahnawakes to remain neutral — first by threats and then by a substantial cash bribe[45] — he decided not to approach them for assistance and was able to collect only about eighty Kanehsatake Mohawks. Nonetheless, he amassed a respectable force of 130 Regulars and Emigrants and eight hundred Canadien militiamen.

The Chevalier de Lorimier was appointed to command the Canadiens, and he assigned his brother, Verneuil, to command the warriors and some habitant friends. Orders had been expressed to Maclean at Sorel to march along the south shore toward Longueuil to catch the rebels in their eastern flank. The rebels were commanded by Vermont's Colonel Seth Warner, who had some three hundred men of his Vermont regiment and detachments of two New York regiments.

Carleton's men took to their boats to make the crossing. When the Chevalier de Lorimier had his craft organized for the assault, La Corne Saint-Luc made a grand gesture and passed across the front of the Canadien brigade standing in a canoe's prow and singing his war song. De Lorimier took this as a signal to commence the assault and ordered the boats forward.

The rebels were fully alert and engaged the boats with musketry and solid and canister shot from the guns captured at Chambly. Verneuil's warriors sped their canoes across the river, made a landing on the flank and dashed forward from sandbank to sandbank, rock to rock. The chevalier's boats were slower and, before their landing could be made, one of his men shouted that Carleton had already signalled a withdrawal. The Canadiens successfully executed the retirement, but a boatload of Regulars foundered and the men were taken.

Abandoned ashore on their own, the Natives were heavily engaged and made a fighting withdrawal, some to their canoes, others into the bush. The chevalier's great friend, the Akwesasne chief Hotgouentagehte, died of a bullet wound in the leg and two other Indians were killed. The next day, the rebels made prisoners of two stranded Indians and a pair of Canadiens.

The New York major, Henry Livingston, wrote in his journal that Carleton had been repulsed "with disgrace" and had kept his Regulars "farthest distant from the danger" during the whole action.[46] That such a small force of rebels was victorious over Carleton's thousand-man force was a clear sign of weakness that again shook the Canadiens.

When Maclean heard that Carleton had cancelled the attack, he turned about and marched back to Sorel.

FORT ST. JOHN'S FALLS

On November 1 General Montgomery sent one of the Canadiens captured at Longueuil into Fort St. John's to report to the garrison that Carleton's relief had been defeated. The fort fell two days later after fifty-five days of dogged resistance. In addition to the Regulars and Provincial Highlanders who went into the bag, there were ninety-one[47] Canadians, primarily francophone, and two Natives. The dogged valour of Preston's garrison and the ineptitude of the besiegers had greatly upset the invaders' timetable. Although the garrison's resistance reflected the highest honour on all ranks their loss was disastrous, as the haul included eighty percent of the Regulars in Quebec and almost all the trained artillery men. When the garrison marched out with the honours of war, drums beating, and colours flying, there were over 650 men at arms, including twenty-three wounded. Twenty men had died, over half of them Natives and Canadiens. Although Preston wrote derisively in his journal about his opponents' performance, the fact was, the fort had fallen.

ST. JOHN'S, ON THE RICHELIEU OR SOREL.

Engraver, Benson J. Lossing, Pictorial Fieldbook of the Revolution (New York: Harper Brothers, 1851).

St. John's on the Richelieu River or Sorel.

The disasters to British arms at Chambly, Longueuil, and now St. John's paralyzed militia recruitment and spread a spirit of detachment across the province.

JOHN PLATT'S REWARD FOR LOYALTY

John Platt, the New York loyalist who had independently dared to spy on the rebel army, returned to Saratoga in late October and found "that his home was pillag'd & Robb'd of every article by the Rebels, and his Wife & family obliged to fly ... in the utmost danger of their lives." It is unknown where he spent the following year, but when Burgoyne's army made its appearance in 1777 he once again left his family and joined as a Volunteer.[48]

5

THE REBELS LAY SIEGE TO QUEBEC CITY

The Worst of Banditti

GOOD FORTUNE AT QUEBEC CITY

Lieutenant Governor Cramahé enjoyed good fortune on October 28 when two of Colonel Benedict Arnold's letters were intercepted. These had been written fifteen days before when Arnold's force was 160 miles southeast of Quebec City. One message was addressed to a prominent city businessman informing him of the approach of two thousand men and asking whether their march was known of, and about Canadien attitudes, and the size of the garrison. The second was a progress report intended for General Schuyler. Cramahé had the merchant seized and stowed in a ship offshore, which resulted in great alarm among the commercial community, which sent a deputation to enquire about this shocking occurrence. The lieutenant governor put them off until the next day, when he brought the captains of militia together to inform them of the cause.

Greater efforts were now made to improve the fortifications, as Arnold would likely appear in a few days' time. Once again Cramahé was blessed with good fortune when, against all odds, the Emigrant's captains, Malcolm Fraser and Alex Campbell, arrived with ninety recruits in a schooner and sloop from Newfoundland and Ile Saint-Jean, followed the next day by a second ship from Newfoundland carrying a party of thirty-two artificers and carpenters. Then, yet another blessing — the frigate HMS *Lizard* appeared in the basin with a cargo of uniforms and accoutrements from England for six thousand men. While the crew and tenders unloaded this bounty the frigate's thirty-five-man Marine detachment was landed to add their martial skills to the city's defence.[1]

When word of Fort St. John's capitulation reached Governor Carleton, he realized he had no choice but to retire to Quebec City, as Montreal's fortifications were weak, his troops few, and local support insufficient. Adding to his anxiety was intelligence of Arnold's army advancing on Quebec City through the Chaudière River wilderness. Yet, despite the risks of delaying, Carleton strangely tarried, which gave the Chevalier de Lorimier the opportunity to wait on him. At first, the chevalier agreed to join in the retreat to Quebec City, but, after some thought, changed his mind and proposed to go into the upper province and live among the Natives, where he would gather a war party and await an opportunity to make a useful strike against the rebels. This plan was accepted.

Arnold Arrives at Quebec

Arnold's ragged, half-starved army arrived at Pointe-Lévy opposite Quebec City on November 8.[2] The colonel found a letter waiting for him from Montgomery with the news of the fall of Chambly and the imminent capture of St. John's. He immediately sent a dispatch to the general announcing his arrival and his plan to cross the river to attack the city.

Four days later Cramahé and all the royalists in the city were greatly heartened when Lieutenant-Colonel Maclean arrived from Sorel with two hundred Emigrants and Royal Fusiliers. Maclean immediately set about reorganizing his battalion into six companies and making preparations for drawing the clothing brought by the *Lizard*. Picket duty for that night was given to Captain John Nairne, who had joined the Emigrants upon Maclean's arrival, and Sir John Johnson's young brother-in-law, Lieutenant Stephen Watts, with a guard of two serjeants, two corporals, and fifty private men.[3]

Arnold discovered that all of the watercraft had been removed from the south shore; however, the arrival of forty birch canoes in the hands of friendly Indians (likely Bécancour and St. Francis Abenakis) provided a solution and, with their assistance, the crossing was made on the night of November 13. Arnold found that Canadiens on both sides of the river gave his men a warm reception, caring for his sick and providing provisions, which no doubt was reassuring.

In the meantime, Cramahé had taken further action by placing an embargo on all the shipping in the basin, so that their guns would provide additional firepower for the defence, and offering a £3 bounty to all commercial seamen willing to do military duty ashore. An accounting was made of the provisions in the city, the supply of firewood, the exact strength of the militia, and the number of the city's citizens.

Once Arnold's troops were across the river, the colonel set his headquarters in the Sainte-Foy manor house of Henry Caldwell, the colonel of the garrison's anglo-militia battalion. His troops occupied nearby farms, and, while the exhausted men slept, a British patrol nabbed a dozy sentry from Captain Daniel Morgan's rifle corps. When his loss was discovered shouts of alarm roused the rebels and they rushed to form up in expectation of a sortie from the city; however, none came. So Arnold marched his bedraggled host to the walls, where they stood under the curious eyes of "hundreds of gaping citizens and soldiers" who lined the parapet. The rebels then gave three resounding cheers, which were answered by canister shot from the city's artillery, which sent them scampering.[4]

Arnold boldly sent forward a truce party to demand the city's surrender, which was spurned by being fired upon. The next day his second truce party was received and delivered the usual demands and threats, but to no avail. Failing in these attempts, and recognizing he did not have sufficient strength to force the walls, Arnold withdrew upriver to await Montgomery's arrival. His men distributed copies of Washington's letter to the Canadians in which he had made the clever observation that the British imagined the Canadiens were incapable of recognizing the difference between slavery and freedom and, by their appeal to the vanity of the noblesse, that the people would be satisfied, which was precisely what a great many of them were inclined to believe.[5]

Within the city there was considerable distress among some elements. A town meeting was held to discuss how to proceed and some agitators went so far as to prepare articles of capitulation, which had the advantage of exposing likely rebel sympathizers.[6] Cramahé despaired when he found that neither militia battalion could be trusted on guard duty, so he employed a carrot-and-stick measure to improve performance. For the anglo-militia, he ordered eight men from each of the six companies to appear on parade without arms while being observed by an armed party of Marines. Each man was given a shilling and a pint of porter to encourage him in his duties. How much this affected the militias' performance is unknown, but certainly they would have recognized the not-so-subtle threat.[7]

CARLETON DEPARTS MONTREAL

On November 11 Carleton, with his remaining Regulars and the political prisoner Moses Hazen, embarked in three armed ships and some smaller craft at Montreal and set sail for Quebec City; however, one of the ships ran aground, and the small fleet had to halt to refloat her. Soon after that was accomplished, the wind fell and the vessels were forced to anchor not far from Sorel. They were still becalmed there on the fifteenth when a flag of truce appeared with a demand that the troops and fleet surrender. Carleton was affronted. Major John Brown then made an appearance and threatened to blow the fleet out of the water with a battery of 32-pdrs that he had just emplaced at Sorel. He stated that guns had been mounted on the north shore at Berthier and on a floating battery in the river. The governor held a council of war which decided it was vital for him to get to Quebec City. Jean-Baptiste Bouchette, a well-known, skillful mariner, volunteered to conduct the governor downriver in a whaleboat. The governor instructed Brigadier Prescott, who was to be left behind with the ships and troops, to destroy all useful arms and supplies if he found surrender his only option. Then, in the dead of night, Carleton went over the ship's side into Bouchette's boat disguised in a toque and a capote cinched with a ceinture fléchée.

With Bouchette navigating, the whaler was propelled with muffled oars and, when near Sorel, the oars were shipped and the crew and passengers paddled with their hands in the frigid water, slipping silently past the rebel sentries. On the afternoon of November 17 Carleton, his faithful aide Charles-Louis de Lanaudière, and the distinguished sexagenarian veteran Chevalier Joseph Boucher de Niverville,[8] went ashore at Trois-Rivières, where de Tonnancour advised the governor that he was still not safe, as there were rebels between the town and Quebec City. The governor could scarcely credit this intelligence, but, leaving Niverville in Trois-Rivières, he once again placed himself and Lanaudière in the hands of Bouchette, who continued downriver and soon had him aboard the snow *Fell*. The vessel made landfall at the city on the nineteenth "to the unspeakable joy of the garrison," who feared he had been lost. Carleton recognized it was Bouchette's skill and nerve that had saved him from capture, and he rewarded the mariner with command of a militia artillery company during the siege, and, afterwards, of an armed sloop.[9]

In Carleton's dispatch to London he complimented Cramahé's efforts, stating, "everything has been done in my absence for the Defence of this Place." Despite Carleton's praise, Captain Thomas Ainslie of the British militia thought that Cramahé had been "weak and diffident," which likely reflected the captain's more bellicose, intemperate nature. Lieutenant-Colonel Maclean assumed military command of the garrison and immediately suppressed all talk of negotiation or surrender, while Carleton concentrated on political affairs. A rebel officer wrote of Maclean's activities, "This Villain has worked up the People against us, by representing us as the worst of Banditti…. This has caused the People to resist"; however, it took very little to persuade the merchants of what would occur if the starving, disease-ridden rebels got loose in the city.[10]

The Emigrants' regimental orders betrayed considerable frustration among the officers. It appears that the rank and file were selling or trading their necessaries for drink. A general inspection of same was ordered to be held every Monday and Thursday, as many of the "Soldiers [were] such Compleat Scoundrels, that the Capts. must be all ruind if Every man found Guilty of making away with his Necessary's is Not Severly Punish'd."[11]

After being informed there were traitors among the citizens, Carleton had a proclamation posted on November 22 stating that any male refusing to join the militia must leave the city and environs with his family within the week. After December 1, those not on militia rolls would be treated as rebels and spies. About 170 men left, among them two migrants from the lower colonies — Edward Antill, a New Jersey lawyer, and Udney Hay, a Poughkeepsie merchant. Both were to become significant officers in the rebel army.[12]

The Canadien militia now numbered 533 and included a company of young students and less active men, which guarded prisoners and performed other useful duties. In addition, the Navy's bluejackets and the merchant seamen provided a force of 450 men. James Thompson,

Detail from a watercolour by Millicent Mary Chaplin (Library and Archives Canada, C-000856).

St. Roch Faubourg and River St. Charles from St. John's Gate.

a former serjeant in Fraser's Highlanders, had the direction of 120 artificers and was prominent in improving the fortifications protecting the land approaches to the city's Lower Town.[13]

On December 5 the rebel Canadian Jeremiah Duggan and his men disarmed the inhabitants of the St. Roch suburb, which lay outside the city walls.[14]

POLTROONERY AT LONGUEUIL

As to the ships and troops that remained behind off Longueuil, the whole was disgracefully surrendered by Brigadier Prescott, including the vessel captained by William Friend, whose Lake George property had been earlier looted by Allen and whose sloop *George* had been taken by Arnold at Fort St. John's.[15] It was shaping up to be a nasty war for Mr. Friend. The political prisoner, Moses Hazen, was freed, and the course of his career for the balance of the war was sealed.

Prescott had failed to take the precaution of destroying the guns, small arms, and supplies of provisions, let alone scuttle the vessels, despite Carleton's specific instructions. Fortunately, ship's captain François Bellet[16] denied the rebels a complete victory by throwing the powder overboard.

Montgomery — the former British officer — crowed to his wife in a letter, "The other day General Prescott was so obliging as to surrender himself and fourteen or fifteen land officers, with above one hundred men, besides sea officers and sailors, prisoners of war! I blushed for His Majesty's troops! [S]uch an instance of base poltroonery I have never met with."[17]

MONTREAL OCCUPIED

Montreal Island was the thriving centre of the fur trade and the merchants' warehouses were packed with peltry and trading supplies. Recognizing they had everything to lose, the traders knew they must come to an accommodation with the invaders. A body of citizens of all political stripes met with the Montrealer Jacob Price, who was serving as Montgomery's advisor, banker, and later his engineer, and drew up terms of capitulation. Montgomery, who had occupied Ile des Soeurs and landed troops below the town, had the whip hand and need not have paid any attention to this business; however, he chose to be magnanimous and bring the citizens "liberty and security." The fur merchant François Cazeau came to the fore again by supplying the rebels' troops and sheltering some of their officers, and busying himself distributing new messages from Congress. Joseph Bindon once again revealed his true colours and warmly welcomed the invaders.

Montgomery did not linger in Montreal for long, as he recognized the British were not truly defeated until the fortress of Quebec was in his hands. Leaving General David Wooster, a Connecticut veteran of the old wars, in command of Montreal with five hundred troops, he sailed downriver with three hundred men in the vessels of the captured fleet and occupied Trois-Rivières. While there, he gave James Livingston a colonel's commission to raise a regiment of Canadians for Congress, and placed orders for iron guns and solid

Oil painting by Henry Richard S. Bunnett, 1885 (© McCord Museum M405).

Montgomery's Montreal headquarters.

shot with Christophe Pélissier, the foundry manager of Les Forges du Saint-Maurice, Quebec's principal manufacturer. Loyalists, such as the Chevalier de Niverville, were disarmed, but otherwise ignored. Setting sail again, he joined Arnold at Pointe-aux-Trembles. Their combined army numbered about a thousand rebel Americans and two hundred Canadien volunteers.[18]

Montgomery wrote Schuyler on December 5, advising that he had arrived at Point-aux-Trembles "with the vessels Mr. Prescott made us a present of." As Quebec's works were so extensive, he was confident the city could not be defended. He was greatly impressed by Arnold's corps, which he thought was "an exceeding fine one, inured to fatigue.... There is a style of discipline among them much superior to what I have been used to see this campaign," and, of Arnold himself, he was described as "active, intelligent and enterprising." As to the defending garrison, it was composed of the unlikely combination of

"Maclean's banditti" and various sailors, and citizens who were obligated to take up arms. He would amuse Carleton by erecting batteries, but his real intention was to mount an assault into the Lower Town. He had issued Arnold's and his own men "with a year's clothing of the 7th and 26th" regiments, which had fallen into his hands.[19]

Carleton's Resolve Stiffens

Governor Carleton's narrow, perilous escape from Montreal had shaken him awake and stiffened his resolve, and he adopted a purposeful, tenacious manner, which was exactly what the city and garrison required.

One of General Montgomery's first actions was to send a summons to the governor brimming with bluff, bluster, threat, and insult, which seemed quite out of character for the man and perhaps reflected rash confidence, or Arnold's influence. Having been apprised of Carleton's earlier refusals he sent his missive in the hands of an elderly woman, but again there was no reaction. Montgomery had no idea that Carleton had arranged for the letter to be burned, unread. In addition messages were directed to the citizenry, replete with lurid descriptions of carnage and destruction. These were wrapped around arrows and lofted over the walls, again to no obvious effect. In these various missives the rebels did little to assist their cause; they insultingly described the garrison as motley; the Emigrants, miserable; the works, wretched; and, finally, they threatened to plunder the city. On the twentieth, Lieutenant Patrick Daly of the Emigrants noted in his journal that Montgomery had told his men he would dine in the city on Christmas day, or in hell.[20]

In Montreal, Wooster attempted to raise Canadien volunteers to reinforce Montgomery by distributing three hundred copies of Washington's letter, but response was poor. Resentment was building to the occupation, the paper money and promissory notes, the frequent commandeering of various supplies made worse by the excesses of the ill-disciplined soldiery. Having been released from confinement the anglo-rebel Thomas Walker exerted himself to raise men, but even his francophone friends demurred.[21]

REBEL ARTILLERY AND RIFLEMEN AT QUEBEC

The rebels had captured a substantial train of medium artillery at Chambly, St. John's, Longueuil, and Montreal and were able to erect several batteries overlooking Quebec City, but their guns no sooner opened fire than the garrison's heavier pieces dislodged them. On December 10 they set up a mortar battery hidden behind houses in the St. Roch suburb, but its shells were too small to be effective. Despite these disappointments Morgan's riflemen made bloody work by sniping any sentry or curious individual who showed a head above the ramparts. This "American way of making war" disgusted many in the garrison. Captain Ainslie of the British militia noted, "they are worse than Savages, they will ever be held in contempt with men of courage. Lie in wait to shoot a sentry! A deed worthy of Yanky men of war."[22] Indeed, this was war in America and far worse was yet to come.

The besiegers worked diligently to build five hundred scaling ladders, but their attempt to use them was foiled by a heavy snowfall, much to the merriment of the defenders.[23]

THE REBEL ASSAULT

The besiegers were greatly weakened by the onset of relentlessly frigid weather overlaid with the horrors of a smallpox outbreak, yet Montgomery and Arnold remained resolute. On December 22 Joshua Wolf, Colonel Caldwell's servant, attempted to retrieve something of importance from the ruins of his employer's manor

house. He returned to the city with a rebel deserter and the intelligence that an attack would be made the next night. The following
day, a second deserter brought news that the assault had been
postponed because of the escape of the first two; nonetheless, the
garrison remained on high alert, as it was clear an action would
occur soon. Every man had his post in case of attack and, when off
duty, slept near his arms. Both the anglo- and franco-militia were
said to be brimming with zeal.

Tension inside the city was high. Emigrants coming off duty
had been accustomed to unload their firelocks by discharging in

Four attacks on Quebec, New Year's Eve, 1775 — Arnold's and Montgomery's
thrusts into the Lower Town and Livingston's and Brown's feints against the
St. John's Gate and the Citadel.

the streets, but, with an attack being imminent, this practice was considered too alarming and orders were issued that an officer was to take any men needing to unload to the riverside or the ramparts between the hours of eleven and one only, and have them fire at a mark, thus gaining an extra benefit from the procedure.[24]

Christmas dinner came and went and, despite Montgomery's prediction, he was still not in the city. An officers' council was held to discuss how to proceed, and there was much to and fro about how and where to assault the walls. It was decided to wait for the promised delivery of bayonets, axes, and hand grenades to come downriver.

When Montgomery's chief engineer, Edward Antill, and his assistant, James Price, arrived from Montreal, they recommended striking into the Lower Town, a concept already in the general's thoughts. They theorized that the merchants would be so distraught over the danger to their warehouses and inventories that they would force Carleton to capitulate. This was a risky strategy, as the Lower Town was entirely dominated by the heights above and the rebels had little idea of the strength of the defences they would need to overcome; however, the two anglo-Quebeckers were persuasive and Montgomery agreed. Poor weather caused continual postponements and the general became extremely worried because the smallpox continued to spread. As well, the terms of service of a significant number of his New England troops would expire on New Year's Eve and they were adamant they would stay no longer.

A two-pronged night assault was planned. Montgomery would lead one branch along the St. Lawrence shore under the steep cliffs of Cape Diamond and into the Lower Town. Arnold would lead the other through the St. Roch suburb and along the St. Charles River shore into the other end of the Lower Town. Two diversionary attacks would begin the dance — one against St. John's Gate by Livingston's 160 Canadiens[25] and the second against the citadel's bastion by Major John Brown's Massachusetts detachment of odds and sods. An elaborate signal system of lanterns, fires, and rockets was contrived to coordinate the effort. It was these pyrotechnics that would alert the garrison.

———————

At about five o'clock in the morning of New Year's Eve, Emigrants' captain Malcolm Fraser, the main guard duty officer, observed several lights flashing. When he spotted an arcing pair of rockets, he was convinced something was afoot and raised the alarm. Musketry suddenly erupted outside St. John's Gate and the Cape Diamond bastion and shells began to fall into the city. He ran down St. Louis Street shouting so loudly for the guards to turn out that even Carleton was alerted in his quarters in the Recollects' convent.[26]

Now the cathedral's great bell rang out the general alarm, joined by all those of the other churches, and duty drummers beat to arms. Daly noted that "the morning was so boisterous and snowy that at some of our Posts neither bell nor drums were heard, but they were sufficiently alarmed by the flashes as the enemy began firing."[27]

Maclean requested that Colonel Caldwell take a detachment of his anglo-militia to Cape Diamond to investigate the firing. If it proved to be a diversion he was to leave a party there and return immediately. Caldwell complied and returned by way of the St. Louis Gate. He was then sent to reinforce the Lower Town, which he approached via the rear of the Hotel-Dieu, where he encountered the field officer of the day and received his permission to take Captain Nairne and his detachment of Emigrants.

———————

The temperature had plummeted and a driving snow fell as Montgomery's eight-hundred-man column of New Yorkers and a handful of rebel Indians under Louis Atayataghronghta forced their way through deep drifts. The St. Lawrence shore was choked with randomly strewn slabs of ice thrown up by the tide that narrowed the column's head to four or five abreast. With the general in the lead, the column stopped twice to wait for pioneers to saw down pickets. After stepping through the second gap, the leaders halted only fifty yards from the Près de Ville barrier, which protected entry into the Lower Town. Montgomery gave an encouraging shout and strode forward into the path of a discharge of canister rounds from a four-gun battery. These explosions were followed by shrieks and groans, in turn smothered by flashing musketry from the upper level of a house fired by thirty-five Canadiens commanded by Captain Joseph Chabot and Lieutenant Alexandre Picard. Their fire drove off the rest of the column, which abandoned a dozen corpses staining the snow. This decisive repulse was followed by panic at the barrier when an elderly woman cried into the deafening silence that rebels had forced the barricades at the Sault-au-Matelot, but order was quickly restored.

The battery had been manned by an artillery serjeant; a merchant sea captain, fifteen sailors, and a volunteer named John Coffin — Carleton's motley crew had blunted the attack.[28]

Arnold's division of about 650 New Englanders and Captain Morgan's Pennsylvania and Virginia riflemen formed up in the St. Roch suburb. John Henry, a Pennsylvania Continental, recalled that "the storm was outrageous, and the cold wind extremely biting. In this northern country the snow is blown horizontally into the faces of travelers."[29] The attackers moved forward resolutely at four in the morning against the background of the muffled firing of the diversionary attacks against the western gate and bastion. When the sentinels spotted their column from above they threw down fireballs as illumination and musketry played along their column's length. Arnold fell with a wounded leg and command devolved upon Morgan. Arnold withdrew, dragging his leg through the snow for nearly a mile to a hospital while under continual fire from the walls. At times the marksmen were at no greater distance than fifty yards and several of his attendants were shot down at his side.[30]

Clipart.

Captain Daniel Morgan, famous leader of riflemen.

When Caldwell arrived at the Sault-au-Matelot's second barrier, he found the Canadien militiamen were hesitant to step forward; however, the arrival of the anglo-militia with Nairne's thirty Emigrants and fifty bluejackets energized them. Assisted by Colonel Noël Voyer, Caldwell strongly posted the barrier and its environs, placing marksmen in the houses commanding the street. A detachment of Royal Fusiliers was set behind the barrier with fixed bayonets.[31]

There are conflicting versions of the rebels' taking of the Sault-au-Matelot's first barrier; some claimed the sentries had been in liquor, others that there was a brief, intense firefight.[32] Whatever the case, Morgan's troops poured over the obstruction and crowded into the narrow, house-lined street where they seized some seminary students who were on their way to reinforce the second barrier, and presumably pushed them to the rear. That done, the attackers began to advance the two hundred yards to the second obstacle; however, Colonel Voyer's Canadiens and a detail of 7th Fusiliers were fully alert and discharged cannon and musket fire into the packed throng. At the same time another Canadien party opened fire from a house's windows. The rebels were clothed in British uniforms taken at Chambly and St. John, and to prevent a close quarters' recognition problem had stuck identifying signs in their hats, but there was no doubt — those in the street below were invaders.[33]

James Pattison Cockburn, 1830 (Library and Archives Canada C-040038).

The Continentals' view looking down the Sault-au-Matelot with the Upper Town's fortifications looming above.

Some intrepid souls advanced right up to the barrier and placed a scaling ladder against it, but Charles Charland, a bold, quick-thinking Canadien giant, pulled it up while a swarm of rebel balls buzzed around him. Caldwell saw that other rebels had gone into an adjacent house that commanded the rear of the barricade. He had the ladder propped against the gable end and Nairne's lieutenant, François Dambourgès, instantly climbed up, broke in the window with his fusil butt, and pushed inside. By the time that Nairne and his Highlanders scrambled up, they found Dambourgès surrounded by rebels, whom they drove out at bayonet point.[34]

Nairne later wrote to his sister:

> It was the first time I ever happened to be so closely engaged, as we were obliged to push our bayonets. It is certainly a disagreeable necessity to be obliged to put one another to death, especially those speaking the same language and dressed in the same manner with ourselves.... These mad people had a large piece

Seigneurs, 1908.
Right: Unattributed engraving from A Bard of Wolfe's Army, *James Thompson, Gentleman Volunteer, 1733–1830.*

Left: Lieutenant François Dambourgès, RHE.
Right: Captain John Nairne, RHE.

of white linen or paper upon their foreheads with the words "Liberty or Death" wrote upon it.[35]

The fighting continued in driving snow in the street and houses with the flash of guns and musketry and the crack of hand grenades. From occupied houses the rebels exchanged fire with the defenders in the Sault-au-Matelot from the front windows and out the back onto the adjacent street and wharf. Caldwell had a narrow escape just at daybreak when he went to reconnoitre the wharf area and was suddenly challenged, "Who is there?" Thinking the challenger was one of Nairne's men, he replied, "A friend — who are you?" to which came the response, "Captain Morgan's company." Thinking quickly, he assured them they would soon be in the town, then ducked behind a pile of boards and made his way off.[36]

Meanwhile, Carleton had dispatched a large detachment of Emigrants from the Palace Gate under Captains George Lawe and Alexander Fraser to cut off the rebels' rear.[37] They were joined by a party of bluejackets from the *Lizard* led by a sea captain. When the Provincials and sailors entered St. Roch, they collided with rebel major Henry Dearborn's[38] company, which had missed Arnold's rendezvous. After some skirmishing in and about the houses, Dearborn's men were routed and fled. Lawe detached a party to burn down the St. Roch houses that were giving cover to the rebels' battery and to bring off their cohorn mortars, while the main party continued round to the Sault-au-Matelot. Impulsively, Lawe got too far ahead of his men, rushed over the first barrier, and was

John Nairne's Highland dirk.

captured. Captain John Nairne rushed to his aid and killed a rebel who was threatening him and captured some others.[39]

Caldwell had manoeuvred a 9-pdr gun onto the wharf behind the rebel-occupied houses and its first discharge killed one and wounded another. Within the rebels' hearing, Caldwell called out to Nairne to let him know when he heard firing on his side. The rebels realized they were surrounded and many threw down their arms and capitulated, while others, primarily Canadiens and Natives, risked their lives by escaping over the treacherous St. Charles ice.

Captain Morgan, who had received a vicious, humiliating flogging from British officers during the Seven Years' War, refused to surrender until he spotted a Canadien priest to whom he gave his sword. A total of 426 prisoners were taken and another hundred were killed or wounded.[40]

THE CONTINENTAL ARMY'S FIRST DEFEAT

The Continental Army had suffered its first thorough defeat. Their commanding general was dead; their second-in-command, badly wounded; and two majors and one of their most promising captains and seven others of that rank were captive. To contemplate taking the city was now impossible, at least until major reinforcements arrived.

Captain Ainslie wrote in his journal, "Every power of Col: McLean was exerted on this occasion, he had his eye every where to prevent the progress of the attackers; his activity gave life to all who saw him…. The Canadian militia shew'd no kind of backwardness." Such a compliment from an anglo-militia officer![41]

MONTGOMERY'S CORPSE

On New Year's Day a party went to investigate the bodies buried in the snow at Près-de-Ville. A single arm rose out of a bank and indicated where the corpses lay. A young drummer uncovered a sword nearby, and James Thompson persuaded him to surrender the trophy, for which he later paid the youngster a small finder's fee. Thompson believed the sword belonged to General Montgomery, which was confirmed when his body was identified by Mrs. Prentice, whose husband Miles, the city's provost marshal, kept a tavern often visited by him during his business trips and used at the time as Maclean's orderly room. Carleton instructed Thompson to have Montgomery decently buried in a private manner.[42]

General Orders recorded on New Year's Day in Captain Fraser's Orderly Book indicated the governor's satisfaction with the garrison.

> His Excellencey Generl. Carleton Returns his Thanks, to the officers and Men, of the Garrison for There Gallont and Sperrited Beheaver yesterday. The Generl. Was perticklerly Plesed, to See the alertness and Sobertriety of the Different Corps, Which Greatly Contributed to the Suctsess of the Day, — he Makes know Doupt, but they Will Persevere in a Conduct Which Redounds so much to there honour and Suckiterety [security], and Which is so Benificl to the Kings Servis. [A] Return of the Kiled and Wounded, to be given in to Morrow in the several Corps to the Bridge. Majr. [brigade-major] at orderly Time. The armes and accoutments taking from the Ribbils to be Giving in to Mr. Ramsay.

Lieutenant-Colonel Maclean later offered a tribute to Volunteer John Coffin, who had served at the Près-de-Ville barrier.

> To your resolution and watchfulness … in keeping the guard at the Pres-de-Ville under arms, waiting for the attack which you expected; the great coolness with which you allowed the rebels to approach; the

spirit which your example kept up among the men, and the very critical instant in which you directed Capt. Barnsfare's fire against Montgomery and this troops, — to those circumstances alone do I ascribe the repulsing the rebels from that important post.[43]

The rebels' first reaction to their shattering defeat was to tell the locals that the garrison had lost six hundred men during the assault against a mere fifteen of their own. They claimed they were in possession of the Lower Town, which resulted in a mob of Canadien opportunists congregating in St. Roch, expecting to share in the loot Montgomery had promised. When Carleton's aide, Charles-Louis de Lanaudière, left the city to collect the baggage of the rebels' commissioned prisoners, he saw this collection of "canaille" and became worried that he might be seized, and turned back. After the mob spent the night waiting for permission to enter the Lower Town, the truth became evident and word of the rebels' defeat spread far and wide.[44]

ALLOWING THE SIEGE TO WITHER

Carleton fell back on his earlier pattern of caution and chose not to take the initiative. It was obvious to the garrison that a sally from the city could overwhelm the besiegers, who were sick with disease, undersupplied, and faint of heart, but the governor remained behind the walls where his men had the advantages of secure supplies and relatively good health. Clearly, he intended to allow the siege to wither and fail.

Some historians laud Carleton for his prudence, while others criticize him severely for his lack of action at a moment when he could have sent the rebels packing and relieved the countryside from the weight of the occupation. Yet others say that he held hopes of negotiating with the rebels and did not want to humiliate them. Likely, a blend of all these considerations was at play.

Questionable Recruits

Seven days into the New Year ninety-four rebel prisoners, primarily of Irish extraction, volunteered to serve in the Highland Emigrants. After being counselled to consider their decision with great care, they took the oath of allegiance to the King. Many in the garrison were unimpressed by this supposed conversion and laid wagers that most would run at the first opportunity. The first three desertions came late in the month and were soon followed by several more, until Carleton put a stop to the leakage in mid-February by incarcerating the remaining eighty-four in a ship's hold in the harbour. These events would have future repercussions for the regiment.[45]

There were several days of brutal winter weather and parties were dispatched to bring in firewood under the cover of a 3-pdr gun, or alternatively, a 6-pdr on a sleigh. By mid-January, intelligence was received that two hundred rebels had deserted since the failed assaults.[46]

RELIEF ARRIVES

Congress had deceiv'd them

ENEMIES TO LIBERTY IN MONTREAL

Montreal's rebel commandant, General David Wooster, was concerned that intelligence would get passed to the British garrisons at Oswegatchie and Niagara and result in an attack in his rear. To prevent this he proscribed all communications with the upper country, a restriction that greatly interfered with the trade upon which so many of the city's businessmen relied.

Wooster was a rigid New England Protestant, so, in anticipation of possible problems, his superiors had instructed him to avoid any conflict with Roman Catholics. Yet, the clergy's open support of the Crown led him to threaten deportation of some of the more virulent priests to the lower colonies, which precipitated a major uproar. In retaliation for their obstinacy he closed the churches on Christmas Eve, which was a great affront to all Catholics, both practising and nominal.[1]

By early January Wooster had prepared a list of sixty-four inveterate loyalists. He arrested twelve, principally Canadiens — among them the notary Simon Sanguinet and his two brothers — again with the intention of deportation. When citizens of all stripes protested vigorously he released the prisoners, but, to offset this policy defeat, he had the militia officers post a threatening notice on parish church doors. It read, in part:

New York Public Library Digital Gallery, Record 831339.

MAJ. GEN. DAVID WOOSTER.

David Wooster, the Protestant extremist.

> Any citizen or other inhabitant of Canada ... prejudicing the interest of Congress or the progress of our arms, whether by injurious speech, seduction of loyal subjects, or protection of deserters, as well as any person suspected of furnishing food and maintaining or promoting communication with the city of Quebec, likewise any person guilty of disobeying officers created by us, will be declared by us enemies of liberty and traitors to their country, and as such will be severely punished, imprisoned and even transported from the province if such action be necessary.[2]

By mid-January, three Montreal suburbs were wavering in their support of the rebellion and Wooster had their citizens disarmed. When they were ordered to turn over two suspected loyalists as hostages for their future behaviour they refused, which signalled a growing resistance to the occupation.

Moses Hazen was unimpressed by Wooster's methods and commented that the Montreal district's habitants were "waiting an opportunity to join our enemies," and that the "better sort of people ... would wish to see our throats cut, and perhaps would readily assist in doing it."[3]

Although Congress had recognized Arnold's services by promoting him to brigadier-general on January 10, he was dispirited with the failure to take the city and the loss of "his truly great and good friend," Richard Montgomery.[4] Added to his despair was the pain caused by a fall from his horse. He notified the army of his intention to step down as deputy commander, but his officers would hear none of it.

Wooster had assumed command of Congress's army in Canada after Montgomery's death, and Arnold sent his adjutant, the anglo-Quebecker Edward Antill, to appeal to him for reinforcements, mortars, howitzers, and shells. The general told Antill he was unable to spare any men from his small garrison, so the adjutant decided to seek help in the south and set off on a gruelling trip down the ice of the Richelieu and Lake Champlain to Albany. He found Schuyler

Painting by A. Panet, 18th Century (© McCord Museum MP-1988.40).

Edward Antill, Montgomery's anglo-Canadian chief engineer.

and the town trembling in fear over Sir John Johnson's seven hundred armed Highlanders, which the baronet had raised from among his Mohawk Valley tenants. Undismayed, Antill plunged on to Philadelphia with the news of the disaster at Quebec and the need for more troops. Although the congressmen were genuinely concerned, it took months before a flood of reinforcements moved north.

In fact, Congress persisted in the belief that the Canadiens would support their cause and on January 24 — probably as the result of Antill's urgings — Moses Hazen was given a beating order to raise a second Canadien regiment as its colonel, with Antill as lieutenant-colonel.[5]

EBENEZER JESSUP TAKES ACTION

That January, Ebenezer Jessup, an influential, wealthy land speculator from the upper Hudson River, applied to New York's royal governor, William Tryon, "for Permission to Raise Men to bear arms in support of His Majesty's Government in America." Approval was granted and the Jessup brothers and their close associates began to secretly recruit.[6]

TORIES — ENEMIES TO THEIR COUNTRY

Recognizing that many loyalists were conspiring against the rebellion, the Albany County Committee of Correspondence resolved on March 6 that, "[W]hoever shall act in opposition to the Resolves of the Continental Congress or shall endeavour to obtain redress of Grievances by means not warranted by the said Resolves shall be deemed Violators of the Association and an Enemy to his Country."[7]

Under the committees' orders the militia had the duty to apprehend those against whom a complaint had been entered. Schenectady historian Willis Hanson notes that:

These complaints and subsequent arrests were incited by a variety of causes: aiding the enemy in any way; associating or corresponding with Tories; refusing to sign the Association or violating its provisions; denouncing or refusing to obey congresses and committees; writing or speaking against the American cause; rejecting Continental money or drinking the King's health, and even mere suspicion was not infrequently deemed sufficient to justify a man's seizure.[8]

CLEVER PLOYS

Without reinforcements from Montreal, Arnold realized he would have to rely on Canadien recruitment and cleverly co-opted a rogue Catholic clergyman, the Abbé Louis de Lotbinière, to act as his chaplain to swear in his new troops. This was of some help in settling the wavering confidence of his Canadiens.

Hazen had a similar inspiration while he was recruiting in Montreal in competition with James Livingston and enlisted the Jesuit Pierre-René Floquet, a clergyman who had earlier been persuaded to the cause by Montgomery. Even so, Hazen suffered forty percent desertions in one of his companies. In his opinion the Canadiens' disaffection to the cause was in part prompted by the bad behaviour of the rebel troops.[9]

By late month a few men arrived in Quebec City from Montreal and a trickle more from the lower colonies, but Arnold made no further attempt on the city.

MASSACRE THEIR COMPATRIOTS

In fact, the only combat that occurred was between Canadiens when the Sieur Liénard de Beaujeu,[10] a former Metropolitan Regular officer and "partisan of tried fidelity," raised a loyalist detachment of 106 men from the St. Lawrence parishes below Quebec City at Carleton's request. De Beaujeu marched on March 23, intending to surprise the rebel post at Pointe-Lévy, but was delayed by bad weather. A second detachment of sixty-six men joined him on the twenty-fifth, and he sent a vanguard ahead, which arrived at Captain Michel Blais's house in Saint-Pierre-de-la-Rivière-du-Sud and hoisted a Grand Union flag.

The rebels had been warned of this threat two days before, and Arnold had dispatched 150 men with artillery under Major John Dubois, who was joined by 150 Canadiens recruited by Pierre Hayot from the Saint-Pierre area. This force surprised Beaujeu's men at Blais's house and poured musketry and cannon fire into the building, killing three loyalists and wounding several others before the party surrendered. De Beaujeu was forced to go into hiding after this confrontation. Quebec historian Lanctot writes,

> Thirty-eight were taken and only a few escaped. Men from the same parish found themselves in rival camps, and families were divided, with sons on one side and fathers on the other. In their rage ... the furious pro-rebels might have made good their threat to massacre their compatriots, but fortunately the Americans intervened to avert any such disaster.... Some of the loyalist prisoners were released, but twenty-one were sent to the camp at Quebec under Canadian guards who treated them roughly and jeered at their misfortune.[11]

By March 30 Arnold's army had grown to 2,850, although 790 were unfit for service, primarily due to smallpox. The weight of metal his artillery could throw continued to be insufficient and, without competent engineers, he despaired of ever mounting an effective bombardment. Although Livingston and Hazen had recruited almost five hundred Canadiens, they worried that their men would turn against them if the populace did so openly.[12]

RELIEF ARRIVES | 127

MONTREAL'S MERCHANTS TAKE ACTION

In early February several of Montreal's merchants reacted to Wooster's embargo on the western trade by sending the city's first, and only, petition to Congress to request the reopening of communications,[13] which resulted in the rebel administration issuing special permits to those traders they decided were trustworthy.

Understandably, the Chevalier de Lorimier had behaved cautiously while he remained in the city, as his role in the province's defence was widely known; however, he was emboldened when Wooster, who knew his family from old, sent assurances that he would not be sent captive into the colonies. Reassured, de Lorimier decided to attend an assembly of the town's affluent citizens hosted by Price and another businessman and, when the pair urged the captains of militia to surrender their Crown commissions and accept new ones from Congress, the chevalier protested:

> Listen, brave citizens! I too was conquered by the British, and I still hold two commissions from the King of France, but the British government never bothered me to surrender them. I never had the honour of receiving one from King George, but if I did have one, not one of these lousy Americans would ever lay a hand on it!

After this rash outburst he went into hiding, convinced that he would be arrested and sent south. Employing his celebrated charm, he persuaded an acquaintance, Louise Schuyler, a relative of the rebel general, to help him escape the city limits. With her assistance, and after a few adventures, he and two fellow loyal Montrealers, Richard Walker and James Stanley Goddard — the latter a western fur-trading merchant who had been Sir William Johnson's Inspector of Native stores — arrived at Akwesasne, where de Lorimier's friend Francis Thehonahogen provided assistance. Two and half days later the fugitives were at Oswegatchie where they met with Captain George Forster, 8th Regiment, whose Light Infantry company composed the garrison. De Lorimier proposed a plan to destroy a rebel flotilla or, alternately, an action against Montreal. Forster was intrigued, but it was March, and he said he could not act until navigation on the river opened. The captain provided de Lorimier and a Native companion with a supply of powder and ball and they left for the upper country to raise a Native war party. For his part, Goddard began the long, long trek to Fort Niagara where he hoped to persuade Lieutenant-Colonel John Caldwell to support Forster's strike into lower Quebec.[14]

Congress's Commission

Congress had never abandoned its belief in the importance of converting Canada to the cause. The declining fortunes of their army raised substantial alarm and led to the creation of a political commission to visit Quebec to sell the rebellion's virtues. The delegation's leader was Benjamin Franklin, America's foremost thinker and scientist. He was an excellent choice, as he was thoroughly bilingual and the former postmaster of Canada. Samuel Chase and Charles Carroll were the other two official commissioners and Charles's brother, Father John, travelled as an associate. The Carrolls of Rhode Island had been brought up in France and had the benefits of language and religion to recommend them. There was an inexplicable delay of two and a half months after their time of appointment before they arrived in Montreal and took lodgings in Thomas Walker's house, which Carroll described as "the best built, and perhaps the best furnished in this town," suggesting that the damage from the fire had been repaired.

From the very outset of the mission Father Carroll discovered that most Canadiens were as ill-disposed toward helping Congress as they were to assisting the Crown. They had not even objected to what he thought was "their present restrictive constitution" and, by and large, were unaffected by the reasons that motivated the lower colonies to rebel. After the Canadien clergy declined to receive him the priest refrained from involving himself any further.

Portrait by François Beaucourt, 1794 (© Musée du Québec, 67.197).

Thought to be Fleury Mesplet, the Commission's French printer.

Congress also recruited Fleury Mesplet, a French immigrant who had been running a printing press in Philadelphia. He was instructed to take his machinery to Canada, where he would publish the commissioners' words of persuasion and encouragement. Upon arrival Mesplet began to erect his press in the basement of the Château Ramezay, where Arnold had located his headquarters.[15]

JOHN PETERS MAKES A MOVE

John Peters of Moortown decided that his health was faltering under the pressure of his neighbours' hostility and planned an escape to Canada. He approached his "old and steady friend," the New Hampshire colonel, Timothy Bedel, for assistance. Bedel was home from Canada to recruit his ranger company up to a full battalion of eight companies and agreed to take Peters with him after obtaining the consent of the local Committee of Correspondence. The pair departed Moortown in March, but before they left Bedel agreed to make no demands on Peters to bear arms. Why the Tory was permitted to tag along is a mystery.

W.H. Bartlett, 1842 (Canadian Scenery [London: 1840–42]).

Nineteenth-century view of The Cedars village.

When they arrived in Montreal they discovered that the flight of de Lorimier, Goddard, and Richard Walker had intensified fears that the British Army and its Native allies would launch an attack out of the west. To counter this threat Bedel was ordered to take his regiment up the St. Lawrence to a village on the north shore called The Cedars and establish a blocking post. Bedel marched with two 4-pdr guns and 390 men composed of his newly expanded New Hampshire ranger battalion and a detachment of Connecticut Continentals.[16]

As the army's de facto Indian agent, Bedel was instructed to pay particular heed to cultivating "a friendship with the savages," which one of his detachments immediately threatened by peremptorily searching Native canoes that were heading for the Lake of Two Mountains villages.[17]

Peters overheard that Bedel had orders to burn The Cedars hamlet and persuaded him against it. The troops were set to building a stockade fort and, while that was underway, Peters somehow snuck away to the British post upriver at Oswegatchie[18] where he met with Captain Forster to give him intelligence about the rebel positions. Having received the captain's promise that an attack would soon be made, he returned to The Cedars and warned his friend that a confrontation was imminent, which he claimed later led to Bedel leaving the post. Yet, according to historian Paul Stevens, Bedel went to Kahnawake to recruit warriors as a security screen for his new post. Whatever the case, the colonel's absence at a critical moment would later be held against him.[19]

NIAGARA SENDS REINFORCEMENTS

James Stanley Goddard had arrived at Fort Niagara in early May and obtained Lieutenant-Colonel Caldwell's blessing for Forster to mount a strike, which was presumably conveyed to the captain. He also received the promise of a small reinforcement, which John Butler, the Six Nations' deputy superintendent, organized with the assistance of various tribal representatives who had congregated at Niagara. Although Butler had no formal success with the Confederacy's hierarchy, he was successful in recruiting a few adventurous war captains, among them the Onondaga Kaquatanawji and the Seneca Kanughsgawiat, and some fifty young men, mostly Senecas with a few Cayugas, Onondagas, and Mohawks, and a smattering of Ottawas and Ojibways who had recently arrived on a supply ship from Detroit. Sir William's eldest half-blood son, Tagawirunta, known to the whites as William of Canajoharie, and several Indian Department rangers, accompanied the reinforcement when it embarked on May 10.

Goddard obeyed Butler's further instructions and began another arduous overland trek to Mackinac to raise a Native force from the Lakes and western Nations for the relief of the lower province.[20]

THE REBEL FIRE SHIP

Yet another New York loyalist had chosen to risk travelling with the rebel army as a spy. As noted earlier, in May 1775 Joseph Anderson was listed in the Albany Committee's minutes as a representative for Rensselaerwyck Manor.[21] Yet he and his elder brother Samuel had been secretly recruited by Sir John Johnson as officers for his loyalist battalion, and, because both men were Seven Years' War veterans, Samuel was appointed a captain and Joseph a lieutenant. But there was another side to their story. As the brothers were well-established, highly regarded farmers and landowners in Pownal, the rebels offered Samuel command of a Continental regiment and Joseph a majority, which both declined, thereby raising suspicions.[22]

Joseph, in conjunction with two of Sir John's chosen officers, James Gray and Thomas Gumersall, hatched a plot to burn the rebel shipping at Ticonderoga. When that scheme fell through he shifted to the second part of the plan and went to Quebec City to take the measure of the rebel army and determine Arnold's intentions so he could pass intelligence to Governor Carleton.

> I ... arrived at St. Foys where Genl. Arnolds Army were then Quartered on the 26th day of March 1776 and there fell in with one Colonel Maxwell of the Rebel Army an old acquaintance of mine, and his Adjutant a Lieut. Anderson[23] formerly an officer in the 44th Regt. who was likewise an acquaintance of mine[. T]hey Invited me to remain with them in their Quarters during my Stay at St. Foys which I gladly accepted of, it answering my purpose in every respect as I could wish: for Colonel Maxwell I knew was one of the Genls. Counsellors, and knew every thing that was going on at Head Quarters[;] all the Genls. most secret Designs were known to him. The Adjutant frequently shew me his orderly Book and particularly after Receiving any material orders he acquainted me with the Strength and State of their Army. After Supper in the night of the 4th of April they reposing great confidence in me acquainted me with everything that was intended by the Genl. to be carried into Execution, they even told me the

day on which their designs were to be put in force which was to be on the 7th day of April should the River prove Clear enough of Ice, but if not on that day as soon as it should. A fire Ship was to be sent down from Wolfes Cove to set the Kings Shipping &c on Fire that lay in the Docks of Quebec which if effected they were immediately thereupon to storm the Town. I began at this time to be much alarmed and very anxious to get a person to go in to Quebec with this Intelligence to Genl. Carleton which I was determined to do at any Risque and price, at length happening to meet with one Alexander Chaucer,[24] whom I had formerly been acquainted with, we had been Officers together in the same Provincial Regiment in the late war and upon Service together at the Havannah in the year 1762 but was at a Loss to know at this Juncture what his Sentiments were whether Loyal to the King or not However entered into discourse with him & after little while I asked him how much money I should give him to go into Quebec with some Intelligence to Genl. Carleton, who replied that it was so exceedingly dangerous he did not like to attempt it but upon further discourse I perswaded him to go in by promising to give him 40 pounds to him in Montreal in the year 1778.

Chaucers orders from me were to go into Quebec on the 6th day of April 1776 and acquaint Genl. Carleton that Genl. Wooster had the day before joined Genl. Arnold with a Reinforcement of troops &c. and that I had learnt from Head Quarters at Holland house that on the 7th day of April (or at least as soon as the River was clear enough of Ice) he might expect a Fire Ship would come down from Wolfs Cove.... Chaucer accordingly went into Quebec and I sett off from St. Foys on my return to Albany on the said 6th day of April.[25]

Captain Ainslie of the Quebec militia noted in his journal on April 6 that the "Rebels stopp'd two Gentlemen from N York on suspicion — they wou'd not allow them to proceed to Quebec: they had letters for Gen: Carleton, but no papers were found with them."[26] This was likely Joseph Anderson and his friend Chaucer, but, whatever the case, Anderson escaped from Sainte-Foy that day before his activities caught up with him. He was none too early, as General Wooster sent a man after him in hot pursuit. Somehow, Anderson kept ahead of the fellow.

Three days later Ainslie recorded:

A decent looking man calling himself Chaucer came in to day — he talks a great deal, we gather from him that he is or was a butler — he says that Gen: [Charles] Lee was on his march hither — but was order'd to N York to take the command there — the Rebels are about 1800 near Quebec of whom between six and eight hundred are in hospitals.

They talk of storming the Town at Pres de Ville, Sault au Matelot & at Cape Diamond before the 15th. on which day the engagements of many of the men will finish.

The N Yorkers are very highly incens'd at the behaviour & conduct of those they call the Yankeys — they mean the people of the 4 N England provinces, who they say affect a disgusting superiority, taking the lead in every thing.

They are soon to open a battery against Port Louis at 500 yds distance, of 5 guns – 9 & 12 pounders & they are to bombard us with 5 howitzers from the ferry house.

They have two Gondolas afloat — they are busy preparing a fire vessel to burn the shipping in Cul de Sac.

The Canadians are dissatisfied with the Rebel payments, they by no means take the Congress Paper, they are glad to exchange a handful of it for a dollar.

They have punish'd a Canadian in an Arbitrary manner for speaking in favour of the Royalists.

They have put Mr. Evans[27] in irons for caning 2 or 3 insolent Montrealists who were holding forth in favour of the invasion of Canada. He was formerly an officer in the 28th Regt: he threaten'd to chastise some of the Rebel officers, they complain'd to their leader, & Mr. Evans was sent prisoner to Hartford....

Arnold is to leave the Camp tomorrow to hasten down the long look'd for reinforcement. The rebels have no shoes; In the present state of the roads he cannot reach Montreal in less than 3 or 4 days & a body of men will require 8 or 10 days to march down from thence unless they can be sent in Batteaus, at any rate they cannot be here before the 15th — on which day or rather before they threaten to storm us.

Anderson had accumulated an astounding volume of accurate information. Ainslie further reported that "we are ready to receive them. We now guard on the river every night. Our wharfs are garnish'd with guns — we have cannon in some vessels in the Cul de Sac, & strong guards in the Lower Town. Our voluntary Picquets continue, no man sleeps at home — we assemble every night together ready to repulse wherever attacks may be made. [As] Mr. Chaucer is suspected, he will be properly taken care of."[28]

On April 18 Ainslie recorded the arrival of two deserters with interesting information about the deep unrest among the Continentals:

[T]he N Yorkers to the number of 300 had been assembled on the 15th – every argument had been us'd to persuade them to renew their engagements, but these men predetermin'd every solicitation, were immoveable.

To all the entreaties used, they answer'd, that the Congress had deceiv'd them — they as yet had no pay — they had in a manner been forc'd to renew their first engagements, but they had resolv'd not to enter into a third, they see their error, & are firmly determin'd never to fire a shot against the Kings friends — their spokesmen ended with a God Save the King which was echoed by one & all of them with three chears.

Immediately their drums beat to arms[;] orders were given to secure the Mutineers — they were seiz'd, very ill used & confin'd; the rebellious Canadians were the most forward in this service.[29]

Arnold had reinjured his wounded leg when he took a tumble from his horse and found it necessary to retire to Montreal to heal his wound. Wooster came downriver to Quebec City to take command of the siege, leaving Colonel Hazen in command at Montreal, but the commissioners' reports of Wooster's administration in Montreal had earned Congress's disapproval and Major-General John Thomas, whose performance during the siege of Boston had been questionable at best, replaced him on May 1.[30]

When Arnold arrived in Montreal he instructed Hazen to take command of the posts at Chambly and Fort St. John and, with foresight, to prepare the rebel army's route of retreat down the Richelieu valley.[31]

The Fire Ship Sails

As it transpired, the fire ship could not be launched until the evening of May 3. It was carried on a northeast wind and as soon as it came in sight the city's batteries opened fire, which caused the crew to abandon ship too soon. The current caught the vessel and carried it to the middle of the river where its cargo of grenades and bombs exploded harmlessly. All thoughts of assaulting the city were abandoned. This was the last action of the siege and two days later fires were lit by the Canadiens downriver signalling that a British relief fleet had been sighted. General Thomas ordered his army to abandon the siege the following day.[32]

THE RELIEF FLEET ARRIVES

On May 6 the citizens and garrison crowded the city's ramparts to watch a warship enter the basin. To everyone's joy and excitement, she displayed a Union flag. The ship was the frigate *Surprise* with part of the 29th Regiment aboard. Soon after, the commander of the relief fleet, Commodore Charles Douglas, with his pennant flying from the *Isis*, fifty guns, entered the harbour with the sloop *Martin*.[33]

Douglas had been fully aware of the importance of raising the siege as quickly as possible and took his responsibility most seriously. He had set sail from England on March 11 and made landfall off the French island of St. Pierre south of Newfoundland a month later to the day. In a remarkable feat of seamanship, he forced the fleet's way through nearly sixty leagues of massive fields of thick pack ice and arrived off Anticosti Island on the twenty-first, entering the St. Lawrence River that same evening. By May 3, Douglas was off Isle-aux-Coudres and, three days later, his ships entered the basin.[34]

One hundred men of the 29th Regiment, the *Surprise*'s Marine detachment, and eighty sailors were the first to disembark. They marched up to the citadel while the landings continued. The drums had beaten and the city's garrison formed up on the parade. Captain Ainslie reported about the two militia battalions:

[A]lmost to a man both corps were anxious to be led
to action. The general at the head of about 800 men
marched out at 12 oclock; the little army extended
itself quite across the plains, making a fine appearance. The rebels saw us as very formidable. A few
shots were exchanged by our advanced party and the
rear guard of the enemy; their balls whistled over us
without hurting a man. They fled most precipitately
as soon as our field pieces began to play on their
guard houses and advanced posts. They left cannon,
mortars, field pieces, muskets and even their cloaths
behind them.

In the late afternoon the *Surprise* and *Martin* sailed upriver in
pursuit of rebel boats. Next morning they came up with the bateaux,
but the turning tide forced the ships to anchor; however, they were
within range and opened fire, forcing the fleeing craft hard up
against the shore. To lessen their drafts the rebel bateauxmen abandoned numbers of sick men on the beach, scandalizing the crews
and observers aboard the ships.

This was scarcely the orderly withdrawal Thomas had anticipated. It was done; the siege was over.[35]

The Distant West

In far-off Michilimackinac, Captain Arent DePeyster was starved for
information. The first word he had of the rebel invasion had been
brought by three traders from Detroit who had boated and walked
their way and arrived on May 10. Local residents were astonished to
hear of the rebel occupation of the lower country. DePeyster heard
nothing more until some local Ojibway and Ottawa visitors arrived
later that month bringing letters from two Lake of Two Mountains
Fathers, Jean-Claude Mathevet and François-Auguste Magon de
Terlaye,[36] and wampum strings from the Nipissings. The priests
wrote that the rebels were in possession of Montreal and the Canada

Indians needed help from their western brethren or the English might be driven from Canada. The visitors wanted DePeyster's advice on how to proceed, and he advised them to continue with their hunt until instructions were received from the governor. Then in early June James Stanley Goddard arrived from Niagara with orders from Lieutenant-Colonel John Caldwell and Deputy Agent John Butler and wampum messages from the Six Nations asking the Lakes' Nations to assemble at Kanehsatake at Lake of Two Mountains.

When the first trade canoes arrived at Mackinac from Montreal DePeyster was shocked to find that their owners' permits were issued by rebel authorities, and he barred them from trading with his garrison. This startling revelation spurred him into action, and he ordered his interpreter, Joseph-Louis Ainsse, to take charge of Mackinac's and Saginaw Bay's Ojibways and Ottawas and take them to Lake of Two Mountains. They were to consult with the two priests and then join with John Butler or the nearest senior British officer. He then sent an officer to La Baye to instruct Charles de Langlade to assemble volunteers from among the Menominees, Winnebagoes, Sauks, Foxes, and Sioux and dispatch them to the relief of lower Quebec.[37]

OTHER NEW YORK LOYALISTS

On May 23 Captain Daniel McAlpin, a retired captain of the 60th Royal Americans who was a wealthy landlord living near Saratoga, and Lieutenant Thomas Swords, formerly of the 55th Regiment, were brought before the Albany Committee with two other suspects to hear the charges that had been brought against them. McAlpin and Swords were ordered confined to their lodgings with a sentry at the door.

Somehow Joseph Anderson, on the run after escaping at Sainte-Foy, kept ahead of his pursuer and after two and a half weeks arrived at James Gray's house near Albany on May 24; however, the very next morning the two conspirators were taken prisoner by order of the Committee. Their papers were confiscated and examined, but nothing incriminating was found in Anderson's correspondence to prove Wooster's suspicions. Yet neither man was released; they were held in the city's prison with many other men who later became prominent loyal Provincials, among them Daniel McAlpin, John Munro, Joseph's brother Samuel, Simeon Covell, and Alexander Campbell.[38]

In early June McAlpin, Swords, and Munro were removed from their temporary lodgings and put in the fort's jail. Late the next month McAlpin gave his parole to not leave the city limits without the Committee's permission and was liberated, but eight days later he was taken up again and a decision was made to send him to Connecticut. Then he was suddenly set free again. General Schuyler agreed with this last decision, reasoning that McAlpin was so old that "little or no Harm might be expected from him."[39]

The Cedars

Opening the western communication

The Attack

Captain George Forster had gathered a sizeable, disparate force at Oswegatchie by May 12. He had forty of his own Light Infantrymen, eleven franco- and anglo-loyalist traders, a few rangers of the two Indian Departments and 160 warriors of the Mississauga, Canada, Six and Lakes' Nations.[1]

Forster's primary assistant had been the Chevalier de Lorimier, who had travelled to Gananoque to enlist warriors, primarily Mississaugas. De Lorimier instructed them to be at Gananoque when the April moon was full with as many others as they could persuade. That done he went back to Oswegatchie, deeply concerned there would not be enough provisions for all the Natives he expected. After consulting with Forster he disguised himself as an Indian, and, with a Native boy, went downstream to The Cedars to ask two close friends, a M. Denis and *Curé* Deneau, to gather a fortnight's supply of provisions for three hundred men and have it available when the river's ice broke up. He arrived back at Oswegatchie just as the ice went out and turned about again for The Cedars, taking three bateaux, their crews, and a squad of the 8th's Light Bobs.

Particular survey of the Isles of Montreal.

After hiding his boats and men de Lorimier made his way to the *curé*'s house in his Native disguise to enquire if the provisions were ready, but there were complications. The house was posted by a rebel serjeant's guard of seven men and a comic dance ensued between Deneau, de Lorimier, and the serjeant over a bottle of rum and some ducks that the chevalier had managed to bag on his way downriver. This clever farce allowed de Lorimier to meet privately for a few moments with the priest and get the information he needed — to wit, the provisions were safely hidden at Coteau-du-Lac, not far above The Cedars. That accomplished, the *curé* perfunctorily dismissed him from the house and he made his way to Coteau where he met Deneau's friend André Lalonde and arranged for the provisions to be brought to his hidden party. At sunrise the next day the goods were loaded onto the bateaux and three days later were off-loaded at Oswegatchie.

Upon arrival at the post de Lorimier sent a messenger to Gananoque to gather in his Native volunteers. Within days about 140 men arrived, accompanied by John Butler's twenty-two Six and Lakes' Nations warriors from Niagara, whose addition energized everyone.[2] Although de Lorimier makes no mention of John Peters's contribution, and assuming the New Yorker was not indulging in flights of fantasy, he must have appeared at Forster's door about this time with details of the rebel force and their fortifications.

Forster's little army set off on May 12 and halted to camp at Rapide Plat on the first night. They were met there by a senior Akwesasne chief who claimed that a rebel army was on its way upriver and urged the Natives to turn back or face slaughter. De Lorimier boldly rose to the occasion, thanked the chief for his warning, and artfully persuaded him to join with the party and share in the glory. The men took to the boats the next day and, when they arrived at Akwesasne about two o'clock, discharged an impressive fusillade and gave choruses of war shouts before landing. An ox was roasted and many warriors sang their death songs — the upshot, another fifty-four warriors joined the expedition and the canoes and boats travelled on to make camp at Pointe des Nègres.

Next morning, de Lorimier set out on a reconnaissance with four Native comrades and fell in with his friend Pierre La Fleur, who warned that three thousand rebels were coming upriver the next day to take up the positions Bedel's three hundred troops had prepared around The Cedars church. Bedel's men would then move further upriver and entrench a second position at Pointe-au-Diable.

As there was no large body of rebel troops on the march upriver it would seem that this intelligence was deliberate misinformation designed to halt Forster's advance. That La Fleur had been sub- orned was proven later when he was discovered attempting to sneak off to give information to the rebels.

By May 15 Bedel had received word of Forster's movements from Philip Sanorese's Kahnawake scouts. They had observed de Lorimier's vanguard, but retreated with some precipitation when Forster's flotilla of canoes boldly took to the water.

Near The Cedars Forster's canoes put ashore and the advance continued on shore with de Lorimier and his Native warriors still in the van. When the rebels' entrenchments came into view the chevalier proposed making a quick thrust to cut off their communications, but, to his surprise, his companions demurred, saying that such action was properly the role of the Regular troops, whom they wryly observed had hung back. This alarmed the chevalier, as these warriors were his personal recruits and most of the Niagara contingent had already chosen to remain with Forster. De Lorimier chided his men, reminding them they had sung their ritual death songs, but the only one to rise to the challenge and step forward was the Mohawk William of Canajoharie, Sir William Johnson's eldest son.[3]

The pair boldly advanced and, upon nearing a farm, William spotted two rebels taking aim at them over a rail fence. He shouted a warning and he and de Lorimier dove into a ditch as the balls whirred overhead. Springing up, they sprinted toward the fence, forcing the rebels to abandon reloading and take to their heels. The chevalier and William each picked a target, took careful aim, and fired; one rebel was struck in the shoulder, the other in the thigh. Ironically, de Lorimier knew the man he had felled.

The rest of the Indians had rapidly followed their spirited leadership and all ran forward. In a sharp skirmish they cut off the rebels' roadway to the settlements below. Twenty rebels who had just arrived from Les Cascades ran into a house outside the fortification and delivered a sharp fire from the windows, killing Bonneur, one of de Lorimier's Natives. Enraged, his warriors assaulted the house, ignoring the musketry coming from the adjacent rebel works. Inside, the rebels climbed a ladder into the attic, tore open a gable, and escaped. Thinking they had the men trapped inside, the Indians were shocked when a solid shot passed through the building and they retreated to a nearby ravine to await the arrival of Forster's Regulars.[4]

While this skirmishing was underway Forster received couriers from Quebec City who brought the momentous news that reinforcements had arrived from Britain, the siege of the city was raised, and the rebel army was fleeing in panic.[5]

BEDEL GOES FOR HELP

At Kahnawake, Bedel had been receiving constant reports of Forster's progress from Sanorese's scouts and he crossed the river to Montreal to advise Arnold that a British attack on The Cedars was underway. Word that British reinforcements had arrived at Quebec City had shocked Montreal and an evacuation was underway with the pro-rebel merchants falling over themselves to get away. Congress's commissioners had already departed, Franklin in a boat with Thomas Walker's wife.[6] Bedel was told that Arnold was at Sorel and there were only about 150 troops remaining in the city. So he sent a dispatch to Arnold and a brief delay ensued before the brigadier was able to send a 140-man First Massachusetts detachment under Major Henry Sherburne to march to the relief of The Cedars. The major marched on May 17 and, after experiencing some difficulties crossing Lac St. Louis, landed about nine miles below The Cedars the next day.[7]

THE CEDARS SURROUNDED

Much had occurred in the interim. De Lorimier had become alarmed when 180 rebels sortied out their stockade, as he only had about eighty warriors to block them; however, his fears were for naught, as their only goal was to set fire to a barn that overshadowed their works. That done, they promptly returned to their fortifications.

De Lorimier went to Forster to persuade him to bring his Light Infantry and the rest of the Natives into action, but the captain chose to remain behind a breastwork of fence posts that had been built by his Lights. The next morning de Lorimier sensed Native unrest and became concerned that the captain's hesitation would result in them drifting off, so he was very pleased to see a party of Kanehsatakes arrive, which raised all their spirits. Bolstered by this reinforcement, he developed a plan to take the rebels' works by assault and went to share his thoughts with the captain.

Forster had become alarmed about the disproportionate size of his Native contingent. He was fully aware of their potential for savagery and had no difficulty recalling Carleton's instructions to avoid excesses. Although the chevalier's plan had merit, it would mean the Natives would be the first into the fort, with all the outrages that would follow. So next morning Forster advanced up a deep ravine with two flags, which he stuck into the gully's lip within musket-shot of the stockade. Then he sent forward First Lieutenant Henry Bird[8] with a flag of truce and a drummer, who presumably beat a chamade. Bird delivered Forster's summons to Bedel's second-in-command, Major Isaac Butterfield, demanding the garrison's surrender and, in time-honoured fashion, warning that there would be no quarter given if the Natives stormed the works. It was proposed that the rebels would be allowed to return to their home country within two weeks if they promised not to take up arms again during the conflict.

After Butterfield made a counter proposal that the garrison should be allowed to retire with its arms, Bird retired. Forster's men began a constant patter of musketry against the works and he put some men to work hewing sham cannon barrels from logs in the hopes that the threat of cannon fire would undermine the rebels' resolve.

About ten the next morning fur trader Jean-Baptiste-Jérémie Testard de Montigny,[9] an in-law of de Lorimier's who had recently

Anishinabe (Ojibway/Chippewa) sword — a typical sidearm, 1775–1800.

had much of his property seized by the rebels, arrived at the head of thirty Canadien volunteers. Like many of Forster's anglo- and franco-loyalists, de Montigny was associated with the upper-country trade that had been badly hurt by Wooster's embargo.

News of the relief detachment coming from Montreal arrived and Forster sent de Montigny and his party to shadow its march.

THE GARRISON SUBMITS

Of course, cooped up as he was in the palisaded fort, Major Butterfield was unaware that help was approaching. He was ill, and the threat implied by the Indians' incessant yelling eroded his resolve. He sent out a flag with an offer to surrender if Forster agreed to protect his men from the Natives. This was no simple request. When Butterfield had spurned Forster's original terms, the Natives had declared they would give no quarter. The captain had far too few Regulars to hold off the Indians, who were agitated by the loss of some friends and the wounding of others, and by their expectation of booty. With the menace of a new rebel force close by, Forster knew he needed to draw the issue to a rapid close. The captain sent a warning to Butterfield that he could guarantee the lives of the garrison only if the works were vacated within thirty minutes. This condition was agreed to, and the Light Infantry and six chiefs were admitted into the fort to formally receive the surrender. The garrison was then marched out and, despite the protests of the British and Canadien officers, the Indians fell on them and stripped their clothing. De Lorimier found that he had to give Butterfield some of his own old clothes, which was ironic, as the major had offered two Kahnawakes substantial rewards for the chevalier, dead or alive. After that demeaning exercise, the Natives had the run of the fort. When avarice was satisfied the rebels were readmitted and confined to their former quarters, which were probably in the village church.

DEFEATING THE RELIEF FORCE

Next morning Forster received detailed intelligence about the character and size of the rebel relief force and ordered de Lorimier and some sixty warriors to assist de Montigny in blocking its progress. Before setting out the chevalier armed and ammunitioned his men from captured stores. Then he was fortuitously joined by his brother the Sieur de Verneuil and Jacob Maurer, who had just arrived with thirty more Canadien volunteers. Maurer was a German-born seven-year veteran of the Royal Americans who had settled into Montreal's Jewish community.[10]

De Lorimier's men confronted Sherburne's Massachusetts Continentals at Quinze Chiens,[11] four miles east of The Cedars. The chevalier immediately sent out scouts to warn of any attempt at a flank attack and then coordinated an assault. His brother was to form a base of fire while he rushed for a barn in the rear of the Continentals to cut off their retreat. This bold assault failed. Just as the attackers reached the barn the Seneca war captain Kanughsgawiat fell dead with seven gunshot wounds, Tsonnotouan was struck in the shoulder, and Misisagué took a ball that tore off part of his nose and upper jaw. His men veered off, running stump to stump, hillock to hillock, and made their way to the river's shore where they were reinforced by eight newly arrived Canadien friends.

The chevalier made a second attempt to cut in behind the rebel column, but found the Continentals were retreating too fast; however, de Montigny's detachment had cut off their escape route by seizing a bridge and putting up a brisk musketry, which caused the Continentals to recoil into the arms of de Lorimier's pursuit. The fighting was over; the Massachusetts men surrendered.

The final phase to the Quinze Chiens victory occurred when the chevalier employed a nasty, but effective, *ruse de guerre* and lured the rebels' sentries and boats from a nearby island to the mainland.

Squabbling broke out when the Natives began to strip the prisoners of their accoutrements, arms, and clothing. Some wanted to avenge their losses and de Lorimier exerted himself to prevent an ugly incident when Major Sherburne became the centre of a custody fracas between de Montigny, Captain Lefebvre of the Quinze Chiens militia, and one of the Natives. The Indian was the biggest threat, as he tried to sneak the major away to scalp him. De Lorimier shamed the Native by reminding him that any such breach of European prisoner conventions would endanger men like John Campbell and Hertel de Rouville who were still in rebel hands. While this argument saved the major's life, it did not prevent him from being stripped of his hat, coat, and waistcoat.

The pillaging continued when Sherburne arrived at The Cedars, the same Indian taking the major's shirt and breeches. De Lorimier came across another incident of vengeful looting when he discovered an Abenaki, Portneuf, stripping a wounded officer. When asked why, he said he did not want the clothes to get bloody when he killed him. Angered, the chevalier grasped the man's throat and forcefully used the same argument as before. Portneuf agreed to release the prisoner if de Lorimier would promise that Hertel de Rouville would be returned. The promise was made and, in fact, Campbell and de Rouville were later exchanged.

The Natives and Canadians had thoroughly overwhelmed Sherburne's relief and had about 130 new prisoners to show for it. As a complication, by tradition many captives were claimed by individual Natives. Most were quickly redeemed with hard cash, although thirteen youngsters and all the black captives were carried off by the Mississaugas and recovered only over time. John Peters wrote that the bereaved Natives had their thirst for revenge assuaged by a gift of "eight yoke of oxen and several cows."

Reports of the number of Continentals killed at Quinze Chiens varied widely from a British estimate of five to Sherburne's claim of twenty-eight. Both sides had reason to obfuscate.

FORSTER ADVANCES TOWARD MONTREAL

Captain George Forster was overwhelmed by success. His force had achieved an almost painless victory and taken over 480 rebels captive — Americans and Canadiens — but he had only forty Regulars and a handful of Indian Department rangers to protect them from harm. The Natives were flushed with victory and set on avenging their losses and injuries, an engrained reaction nurtured over the centuries. When the firing broke out at Quinze Chiens, which signalled the close proximity of rebel reinforcements, the Natives at The Cedars had demanded that Butterfield's men be put to death, yet another custom of Native warfare. Although Forster had managed to talk his way out of that crisis, he recognized the situation was balanced on a knife edge.

On May 21 the captain marched his forces and the prisoners to Quinze Chiens to join de Montigny, who had been reinforced by another body of Kanehsatakes eager to retaliate against the rebels. The next evening, Forster sent de Montigny and his party to occupy Fort Senneville on the trader's property at the west end of Montreal Island.

Before marching on May 23 Forster dispersed the prisoners for safekeeping. About 250 enlisted rebels were sent to de Montigny, who put them on a barren island called Ile-aux-Tourtes. Their officers were parolled and sent into the care of the two priests at the Lake of Two Mountains mission, and all the Canadiens were lodged in barns at Quinze Chiens under guard. Those dispositions made, Forster crossed to Montreal Island and established a camp at de Montigny's Fort Senneville.

On the twenty-fourth, he marched east toward Point Clare, which was about eighteen miles from Montreal. He expected to be joined there by an additional body of Canadiens, but, when he was about three miles above Lachine the next morning, he received intelligence that General Arnold held that community with six hundred rebels and six fieldpieces and was awaiting a reinforcement of two thousand — yet another gross overstatement.[12]

ARNOLD OUTMANOEUVRED

Arnold had come to Montreal from Sorel where he was apprised of Forster's further victories and his advance onto Montreal Island. He threw together a new force of about 350 men, which included the majority of the city's garrison. On the march he was joined by small garrisons from the outposts around the city. He expected a Pennsylvania regiment from Sorel, which would swell his strength to over eight hundred troops.

At Lachine, Arnold was joined by Captain James Wilkinson's company. The ambitious nineteen-year-old captain had come to Canada as part of General Thompson's Continental reinforcement. When he marched through St. John's, he cannily scooped up fourteen stragglers from the main army, which brought his company's strength up to a hundred. Having been ordered to join the army in Montreal, he marched to Kahnawake where Atayataghronghta assisted him to get his men across the St. Lawrence to Lachine.

Wilkinson found that Arnold had 250 men at work "retrenching a spacious stone magazine" in preparation to defy Forster. The next day two of his men were foraging for milk and fell into the hands of loyal Native scouts. One fellow contrived to fall behind, then sprang away to escape. A scout wheeled about, fired, and wounded the Continental in "a tender part," but he got away to give warning that the enemy was near, which was confirmed near sunset when Forster's drum was heard beating.[13]

Forster's Native and Canadien volunteers began to slip away, entirely content with their martial deeds and booty. The captain worried that he would not have enough men to control his prisoners, and there was still no word of the whereabouts of the British Army advancing from Quebec City. Prudently, he chose to withdraw.

Some of his commissioned prisoners had earlier suggested negotiating an exchange for an equal number of British prisoners of comparable rank. Forster decided to pursue this idea and sent Captain-Lieutenant Andrew Parke[14] to Lake of Two Mountains to sound them out. Driven by visions of returning to the safety of home, the officers agreed to the condition that they would not take up arms again during the conflict, and a "cartel" was signed by Parke, de Montigny, and de Lorimier representing the Crown, and Butterfield and Sherburne, the Congress.

Meanwhile, Forster had left Montreal Island and taken up position at Quinze Chiens. He had only eighty men left, although several Canadiens and warriors rejoined by the morning of the twenty-fifth.

———————————◆———————————

Arnold was busily preparing the position at Lachine when a sick Colonel Bedel came across the river from Kahnawake to advise that the village was extremely concerned about Forster's success. After seeing Bedel admitted to the local hospital the brigadier left Colonels John Brown[15] and Williams in charge and crossed the river to buck up his allies. Meanwhile, his little force at Lachine stood under arms until ten o'clock, but Forster did not appear. Double guards were posted and the officers retired to their quarters to indulge in some carousing, but Wilkinson restlessly pondered how to make the best defence. At midnight he sat down to compose a depressing letter to his family friend, General Nathaniel Greene of Rhode Island, in which he claimed that Forster had an army of a thousand men, composed of Regulars from Detroit, Canadiens, and Natives. He lamented, "so astonishingly are matters conducted in this quarter, that notwithstanding the General's most pressing solicitations … we cannot muster more than 350 men." This despondency was offset the next morning when Colonel John De Haas arrived with five hundred Pennsylvania infantry and riflemen.[16]

———————————◆———————————

PETERS MAKES A DISCOVERY

Before Forster's force attacked at The Cedars, Bedel had sent John Peters to Montreal to obtain provisions for the garrison. When there, he dined "with Dr. Franklin and the other Commissioners from Congress; also General Wooster and Col. [Brigadier] Arnold." During the meal Arnold commented "Nothing but Independence would settle these matters, and he wished to God it was now done." Somehow, Peters was able to read a letter that "Dr. Franklin and

General Wooster wrote to Col. Ha[z]en to let him know that Col. De Haws was going round the mountain with 700 men to attack Capt. Forster and [that] Col. Arnold with the main body was to meet Forster at LaChine with four field pieces."[17] Peters sent this information over the mountain to Captain Forster.

At Kahnawake, Arnold was greeted with the threat that the community would join the enemy if they did not receive substantial assistance. Unfazed, the bold, charismatic brigadier won them over with his confidence, and several of their warriors joined him to recross the river.

Arnold sent Kahnawake messengers to Forster's Natives to demand that their prisoners be immediately surrendered, warning that, if they failed to comply, he would kill every Indian that fell into his hands and destroy their towns by fire and sword. Such hubris! Arnold was not in control of affairs; the prisoners were within the grasp of Forster's allies and the brigadier's intimidation attempt was both empty and extremely offensive. The loyal Natives replied with their own threats — to wit, if Arnold attempted a landing at Quinze Chiens they would immediately kill every prisoner and give no quarter to any others who fell into their hands. Here was a threat of substance.

The next day Forster was in the midst of transferring the enlisted prisoners from Ile-aux-Tortes to Quinze Chiens when Arnold attempted a crossing to the mainland with eight boatloads of Continentals, rebel Canadiens, and Kahnawakes. Forster's men lined the shore and engaged the boats with musketry and two 4-pdr guns captured at The Cedars. The cannon were competently directed by a militia captain, Pitre de Boucherville, who succeeded in sinking a bateau. The attackers veered away and were followed along the shore by de Lorimier and some Indians peppering away at them to no avail.[18]

At two in the morning of May 27, Captain-Lieutenant Parke suddenly appeared out of the dark in Arnold's camp with Major Sherburne in tow. Arnold's council of war had just decided against trying a second landing after an acrimonious debate, so Parke's arrival with a completed, signed "cartel" was almost welcomed. Sherburne confirmed that the British Indians were prepared to put all the prisoners to the hatchet and, after a day-long negotiation, Arnold reluctantly accepted the hand he had been dealt, although not until he persuaded Parke to remove the clause about the prisoners not taking up arms again.

By the evening of the thirtieth, all of the prisoners had been released except four officers who were held hostage to ensure rebel compliance and a dozen Canadiens who were suspected of desertion from the militia.[19]

When Arnold withdrew he burned Fort Senneville. Forster and de Lorimier followed him with the intention of occupying Lachine; however, the chevalier came across two trustworthy Montreal merchants who warned him that three thousand rebels were about to arrive there. Forster's force was still terribly reduced and he was alarmed by this information, as his Natives and Canadiens continued to come and go like the wind. De Lorimier suggested that the captain withdraw to the west end of the island with the two fieldpieces while he and three Indians scouted Lachine. The chevalier's patrol captured three men and questioned them about the rebel forces in the town. They swore there were no more than 250. There was no expectation of a relief and, when the rebel officers heard of Forster's approach, they urged a retreat. Obviously, de Lorimier's "trustworthy" merchants had been talking nonsense, deliberate or otherwise, but the damage was done, for Forster had left the island.

When de Lorimier caught up to him to deliver this new intelligence the captain was already at Les Cascades and retreating rapidly toward Oswegatchie. This led to an exchange of harsh words. Forster rashly

Unknown photographer, 2003.

Ruins of Fort Senneville burned by Arnold, 1775.

blamed his withdrawal on the Canadiens' infidelity. In consequence all of his white volunteers up and left.[20] The saga of The Cedars was finished, but not its positive after-effects.

In far-off England, when Deputy Superintendent Daniel Claus read the newspaper accounts of Forster's successes, he wrote a letter to his department's contractors. "The advantages he gained over the Rebells ... [were] small in comparison to the [opening of] the communication to the upper posts and the western Indians.... They on hearing the door of Quebec [is] open for supplies in Trade and [that] an armament agst. the Rebels [has] arrived will flock to our Troops on their own accord." Historian Paul Stevens observes that Claus's "astute judgment proved entirely correct."[21] Carleton was soon to receive a flood of western warriors; indeed, more than he was willing to cope with.

THE HESITANT COUNTERATTACK

Want of Spirit

HIS MAJESTY'S DELUDED SUBJECTS

Rather than seize the opportunity to destroy the remnants of the rebel army, Carleton was deliberately tardy. Four days after the rebel army retreated in confusion from Quebec City, the governor issued a decree which surely puzzled his troops and the local Canadiens.

> Informed that many of His Majesty's deluded subjects of the neighbouring provinces, labouring under wounds and divers disorders, are dispersed in the adjacent woods and parishes, and are in great danger of perishing for want of proper assistance ... [the militia officers are] to make diligent search for all such distressed persons, and afford them all necessary relief and convey them to the General Hospital, where proper care shall be taken of them.[1]

To encourage the Canadiens to assist he promised to pay their expenses and, to calm the fears of men in hiding, he announced "that as soon as their health is restored they shall have free liberty to return to their respective provinces."

Lieutenant-Colonel Maclean, whom a naval officer described as "Beloved, Dreaded and Indefatigable," was clearly unimpressed with the decree and other similar conciliatory measures. In a letter of May 10 he wrote, "I ... hope we have had Experience Sufficient to convince us that our Unactivity and want of Spirit was what greatly contributed to the distresses to which this province had been reduced last year, timidity in the field ... is a dangerous matter."[2]

CARLETON BEGINS TO MOVE

When Carleton finally decided to advance he set out for Trois-Rivières in several vessels with the 29th and 47th Regiments. En route he received intelligence about Forster's successes, but did not press the advantage. Then he received a second message advising that Lieutenant-General John Burgoyne had landed at Quebec with a massive reinforcement of seven British regiments from the Irish Establishment, four batteries of artillery, and several Brunswick regiments under the command of General Baron Friedrich Riedesel. He turned over command of the pursuit to Maclean and returned to the city to welcome the newcomers. When Maclean arrived at Trois-Rivières he landed troops and diligently began to build a fortified camp while waiting for the governor's return.[3]

THE KING'S BIRTHDAY AT ALBANY

In traditional manner Albany's mayor, Abraham Cuyler, retired to Richard Cartwright's tavern with a number of his friends to celebrate the King's birthday on June 4. Cuyler proposed a toast to the sovereign, rashly adding the sentiment, "Damnation to the enemies of the King!" Within days he was removed from office and jailed. With some exaggeration Cartwright recalled that his inn had been "surrounded by three or four thousand people," he was beaten and bruised, and his effects destroyed. Hence, both the venue of the city's first Committee of Correspondence meeting held a year earlier and the man who had assisted the committee in examining firelocks were utterly discredited.[4]

THE ACTION AT TROIS-RIVIÈRES

General David Wooster had again taken command of the Continental Army in Canada after Thomas contracted smallpox. He assembled a council of war at Chambly, during which his officers decided to maintain a position in Canada and set up the army's headquarters at Sorel.

Congress continued to pump reinforcements into the province and Brigadier-General William Thompson arrived in mid-May with four regiments; however, his brigade was immediately disabled by a smallpox outbreak.[5] Thompson was in command at Sorel when he received intelligence that a three-hundred-man British force had taken post at Trois-Rivières. He concluded that a sudden attack before proper defences could be prepared would blunt the enemy's advance and restore confidence among the Continentals.

General John Sullivan now arrived at Sorel to replace Wooster and take supreme command in Canada.[6] Thompson revealed his plan to the new C-in-C and had it approved.[7] Unaware that Carleton had been reinforced from Europe, Sullivan reported to Washington "that I can, in a few days, reduce the army to order, and ... put a new

A 1784 view of Trois-Rivières.

Detail from a watercolour by James Peachey (Library and Archives Canada, C-002006).

face to our affairs here.... If General Thompson succeeds at Trois-Rivières, I will soon remove the ships below Richelieu Falls and after that, approach Quebec as fast as possible."[8]

In the midst of this planning the loyalist John Peters stumbled into Sorel. Sullivan had him taken prisoner on suspicion that he had supplied the enemy with the intelligence that led to the debacle at The Cedars, and sent him to Fort St. John's for safekeeping.[9]

Of course, Thompson and Sullivan were unaware that Carleton had dispatched two additional brigades of Regulars upriver to Maclean.[10] Simon Fraser, 24th Regiment, commanded the first brigade and, when his four regiments landed to reinforce Maclean, the local

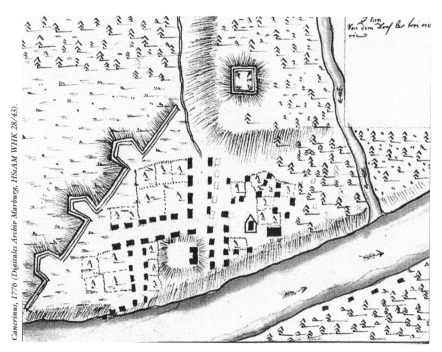

Camerinus, 1776 (Digitales Archiv Marburg, HStAM WHK 28/43).

Plan of the village of Trois-Rivières, 1776 (likely after the rebel defeat).

militia greeted them with three volleys and three cheers of "Vive le Roy." The second brigade, led by William Nesbitt, 47th Regiment, remained on the transports and sailed further upriver.[11]

Thompson led two thousand Continentals, some fieldpieces, and Hazen's and Duggan's Canadiens across the St. Lawrence to Pointe-du-Lac. On the night of June 7 his force began the seven-mile march to Trois-Rivières. Having no personal knowledge of the best route, Thompson's Canadien advisor, François Guillot,[12] persuaded a local named Antoine Gautier to guide the troops through the forest. Gautier recommended avoiding the King's Highway, which he said was swarming with scouts, and took the troops into the woods, subtly adding several miles to the march. He took many detours and led them through a morass of slime and submerged logs. Thompson had divided his men into several columns, retaining Gautier with him as the guide. The column marching nearest the river emerged from the forest onto the shore and was shocked by the sight of Nesbitt's Royal Navy transports and escorts and melted back into the bog.

Gautier had secretly sent his wife to warn Captain Landron of the Pointe-du-Lac militia of the attack. Landron took the direct route along the King's Highway and arrived at Trois-Rivières at four in the morning.[13] Consequently, Maclean was fully alert and posted Chevalier Niverville with a party of Canadien scouts to the west of the town.[14] They scooped up the rebels' advance guard before a signal could be given, and when the exhausted, drenched, and filthy Continentals finally blundered from the woods on the western edge of Trois-Rivières they were greeted by volleys of musketry and gunfire from prepared positions. Forced to retire, the rebels were pursued along the river road by Fraser's Grenadiers and Light Infantry and then cannonaded by the British ships lying offshore. In their flight they lost their fieldpieces and had two hundred men captured,[15] including

General Thompson and a colonel who was taken at Pointe-du-Lac by Captain Rainville and some loyal Canadiens.[16]

Just as the fighting drew to a close Carleton arrived to resume command. Once again he chose not to press his advantage and allowed the remaining rebels to board their bateaux and escape to Sorel. Captain Richard England of the 47th Grenadiers was warned about a fugitive party escaping by a back route and requested Carleton's permission to cut them off. The governor replied, "No, let the poor creatures go home and carry with them a tale, which will serve his majesty more effectually than their capture."[17]

ARNOLD LEAVES MONTREAL

In the isolation of Montreal, Arnold was starved for information about the British advance from Quebec City and sent his newly acquired aide, Captain Wilkinson,[18] with dispatches for Sullivan. Wilkinson was startled to stumble upon British Regulars at Varennes, which was a long way upriver from Sorel. He managed to escape, stole a horse, and

Detail of painting by H.R.S. Bunnett, 1886 (© McCord Museum M309).

Château Ramezay, Arnold's Montreal headquarters and location of Mesplet's printing press.

galloped to Longueuil, where he met with some hostility but was able to seize a canoe and paddle across the river to deliver the startling news to an incredulous Arnold at his headquarters in the Château Ramezay.

Before Peters escaped from Montreal one of Arnold's friends revealed a secret plot to plunder and burn the city and offered him a share of the booty if he joined the conspiracy. Peters thanked the man for his friendship and asked for a few hours to consider it and then went to inform some key citizens, who organized a volunteer watch to disrupt the design.[19]

Once again, it is striking that Peters, a known loyalist, was allowed into these elite rebel circles — strange times, indeed. Perhaps so many men were switching allegiances that everyone's sense of caution was blunted.

Remarking on Arnold's disorderly retreat, the Quebec historian Lanctot writes that it was marred with "extortion, looting, violence, and vandalism," which certainly stained Arnold's name. The rebels were gone in four hours.

Arnold later wrote of his desperate situation, "Neglected by Congress below, distressed with the smallpox; want of Generals and discipline in our Army, which may rather be called a great rabble ... our credit and reputation lost ... and a powerful foreign enemy advancing upon us, — are so many difficulties we cannot surmount them."[20]

Peters's warning had been timely and local citizens were able to extinguish all the fires. The St. Sulpice superior, Abbé Etienne Montgolfier, turned over the keys of the city to militia colonel Thomas-Ignace Trottier Dufy Desauniers,[21] who set up patrols on the streets until the arrival of the Regulars.

SIR JOHN JOHNSON'S ADVENTURE

After leaving Forster, the Chevalier de Lorimier went to his mother's house in the cover of night and discovered the rebels had slaughtered her poultry and livestock and cut down her orchard. They tried to set fire to the house, but were probably in too much of a hurry to succeed. A neighbour complained to their detachment commander that the woman was an old widow who was certainly not responsible for her son's actions, but the officer was undeterred. After viewing that bitter scene, de Lorimier went to Akwesasne and, a short time later, Sir John Johnson arrived from the Mohawk Valley with a party of 180 friends, tenants, and employees. They had suffered terribly, having been reduced to eating beech leaves to survive. Once Sir John was a little recovered from his journey he decided to relieve Montreal and meet the army he heard was advancing from Quebec City.[22]

As Johnson and his regiment are peripheral to this story, his activities will be dealt with in brief. After his two brothers-in-law, Guy Johnson and Daniel Claus, left the Mohawk Valley with their Indian Department entourage, Sir John stood as the most prominent loyalist along the river. He fortified Johnson Hall, the beautiful home he had inherited from his father. It is said he built a stockade around the Hall and the two adjacent stone blockhouses that served as departmental storehouses. His friends, tenants, and employees were well-armed and a significant number had prior military experience. As well, he had his father's pair of fieldpieces. This combination gave the Tryon and Albany County Committees extreme discomfort, and when General Washington was apprised of Sir John's activities he was sufficiently alarmed to order General Schuyler to take immediate action.

In January 1776 Schuyler assembled four thousand Albany and Tryon County militiamen and moved against Johnson. Schuyler coerced the baronet into surrendering his own and his men's arms, then parolled him on his future good behaviour. To ensure compliance Schuyler took eight Highland Scots as hostages, which was a great affront to men accustomed to being dealt with as gentlemen. The measure earned the bitter enmity of the vast majority of Scotsmen in Tryon County and contributed to the inhabitants' suffering over the next six years.

Sir John ignored the parole and by May 19 had replaced many of the confiscated firearms and assembled 170 men and a handful of women and children at Johnson Hall. Schuyler had been monitoring Johnson's activities and decided he must be arrested, and sent a New Jersey Continental regiment to perform the deed. After some tense negotiations with the Fort Hunter Mohawks the regiment arrived in Johnstown to find that the baronet had fled with his friends and tenants. Pregnant Lady Mary Johnson, her children, and her sister Margaret were taken prisoner and the Hall was occupied and vandalized by the Jerseymen. Extensive questioning of the locals did not reveal where Johnson had gone.

The baronet avoided the obvious routes to Canada — that is, east to Lake Champlain or west to Oswego — reckoning that both were too closely watched to be safe, and instead risked traversing the tortuous Adirondacks, guided by some Mohawk friends. As de Lorimier recorded, after nineteen gruelling days the trekkers arrived at Akwesasne and were well received and cared for.

Johnson recovered rapidly. He sent to Forster at Oswegatchie for assistance and the captain supplied firelocks and one of the field-pieces taken at The Cedars. Sir John set out on June 13 with a collection of Canada Indians, Canadiens, and his American loyalists. His ad hoc force grew as he travelled east. By the time Johnson arrived at Montreal the 29th Regiment had relieved the city. After a brief delay, Johnson took his little army across the St. Lawrence to La Prairie to pursue the retreating rebels.[23]

Scattered in Disorder

While Sullivan was preparing to make a stand at Sorel he was undoubtedly distressed to receive a message from Colonel Hazen. "Do not rely on any real assistance from the Canadians whom you are collecting together — I know them well; be assured that, in our present situation, they will leave us in the hour of difficulty.... What are we to expect from a handful of such men, against the well-known best troops in the world?"[24]

Once Colonel Arnold was across the river at La Prairie he sent his aide for information. When Wilkinson arrived at the Richelieu River he was shocked to find that "The front of our retreating army, overwhelmed with fatigue, lay scattered in disorder over the plain, and buried deep in sleep, without a single sentinel to watch for its safety."

———————

The Chevalier de Lorimier met with Governor Carleton, General William Phillips, and Colonel Simon Fraser at Longueuil and, through the auspices of Carleton's aide-de-camp, Charles de Lanaudière, was given command of all the assembled Indians and instructions to cut off the rebels' retreat. De Lorimier was greatly chuffed to be given this honour. He chose a choke point on the Richelieu River north of St. John's where anyone attempting to pass would be within range of a pistol shot; however, his party failed to arrive in time, despite moving at speed.[25]

———————

Although Hazen had predicted the Canadiens' defection he must have been bitterly disappointed to be proven correct when only 175 of his 447 recruits joined in the withdrawal.[26] During Arnold's retreat from La Prairie he destroyed all the bridges behind him, while Sullivan was rallying the rest of the army at Chambly. Sullivan's men were on the move on June 16 after burning the fort, sawmills, surplus row galleys, and other watercraft. When the two rebel leaders held a council of war the next day at St. John's, they decided to retreat to Crown Point. Predictably, Arnold's was the last boat to push off. Louis Atayataghronghta, the ever-faithful Kahnawake, was there to wave him away.

Burgoyne commanded the pursuit out of Sorel. He pushed his Lights and Canadiens ahead, but they arrived just in time to see Arnold's disappearing boat. Only a single Indian was caught, in the process of lighting fire to a bridge. Perhaps this was Atayataghronghta, "performing one last service for a lost cause."[27]

John Peters reported that the rebels "burnt Chambly and St. Johns on their way to Isle la Motte." He had been released after being held on the island for six days, as the only proof against him was a letter from Jacob Bayley of Coös addressed to Sullivan with the warning, "take care of Colonel Peters, who was an enemy to America, and would escape to General Carleton the first opportunity." In the hubbub of the rebel army's setting off for Crown Point, Peters quietly slipped into the island's woods. On the evening of June 28 he returned to the deserted camp and met up with Dr. Joseph Skinner, who had deserted the rebel army. They found a canoe and paddled almost forty miles to St. John's, where they met with the newly promoted Brigadier Fraser, who received them kindly and sent them to General Carleton at Chambly. The governor was satisfied with Peters's conduct and gave him a pass to Montreal, where he was received with "much friendship and thanks for the assistance [he] had given in preserving their town and property." Skinner would later serve in Peters's battalion as the Surgeon's Mate.[28]

When Sir John Johnson's ragtag force arrived near Chambly on June 19 the baronet was received by Carleton, who was impressed with his initiative and the instructions he had received from William Tryon, New York's royal governor. Carleton granted Johnson a beating order to raise a regiment on the frontiers of New York named the King's Royal Regiment of New York. Sir John's following from the Mohawk Valley formed the core of the new battalion, added to which were a few anglo- and franco-Canadians including Jacob Maurer, the Royal Americans' veteran who had served at The Cedars. Two New Yorkers, Patrick Daly and Johnson's brother-in-law Stephen Watts, who had been with Maclean at the siege of Quebec, transferred to the Royal Yorkers; apparently without officially leaving the Emigrants, as they continued to draw double pay for many months.[29]

CARLETON CLEARS THE LAKE

Fire on these damned savages

CARLETON'S DECISIONS

From the very outset of the conflict Carleton had attempted to persuade the rebels of the error of their ways. Before the invasion he had avoided challenging their emissaries and had been soft on their many supporters and sympathizers. As the invasion gained momentum he was often inexplicably hesitant. Then, when their defeated army was fleeing in disarray, he refused to crush it. Despite his senior officers' obvious discomfort, and any evidence of rebel appreciation, he persisted in this approach even after the invaders had been driven from Quebec.

In the opinion of Canadian historian Alfred Burt, "Carleton's inactions when the Americans were scrambling to get out of the country ruined the campaign of 1776 and possibly altered the outcome of the war." Burt notes that the governor had requested an army of ten to twenty thousand and the government had complied,

> But he threw away the means of using it, for he did more than let the American soldiers escape from his grasp. He had only to reach out his hand to seize their boats and the control of Lake Champlain. Then

he might have succeeded in 1776, where Burgoyne was to fail in 1777.... As it was, the large army in Canada was forced to lie idle, unable to stir over Lake Champlain until a fleet was created — fighting vessels to clear the way and transport to use it. This preparation took so long that the great blow had to be postponed for a year.[1]

THE REBEL FLEET

Although Carleton's slow pursuit had allowed the core of the rebel army to escape to fight another day, Burt's claim that he missed an opportunity to seize control of Lake Champlain by capturing the rebel vessels in the Richelieu River is an overstatement. The issue was not that simple, for the rebels had three decked vessels on the lake — Philip Skene's schooner, which they had seized and renamed the *Liberty*; the British sloop *George*, that Arnold had taken at St. John's after Ticonderoga fell and rechristened the *Enterprise*; and the newly built schooner *Royal Savage*, which had fallen into their hands when Fort St. John's succumbed. And they had seized the frames of a row galley standing in the yard's stocks and taken them to Ticonderoga where they completed the vessel.

Yes, the rebels had built a flotilla of bateaux and two gondolas on Lake Champlain for the invasion of Canada. These had been dragged through the Richelieu rapids and used in operations to take Chambly, Sorel, and Montreal and in other waterborne exploits. It was these smaller watercraft that the rebels either destroyed before their withdrawal or used to carry off their beaten army, but their three fully armed, decked ships remained safe on the lake with the row galley and several gunboats, and the British had nothing of comparable strength on the Richelieu.[2]

CARLETON'S PREPARATIONS

Carleton had foreseen that there would be a fight to regain control of Lake Champlain and made early preparations. His naval advisor, Captain Thomas Pringle, had returned to England in November 1775 with the governor's requests that the Admiralty send to Canada in time for the next campaign a number of prefabricated, flat-bottomed boats "ready to be joined together with all their apparatus for rigging, arming &c" and other building materials. These requests had been met.[3]

In a cautionary note of July 8 the governor wrote to Lord George Germain, Dartmouth's replacement as secretary for the American colonies, "The Operations of the Army against the Rebels must now be suspended for some time. Great difficulties occur in transporting provisions, Artillery Stores, &c overland from Chambly, to St. John's and providing [the] Boats and armed Vessels necessary."[4]

Major-General William Phillips,[5] whom Carleton had appointed on June 6 to command the artillery and corps of engineers of the army in Canada, took charge of the military operations in and about Fort St. John's, while Commodore Charles Douglas, the commander of the relief squadron from Britain, supervised construction of the vessels,

New York Public Library Digital Gallery, Record 423916.

Lord George Germain, the new American Secretary.

employing a force of 650 officers and men from his warships and transports. Naval Lieutenant John Schank,[6] and master builder Jonathon Coleman, were given direction of the shipwrights and labourers.

The original plan had been to haul the one-hundred-ton schooner *Maria* overland from the St. Lawrence to St. John's, but the roads were too soft. So the vessel was stripped to the waterline and dragged to the new naval base, followed by its upper structure and fitments. This same procedure was followed for the transport *Carleton*, which was refitted with fourteen 6-pdrs. Naval carpenters took an eighteen-hundred-ton vessel off the stocks at Quebec City and sent its components upriver for movement to Fort St. John's where it was reassembled, armed with eighteen 12-pdrs, and christened *Inflexible*. A recovered rebel gondola was repaired, armed with five 9-pdrs, and renamed *Loyal Convert*. In addition a dozen prefabricated gunboats shipped from England were assembled and added to sixteen newly built Canadian gunboats, each of which was armed with a single gun ranging in size from 6-pdr to 24. Finally, following a Seven Years' War practice, a large flat-bottomed radeau, or raft, named *Thunderer* was constructed, which mounted fourteen 18-pdrs and four eight-inch howitzers. It would be the most heavily armed vessel on the lake and served as the flotilla's depot for powder, shot, and provisions.[7]

Each gunboat was to be crewed by eleven seamen and its guns served by seven Royal or Hesse-Hanau artillerists. In mid-June General Phillips sent the artillerymen to Trois-Rivières to gain experience with

His Majesty's vessels on Lake Champlain.

Pen and ink, Charles Randle, 1776 (Library and Archives Canada, C-013203).

small boats under the guiding hand of a senior naval officer.[8] The army's infantry was spread in cantonments up and down the Richelieu River and maintained a training regimen. The two Provincial regiments, Maclean's Highland Emigrants and Johnson's Royal Yorkers, were sent to patrol the parishes south of the St. Lawrence to watch for spies in the Richelieu region where the habitants had been the most active in the rebel cause during the occupation.[9]

Having been approached privately by Secretary Germain, General Burgoyne reported on June 22, "The Indians flock to us already in swarms, & if it be judged expedient to make use of that arm it is ready & in great strength"; however, Carleton did not find it expedient; he was primarily interested in securing their loyalty to the Crown rather than employing them on scouting missions.[10]

In contrast, during the lull the rebels constantly patrolled southern Quebec. Their most noteworthy partisan was the adventurous Benjamin Whitcomb of New Hampshire, who would play an important role in campaigns to come. On one patrol he sniped and mortally wounded a British brigadier from the cover of the woods, an act which outraged European sensibilities. The next few years would dull such reactions.

On June 20 Carleton relaxed his stranglehold on Native employment and sent Joseph Marie Lamothe with a large party of Kanehsatakes to go up the Richelieu toward Lake Champlain to determine the rebels' positions. At St. John's, Lamothe expanded his patrol base by dividing his men and, the next day, two of his parties took scalps and twenty-four prisoners from a smallpox-ridden camp on Île-aux-Noix. Lamothe's own party overwhelmed a reckless outing of unarmed Pennsylvanians on a fishing expedition and killed, scalped, and mutilated nine and wounded five others. Historian Paul Stevens reasons that these excesses repelled both Carleton and Burgoyne and stiffened their resolve to employ the Natives in a most restrictive manner and to ignore the positive results that Lamothe's efforts had achieved.

MANAGING THE CANADA INDIANS

The governor held a council with the Seven Nations' headmen in Montreal's old Jesuit church on June 24. To emphasize the importance of the occasion the principal British and German officers were in attendance, and Carleton's chief interpreter, Joseph Launière, sat by his side. The three Lake of Two Mountains settlements were represented, as were the Kahnawakes and the Abenakis of Bécancour and St. Francis, a few Lorette Hurons, and some Confederacy warriors. Each language group had its own interpreter, which undoubtedly led to a cacophony of words when the speakers took their frequent pauses. With the British so clearly back in control the Natives recognized they had but two options — either to feign, or to embrace, co-operation. Fingers were pointed at the Kahnawakes for their lack of zeal during the occupation, and their town had wisely sent its pro-British leaders to the council. One of them rose to explain that the rebels had unduly influenced an aged sachem. It was a lame defence, but accepted. The council ended with each community pledging its support and clamouring to be employed against the rebels, which was not at all what the governor had in mind, but he did dispatch a handful of Hurons to track down rebel prisoners who had escaped from Quebec and small parties of warriors to the Richelieu River posts to provide local security.

As Major Campbell and La Corne Saint-Luc were still being held by the rebels in the lower colonies the governor appointed his nephew, Captain Christopher Carleton of the 29th Regiment to lead the Natives in the upcoming movement. He was an ideal choice, as he had lived among the Canada Indians after the Seven Years' War, married a Native, learned the Kahnawake dialects, and become thoroughly acculturated, wearing their clothing and sporting tattoos. During this time he had befriended the de Lorimier and Clignancour trading families, which supplied officers to the Indian Department. The uncle had experienced considerable difficulty prying his nephew loose from the Native life, but now he intended to employ the younger man's knowledge, talents, and influence.[11]

In one of his first actions the nephew persuaded his uncle to allow the Kahnawakes an opportunity to redeem themselves. A party was sent to patrol Île-aux-Noix, where they destroyed a boatload of rebels and took some prisoners. This performance so pleased the governor that he had the Chevalier de Lorimier deliver a general pardon to the community.

When the time for the army's advance arrived Lorimier was instructed to collect the warriors from Lake of Two Mountains and Akwesasne and travel to Fort St. John's where they were to join with the Kahnawakes. There were many tense moments when the loyalist Natives confronted the Kahnawakes who had so often supported the rebel invaders and taken up arms against their Seven Nations' brethren, and the department's officers had a struggle to keep them from being insulted.[12]

THE MILITIA

By the end of June, Carleton had dismissed the loyal militia after thanking them for their zeal and asking them to be prepared to answer a future call for their services. While the naval preparations were underway he returned to Quebec City to fill vacancies in the civil courts. In his dealings with Canadiens who had supported the rebels, his approach was generally as conciliatory as his stance was with the Americans. When penalties were meted out, most were ecclesiastical in nature, which suited Canadien society.[13] Yet all was not sweetness and light. The month before he had appointed three men to investigate infractions and enforce the King's laws in the Quebec City district. All commissions granted by the rebels were collected. Any man holding a King's commission who had not performed his duty was required to surrender it and was replaced by a man of known fidelity. Further, citizens suspected of disloyalty were disarmed while their conduct was under investigation.

The commission concluded that the majority of Quebeckers had been neutral, although often friendly, to the rebels, a stance that had been encouraged by Carleton's failure to take firm action.

This latter finding was not likely reported to the governor. All parishes included a loyalist minority supported by the clergy, but a hostile and vigilant pro-rebel minority had frequently prevented them from taking action. A second commission was appointed to investigate Montreal district and a third to assess the damages to private property caused by the royal and rebel troops, which resulted in some compensation being granted. As to public property, many roads and bridges had been damaged and corvées of twelve hundred men, including several rebels released from jail, were assembled to make repairs. Some men who resisted this unpaid work were arrested and punished by being sent to toil on the fortifications at Île-aux-Noix. Men who had failed to disclose rebel spies were also sent to the island with their hands manacled. While the governor was willing to forgive many past transgressions, he did not abide any fresh offences.[14]

ACTIVITIES IN THE FAR WEST

Captain Henry Hamilton, Carleton's newly appointed lieutenant governor of Detroit, had arrived at his post and successfully taken up his responsibilities, despite some initial sparring with army officers who believed their authority held sway over his. Hamilton was a quick study; he readily absorbed the fine points of Native diplomacy, meeting in council with the headmen of the Lakes' and Ohio Nations and persuading them to follow the somewhat contradictory wishes of Governor Carleton — that is, to remain aloof from the contest but ready to take action when requested.

Some three hundred miles further west at Mackinac, Captain DePeyster had not received any instructions from Carleton. Instead, he obeyed Lieutenant-Colonel Caldwell's orders, which James Stanley Goddard had delivered, and industriously recruited every possible Native to make the trip across Lake Huron and Georgian Bay to the river network that would take them to the appointed rendezvous at Lake of Two Mountains. Goddard travelled further into the interior and assisted DePeyster's recruiting efforts so that by the first week of July the captain was able to dispatch two brigades of close to five hundred Ojibway, Ottawa, Fox, Menominee, Winnebago, and Sioux warriors, accompanied by a handful of British officers, Canadien traders, and volunteers including the accomplished partisan Charles de Langlade and the revered interpreter Joseph-Louis Ainsse. The warriors eagerly made the gruelling trip, recalling former services under the old French regime when their people had received many rewards and achieved great martial glory. Of necessity, DePeyster showered them with presents, purchased vast quantities of provisions for the voyage, and made guarantees to care for their families in their absence. Eight days after the second brigade had left DePeyster received Carleton's belated orders to stop the Natives' march.[15]

NEW YORK TORIES

In the Hoosic region of eastern New York Province, Francis Pfister, a former 60th Royal Americans lieutenant, assistant engineer, and map-maker who had become a successful farmer, teamed up with his father-in-law, John Macomb, an army contractor and Albany County judge; and Robert Leake, the son of the former British Army commissary general, to plan the raising of a regiment.[16]

The behaviour of the two older men came to the attention of the Albany Committee. On July 4 the minutes noted "That this Committee grant a mittimus for Committing John Macombe[,] Francis P. Fister and others to the Tory Goal being persons sent down under Guard by order of the Committee of Hosick." Seven days later Pfister and Macomb were subjects of a secret investigation. The next day Macomb appeared before the committee, refused to sign an association, and was required to tender a surety of £200 for his future good behaviour.[17]

Yet the vigilance of the committees was unable to prevent the three men from pursuing their plans. After General Howe had taken New York City they applied to him for a beating order, which was granted. Somehow, they collected commitments from 650 men, but it was not until the following year that many of them were able to join a detachment of Burgoyne's army on its march to Bennington.

Loyalist activities had increased in northern New York to such a degree that the committees were greatly concerned about "disaffected" groups hiding in the woods. These were men who had been hounded for their expressions of loyalty and refusals to do rebel service, and had gone into hiding after being intimidated by threats of violence and incarceration. On August 8 former Cambridge committeeman Simeon Covell was required to post a staggeringly large bail of £500 in order to gain his liberty so he could find defence witnesses for his next appearance. Covell soon found it necessary to take to the woods to avoid further persecution. James Hewetson was brought in with several other suspects from Coxsackie, interviewed, and set at large. In a few months he would swing from a rope. The next day the committee formed two "ranging" companies with a mandate to hunt down Tories and bring them to "justice." Day after day the committees' relentless meat grinder heard reports, examined, confined, or parolled proven and suspected Tories.[18]

THE WESTERN NATIVES ARRIVE

On July 23 the warriors of DePeyster's second Mackinac brigade arrived at Lake of Two Mountains and were advised that Governor Carleton had no need for their services. This was another instance of the fumbling, confusing British Native policy.[19] Just a few days before, the governor had met with the first brigade's warriors and put the best face possible on his decision not to employ them. He held a major council and invited senior British and German officers to add European dignity to the gathering. He was most generous in his words of thanks and in the presents he showered on the warriors. He assured them that the rebels would not be able to withstand the might of the King's armies; then, in his contradictory fashion, asked that they hold themselves in readiness if he should have a future need to call upon them. Why they might be needed when the King's armies were going to thrash the rebels was unexplained. The

Natives were cautioned to protect their homelands, refuse access to the rebels, and to never acknowledge any rule other than their grandfather, the King of Great Britain.

He asked them to take the Great Lakes route on their return voyage and speak to all the intervening Nations, spreading the good news of the rebels' defeat in Canada and of the opening of the western trade routes for business. In complying with this request they travelled up the St. Lawrence River and missed meeting the second brigade as it descended the Ottawa.

Carleton set off for Quebec City on July 20, satisfied that he had fulfilled his obligations to the western Natives. This left General Burgoyne on his own to receive the shocking arrival of the second brigade. Flummoxed, Burgoyne sent an express inquiry to the governor about how to proceed. Carleton replied that he should use the methods he had witnessed being employed with the first brigade. He was to take every measure "to satisfy them entirely in the Articles of Presents" and to fix them firmly in the King's interest. He was also to "give some mark of the Kings favour" to the Canadien officers and to determine which of them were the "most capable of commanding Indians and the fittest for that service."[20]

Burgoyne performed as instructed. This brief exposure to Native diplomacy represented the sum total of his experience before he took total control of their employment for the 1777 campaign. It would scarcely be enough.

NEWS FROM BOSTON

Ironically, just as Governor Carleton was taking satisfaction in the expulsion of the rebels from Quebec, the *Quebec Gazette* printed an account of the British Grand Army admitting to defeat at Boston and evacuating. Undoubtedly, Carleton knew of this reverse long before it was announced in the press; however, this startling news must have given many Quebeckers pause for thought.[21]

THE CANADA INDIANS RESPOND

It was the Canada Indians who were expected to support Carleton's Lake Champlain campaign, and by early September 641 warriors had assembled to assist the governor. The Seven Nations supplied 560, a large proportion of their full fighting strength. From Lake of Two Mountains came eighty Kanehsatakes, ninety Nipissings, and ninety Algonquins; from Akwesasne, 110; and from Kahnawake, 121, although the two Abenaki towns sent only seventy. As well, there were fifty-six Confederacy warriors, who were operating independently of their Nations' politics, and twenty-four Ottawas.[22]

Brigadier Fraser led a patrol of three British light companies south to Rivière Lacolle and then across the New York border to Isle La Motte, but their movement was so blatant that no intelligence was uncovered; however, a small patrol brought word on September 3 that a rebel flotilla had come north to Pointe-au-Fer and Akwesasne canoeists were sent to investigate. Native parties were now kept out constantly, managed by British officers who were accomplished, ambitious, young professionals seeking advancement. Their names were: Captain Alexander Fraser, 34th Regiment; Lieutenant James Wright, 9th; Lieutenant Thomas Scott, 24th; Lieutenant Richard Houghton, 53rd; and Ensign William Johnson, 29th.[23]

EMIGRANTS EMBARRASSED AGAIN

On May 28 Major Nairne of the Highland Emigrants was mortified to report to General Burgoyne's aide that five men had deserted from the regiment, but worse was to follow. The very next day he was compelled to advise that another eleven had run with their arms and accoutrements. Nairne opined that they would be easily recognized, as they were "mostly Cloathed in Green," and he thought that Canadiens would not dare to accept an exchange of those clothes. The major added, "I am much afraid no trust can be put in any of the men who were formerly with Rebels, of which number all those who sent off are, and we have Still several of them in the Regiment." The sixteen men were all taken up by August 9, but the damage had been done. Next year Burgoyne would request that the Emigrants be left in Canada rather than join his expedition.[24]

THE MARKSMEN

Lieutenant-Colonel Simon Fraser, whom Burgoyne considered the best light infantry commander in America, had a great deal of experience in *petite guerre* operations in Europe. Fraser recommended to Carleton that a specialized company of one hundred select British Regulars be created to operate with the Canadiens and Natives and provide the steadiness and reliability of European discipline when necessary. This oversize company was formally defined in Burgoyne's orders of September 6. Each of the army's ten British regiments was to contribute a serjeant, a corporal, and eight privates chosen for their strength, agility, and marksmanship. They were to be of "good character, sober, active, robust [and] healthy." The brigadier's nephew, the above-noted Alexander Fraser, was chosen as company commander with James Wright and Thomas Scott as his subalterns. Intentionally, the three officers also had duties in the Quebec Indian Department.

The colonel mused about the company's tactical employment alongside the Canadien and Native auxiliaries: "The nature of the country can admit of their turning large corps of the enemy, surprising convoys and making them uneasy in their rear." These roles, and many others, would be fulfilled by the Company of Select Marksmen during the next two campaigns — contributions that were entirely out of proportion to its size.

The formation of Fraser's British Rangers presented a problem. If they were to operate with the Natives under Captain Carleton's direction, young Fraser would be deprived of freedom of action; so to avoid this complex conflict of nepotism an ad hoc solution was adopted. Those Nations most familiar with young Carleton — the Kahnawakes, Akwesasnes, and the three Lake of Two Mountains villages — were put under his management. Alex Fraser was assigned the Abenakis, Six Nations, and Ottawas. The two bodies were expected to coordinate their activities, although, it must be noted, the Natives, who were not slaves to British orders, would follow the directions of their war captains and be guided by the more-familiar and empathetic Canadien officers. Captain Fraser would have his Marksmen, but young Carleton would be without a Regular component, so Brigadier Fraser assigned a Light Infantry detachment to him.[25]

Native Deployment

On September 8 fifty-five warriors arrived at Île-aux-Noix, followed by another twenty-five the next day. Captain Fraser with a detachment of his rangers and Natives had established an outstation at Rivière Lacolle and the new arrivals were allowed to send parties upriver to join him. On the eleventh Captain Carleton, bedecked in Native dress and paint, arrived at Île-aux-Noix with the majority of his warriors, and the next day Lieutenant Wright joined with the balance of the Natives and the marksmen from St. John's.

Pierre Foretier, the primary contractor for the Quebec Indian Department, had completed the outfitting of the Natives for the immediate campaign and also forwarded five hundred capotes and pairs of mittens in preparation for the winter. Now that the British had deployed their Native contingents forward, the Indians were permitted to run continuous patrols as far south as Ticonderoga. In consequence, rebel patrols became less frequent and less effective.

After a company of Regulars relieved the outstation at Rivière Lacolle, Captain Fraser's force set out in canoes to reconnoitre the lake. A Canadien officer set off on the tenth with nine warriors to take prisoners at Ticonderoga, and, a week later, Natives destroyed one of Arnold's bateaux and some others drove off rebel troops from the Onion River area.

On September 19 Captain Fraser's detachment attempted to lure the rebel schooner *Liberty* close to shore. The vessel's captain was sensibly cautious and had his longboat approach the shore stern first, whereupon Fraser's men sprung the ambush and fired on the boat and the ship causing several casualties, but also taking punishment from retaliatory fire. Fraser's canoes continued to dog the rebel fleet for a few more days, but retired to the advance camp when Arnold withdrew southward on September 23.[26]

CARLETON'S VIEW OF THE MILITIA

In preparation for further employment, the governor instructed militia colonels Dufy Desauniers in Montreal, de Tonnancour in Trois-Rivières, and Voyer in Quebec City to draw up lists of men willing to volunteer their services. Two thousand responded, which delighted Carleton, but this expression of zeal probably reflected the heady days following the rebels' expulsion, as it later proved very misleading. Delighted or not, the governor expressed doubts to the American secretary in a letter five days later.

> As to my opinion of the Canadians, I think there is nothing to fear of them, while we are in a state of prosperity, and nothing to hope for when in distress. I speak of the people at large; there are some among them who are guided by sentiments of honour, but the multitude is influenced by hopes of gain, or fear of punishment.[27]

On September 26 Carleton's military secretary ordered Sir John Johnson to bring his Royal Yorkers to La Prairie to be in position to join the troops should the army establish itself "on the other side of the Lake."[28]

It was October 4 before the British fleet was complete and set sail from St. John's to reconquer the lake.[29] As expedition commander Carleton took post in the *Maria*, the schooner named after his lady. He had scarcely five weeks of open navigation in which to defeat the rebel fleet and occupy the Lake Champlain posts of Crown Point and Ticonderoga.

Rebel Preparations

During the long delay while Carleton's fleet was being assembled the rebels had been equally busy, although they lacked similar quantities and qualities of resources and manpower. The indefatigable Benedict Arnold made up for these shortfalls with immense energy and considerable innovation. Rather than building square-rigged ships or schooners, Arnold used his seaman's skills and experience to develop a plan for a single-masted gondola armed with a bow-mounted 12-pdr, a pair of 9-pdrs abaft the bow, and several swivel guns. Eight of these craft were launched in mid-September from the Skenesborough yard and brought to Mount Independence to be rigged and armed. Three lateen-rigged row galleys were also part of this fleet. As a result, together with the three decked vessels taken from the British, the rebels had put together a sizeable armament, added to which was Arnold's firm grip on bold tactics, whether on land or water;[30] however, he was disappointed with his crews. "[W]e have a wretched motley Crew ... the Marines[,] the Refuse of every Regiment, and the Seamen, few of them ever wet with salt Water."[31]

Major-General Horatio Gates, an ambitious and opportunistic former British Regular officer who had retired to live in Massachusetts, after much lobbying had been appointed by Congress to replace Schuyler as commander of the northern army and, bizarrely, the dictator of Canada.[32] His appointment offended both Schuyler and Sullivan, but Schuyler pragmatically struck a deal, which had Gates take command on the lakes while he held command in Albany. In contrast, Sullivan went to Congress to lodge a fruitless complaint.

Gates chose to withdraw from Crown Point, leaving behind three hundred men to retard the British advance. By the fall, he had some nine thousand men spread between Crown Point, Fort George on Lake George, Skenesborough on South Bay, and (the majority) centred at Ticonderoga and Mount Independence. In a display of typical American drive and engineering skill the works at the latter complex were greatly improved and strengthened. Gates's army was composed of several artillery companies, Continental infantry, New England militia, and a company of Stockbridge Indians.[33]

The rebels were first to put their fleet on the lake and by September 1 Arnold was patrolling with twelve sail as far north as the Canadian border, over a month ahead of Carleton.[34]

CARLETON MOVES

When it came, Carleton's advance was typically cautious and well organized. The army's brigades moved in stages from St. John's to Île-aux-Noix, to Rivière Lacolle, then to Pointe-au-Fer with Fraser's Advance brigade leading and Captains Carleton and Fraser with their Regulars, Canadiens, and Natives in the van occupying campsites days ahead of the arrival of the artillery and infantry brigades. For all this due care, no information about the rebels' whereabouts came back to the governor. So on October 5 he sent his aide, Captain de Lanaudière, on a scout southward, followed by a second party on the seventh. That day Colonel Fraser marched to Pointe-au-Fer, with Captain Carleton ahead scouring Isle La Motte and Captain Fraser scouting Cumberland Bay. Still, no rebels!

Outfoxed Twice at Valcour Island

On October 10 the lead elements of the governor's fleet of ships, gunboats, and bateaux set out from Isle La Motte accompanied by Fraser's Natives in birch canoes and Captain Carleton's detachment advancing afoot along the western shore to Cumberland Bay. Burgoyne's line infantry brigade remained at Pointe-au-Fer and Powell's at Rivière Lacolle.

The next morning the British ships were blessed with a favourable wind, and, after picking up Captain Carleton's detachment, they sailed past Valcour Island, which was precisely what Arnold had anticipated when he hid his ships behind it, recognizing that the British fleet would be divided into those who relied on sail and those who did not.

Captain Pringle, the governor's naval commander, had failed to send out scouting vessels, so the British sailed blithely on and Arnold had to dispatch the captured *Royal Savage* to lure them back. When the British spotted the *Savage*, their sailing vessels were faced with the chore of beating back against the wind in order to come into range to engage. On the other hand the crews of the gunboats and gondolas bent their backs over their sweeps and were able to come into position to engage the *Savage*, which they forced to run aground off the island, where it was abandoned and later captured. But now they were in range of Arnold's guns.[35]

In the meantime Carleton had signalled to the scouting captains that the rebel fleet was sheltered behind the island and they swiftly paddled toward the shore. De Lorimier recalled that "M. Charles Lanaudière landed on the island where he silenced the fire coming from one small vessel: his volunteers fired so briskly that not a single American dared appear above deck."[36] The detachments of Captains Carleton and Fraser landed on the New York shore and ran through the woods to come abreast of Arnold's right flank. De Lorimier was with them and recalled:

> As for us, we had our hands full with the vessel commanded by General Arnold himself. We made it so hot for him that all his men flung themselves on the

bottom of the boat and left him all alone on the deck. He was so enraged by their cowardice that it is said that he flung overboard three of his own men who were groaning with the pain of their wounds; but I didn't see him do that. Then he grabbed a speaking-trumpet and hailed another vessel to fire on these damned savages. They carried out his orders to the letter; a cannon ball toppled over a stone and mortar chimney and part of it fell onto Lieutenant de Bleury who livened things up a bit by galloping off as though he had been struck by the whole chimney, which made everyone roar with laughter.[37]

The shorelines of both the island and mainland were sufficiently high that the various marksmen could look down on the decks of the anchored ships and snipe at the exposed crews. Arnold later claimed that they did little execution, but a rebel soldier at Ticonderoga was told that the small-arms fire had been more annoying than the British vessels.[38]

Dr. Samuel Adams, a New York loyalist from Arlington in the Grants, had volunteered under Captain Carleton and landed with him on the New York shore. He had many enemies among the Green Mountain Boys, who had earlier humiliated him by strapping him to a chair and hoisting him to the top of the sign of their favourite tavern. Valcour was the doctor's first military action on behalf of the Crown and a precursor to his activities during Burgoyne's 1777 expedition.[39]

The naval action was prolonged, with the Crown's gunboats carrying the fight to the rebels. The *Carleton* eventually worked into range, only to become the rebels' largest and preferred target and take a terrible beating. At sunset the British vessels withdrew, which was just as well, as the gunboats were almost out of ammunition. Although only one rebel gondola had been sunk, their other vessels had taken a solid pounding.

The British ships and gunboats formed a line south of the rebels' anchorage while being reammunitioned by the radeau; however, in the dead of night Arnold again displayed his tactical wizardry and, in utter silence, led his battered ships past the British line.[40] De Lorimier was miffed, as he had recommended to Captain Carleton that a canoe be spotted ahead of the rebel fleet overnight to prevent just such a movement and had been told it was unnecessary.[41] Governor Carleton was enraged.

Although the British were slow to pursue, they caught up with the rebel fleet just north of Crown Point and used their superior weight of metal to defeat it. After the *Congress* had been repeatedly hulled, Arnold ran her ashore in the company of several other gondolas and the crews set them afire before retiring into the woods. Arnold somehow managed to avoid a Native ambush and arrived at Chimney Point, where he found more of his gondolas. Boarding one, he took the surviving vessels across to Crown Point. They were a mere shadow of his original armament and he saw no point in attempting to contest this post. He destroyed the works and a local sawmill before withdrawing to Ticonderoga.[42]

The schooners *Maria* and *Carleton* in heavy action.

Detail from R. Sayer and J. Bennett, October 1776. (Digitales Archiv Marburg HStAM WHK 28/29).

CARLETON AT CROWN POINT

Carleton's naval elements made an unopposed anchorage offshore Crown Point on October 14 and the two scouting detachments went ashore to secure the area. Two days later the bateaux carrying the line infantry landed. There were now four thousand troops ashore, composed of British and Hesse-Hanau artillerymen, Brigadier Fraser's advance corps of Grenadiers and Lights, line infantry detachments drawn from seven British regiments, and the Canadien and Native auxiliaries.[43]

Many historians believe that Carleton decided against advancing on Ticonderoga because the season was too far advanced. Yet over half his army, including much of his artillery and almost all his German troops, had not been brought forward from the Richelieu camps, which could suggest he had never planned to expand the campaign.[44]

Further evidence along that line are his orders of October 6 to his commanders at Niagara, Detroit, and Mackinac to prepare the

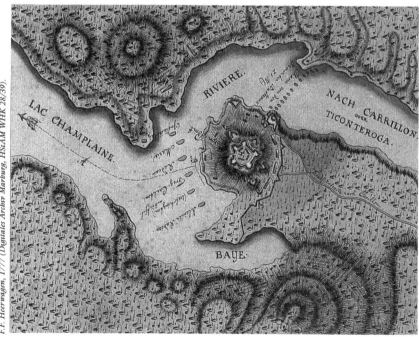

E.F. Heerwagen, 1777 (Digitales Archiv Marburg, HStAM WHK 28/39).

Crown Point surrounded by the Lake Champlain fleet in 1777.

Natives for the next year's campaign. These were written before the clash with Arnold at Valcour Island and entrusted to Charles de Langlade, who had remained in Montreal for this specific purpose after the far western Natives had returned home.

Contrary to this notion is the governor's correspondence with Sir John Johnson. The impatient baronet had written to the governor on October 16 to enquire if his new battalion would be expected to cross the lake to Crown Point. Carleton's secretary replied on October 23 that it was doubtful that Crown Point would be reestablished due to the lateness of the season and declined to order Sir John forward.[45]

NEW YORK LOYALISTS MOVING ABOUT

Joseph Egelston, who lived near the "Large Falls on Hudson's River" reported to the deputy commander of Albany County's 13th Regiment that he and his wife had seen several men under arms passing by their house on October 24. A week later Edward Jessup, Jonathon Jones, John McDoull, and the two sons of Amos Moore passed by the couple's house with more than seventy men under arms and carrying packs on their backs. Presumably Jessup recognized that Egelston was of the rebel persuasion as he told him that his party of about seven hundred men was leaving, but that they had no intention of fighting. Why he would think this news would calm the local committeemen is a mystery. The next day James Hewetson, the previously noted, notorious Tory recruiter from Coxsackie, came to Egelston's house and enquired about Jessup's party and where it had gone. Later that day Egelston came across Hewetson talking to Hezekiah Willis. They told him that they had seen a party, presumably of rebel militia or rangers from Fort Edward, which caused them to return to his house.[46]

The "harmless" Daniel McAlpin and William Edmeston,[47] his close friend who had been brevet major of the 48th Regiment, decided to secretly raise a battalion of "His Majesty's Loyal Subjects in Albany and in the neighbouring Countys." They may not have heard of Ebenezer and Edward Jessups' plans to do the same thing, or may simply have chosen to ignore them, as neither brother had Regular army experience. Whatever the case, instead of approaching Governor Tryon as the Jessups had done, they applied to Major-General Sir William Howe, the new C-in-C North America, who had established his headquarters in New York City. Howe gave them a beating order with "instructions to engage the Men taking care not to appoint more than one Captain[,] two Suballtans[,] three Serjants[,] three Corporals and one Drummer to every fifty Men."[48]

WE TERMINATE THE CAMPAIGN ILL

If Carleton had chosen to attack the Ticonderoga complex, it may have been a tougher nut to crack than his officers anticipated. During the three-month delay to build the fleet the governor had held back his auxiliaries from harassing the rebels' supply columns and construction crews, which allowed Arnold to build his fleet unimpeded and Gates to thoroughly reorganize the fortress's works and rebuild the ruined army's strength to twelve thousand Continentals and militiamen. True, sickness was rife throughout the garrison and only about sixty percent of his army was fit for duty. And it was also true that the militiamen were ill-armed and ill-disciplined, but only four thousand Crown troops, even with strong naval support, may not have been sufficient.

As well, Carleton had no firm grasp of his opposition's strength. He had declined to even reconnoitre the complex until the day after landing at Crown Point, when he dispatched the two scouting captains to Putnam's Creek. Alex Fraser led his British Rangers with thirty Canadiens and interpreter Launière's one hundred Indians to within view of Ticonderoga's entrenchments, but the rebels chose not to make a sally, nor even to fire their muskets. His sole accomplishment was to run off 130 cattle, which at least were very welcome at Crown Point. The two captains continued to worry the rebels with minor forays and took prisoners to Crown Point for examination, but achieved nothing more.

Historian Paul Stevens reasons that Carleton had so constrained the scouting captains with rigid instructions against allowing the Natives a free hand to wage war in their own manner that the warriors became oddly detached. What was there in it for them? No captives to take home, no booty, no glory — just the strange obligation to serve the King.

One event stood out during this bland period. Several Stockbridge Indians had been captured with the sailors from Arnold's fleet and were being held in irons aboard the shipping. The loyal Indians treated them kindly and arranged for their release, which astonished many British officers who expected a demand for revenge instead.

The governor pursued his earlier practice and released all the prisoners taken in the naval battle and by the various scouts with expressions of friendship and admonitions not to take up arms again. It was another grand gesture and might have achieved some traction, except General Gates saw the risk and would not allow any of them to land at Ticonderoga for fear their tales of good treatment would pollute the garrison.

Carleton's other practice of keeping his own counsel led to dissatisfaction among his senior officers, as his decision not to proceed against Ticonderoga had come as quite a surprise. They entirely understood the restrictions of a late season, but the governor's unwillingness to harass the complex with light troops and Natives, or to cut their supply lines to the south, was unfathomable. When he decided to send the two line infantry brigades back to Quebec on October 18, Burgoyne took his leave after obtaining permission to return to Britain to take his seat in Parliament. He took with him Carleton's plans for the 1777 campaign and the governor's request that he personally deliver them to the King.

Four days later Carleton announced his decision not to rebuild or garrison Crown Point; the entire army would retire north for

New York Public Library Digital Gallery, Record 424298.

William Phillips, senior Royal Artillery officer in Canada.

the winter. Major-General Phillips wrote of his disappointment to Burgoyne on the twenty-third, catching him before he sailed to Britain, "Notwithstanding the success upon the lake, we terminate the campaign ill."[49]

A PARTY OF LOYALISTS

On October 27 a party of forty loyalists arrived at Crown Point guided by Justus Sherwood, a substantial farmer, landowner, and surveyor from New Haven in the Grants. Sherwood had been one of Allen's Green Mountain Boys at the attack on Ticonderoga in 1775, but by the spring of 1776 he had a change of heart and was seized by the rebels and given twenty lashes to set him straight.[50] In August armed men again wrenched him from his home, although he managed to persuade the Committee to grant him bail; however, that same night he was roused from his bed and ordered to prison "for the Crime ... of being Enimical to the Country[,] Refusing to take Oaths ... and sending Intelligence to General Carleton." After languishing a month in confinement he was brought before the "Grand Committee," who condemned him to be imprisoned in Simsbury Mines in Connecticut, a frightful place where many loyalists rotted and not a few died. Sherwood managed to escape, and after collecting a dozen men, including his brother-in-law, he set out to join Carleton.[51]

En route his party fell in with twenty-eight men who were Yorker tenants from the Camden Valley in the Grants.[52] These were strange bedfellows for Sherwood's New Englanders, but harsh realities had brought them together. The Yorkers were led by Edward Carscallen, an Irish-born Seven Years' War veteran with twenty years' military service. His companions were Protestants who had escaped religious persecution in Germany and been settled in the Emerald Isle by Queen Anne. They had emigrated from there and taken land in the Camden Valley under a Yorker landlord. It was thought they were tough enough to confront Allen's bullying tactics, but — having suffered repeated persecution, first for being Yorkers, then for their loyalty to the King — they decided to join the British Army, which they heard was on the lake. Finding their way to Crown Point was another matter and they had been lost when they had the good fortune to blunder into Sherwood's party.[53]

These forty loyalists were to serve conspicuously throughout the war, many as commissioned and non-commissioned officers in various Provincial regiments. Sherwood would head Quebec's Secret Service and be given responsibility for wooing Vermont back into the British fold.[54]

A FINAL RECONNAISSANCE

General Phillips finally persuaded the governor to permit a full-blown reconnaissance, and on October 28 five gunboats and several canoes carried five companies of Lights, Canadiens, and Indians to Three Mile Point, from which the Ticonderoga complex could be readily observed. Once there, Phillips and an engineer took a boat to survey the works, and thirteen canoes filled with troops and Indians worked along the shore past the fortifications and were fired on with some round shot, but that was it — by four in the afternoon the whole force sailed back to Crown Point.

ANOTHER LOYALIST PARTY

On November 4 a second party of loyalists arrived at Crown Point, led by Ebenezer and Edward Jessup from the upper Hudson River. Ebenezer presented the governor with his beating order granted by Governor Tryon of New York. Carleton was not very pleased to see the brothers and later wrote to General Phillips, "The plan approved by Governor Tryon, as Mr. Jessop reports seems to me very judicious; it is to be wished the Gentleman and his followers could have remained at their own homes 'till it became practicable."[55] When Ebenezer arrived in Quebec, he explained his predicament in a letter to his friend Sir John Johnson.

> I intended to Send About 1000 Men ... to meet Genl Carlton, & Stay behind myself a little Longer but being unfortunately Discover'd a Day too soon was Obliged to Make the best of my way of[f] with a little more than Eighty Men thinking to Joine the Army at Ticonderoga[.] ... I gave Genl Philips at St. Johns a more General Account of my Intentions, and that myself & Edwd Jessup had Raised Two Regiments.[56]

As with Sherwood's party, Jessup's men provided noteworthy service in various capacities during the war, many as Provincial commissioned and non-commissioned officers.[57]

On November 5 the army boarded the vessels and sailed north, putting an end to a rather insipid campaign. Nonetheless, there were two significant accomplishments. Canada was free of invaders and would remain so until 1812, and northern Lake Champlain was under the control of a strong British fleet.

NOTES

CHAPTER ONE: THE "INTOLERABLE" QUEBEC ACT

1. An excellent resource concerning the Canadien Militia of the French regime, and the reasons for Carleton's difficulties in rallying Canadien support in 1775–77, is René Chartrand, *Canadian Military Heritage,* vol. 1, *1000–1754* and vol. 2, *1755–1871* (2 vols., Montreal: Art Global Inc., 1995); Alfred Leroy Burt, *The Old Province of Quebec,* vol. 1, *1760–1778* (2 vols., Toronto: McClelland and Stewart Limited, 1968), 2, 23–24.
2. Gustave Lanctot, Margaret M. Cameron, tr., *Canada & the American Revolution, 1774–1783* (Toronto: George G. Harrap & Co. Ltd., 1967), 14–15.
3. Arthur Granville Bradley, *Lord Dorchester* (Toronto: *The Makers of Canada* (series). Morang & Co., Limited, 1911). Bradley states that Carleton commanded a Grenadier battalion at Quebec in 1759 and that his wound was not serious; D. Peter MacLeod, *Northern Armageddon: The Battle of the Plains of Abraham; Eight Minutes of Gunfire that Shaped a Continent* (Vancouver: Douglas & McIntyre, 2008), 217, writes that Carleton was very severely wounded.
4. Biography of **Guy Carleton**. *Dictionary of Canadian Biography* [hereafter *DCB*], vol. 5. b.1724, Ireland; d.1808, England. Wife — Lady Maria Howard, eleven children.
5. **Catholic Bishop**: Burt, 84–89.
6. Gage to Amherst, ~December 1859, transcribed in Burt, 13.
7. Biography of **Hector Cramahé**. *DCB*, vol 4. b.1720, Dublin; d.~1788, England. Ensign, 1741 and Lieutenant, 15th Regiment, 1741. Saw South American, West Indies, and European service. Captain, 15th Regiment, 1754. In 1758, at siege of Louisbourg, and 1759, siege of Quebec. After surrender of Quebec City, became Brigadier-General James Murray's secretary, with whom he enjoyed a close friendship. Murray wrote, "There does not exist a

man of more Integrity and Application.... No man has the good of this colony more at heart." Lord Halifax described Cramahé "as one of the best men I know." He left the army in 1761 to serve as civil secretary under Murray, Carleton, and Haldimand until 1780.

8. Carleton to Gage, September 20, 1774. Transcribed in Paul L. Stevens, "His Majesty's 'Savage' Allies: British Policy and the Northern Indians During the Revolutionary War; The Carleton Years, 1774–1778" (6 vols., doctoral dissertation, Department of History, State University of New York at Buffalo, 1984), chapter 4, 259–60.

9. Cramahé to Dartmouth, June 30 and July 15, 1774, found in Stevens, chapter 4, 255. ex CO42/33, ff.56–59.

10. Burt, 56.

11. George F.G. Stanley, *Canada Invaded 1775–1776* (Toronto: Samuel Stevens Hakkert & Company, 1977), 10–11.

12. Burt, 2–3, 44.

13. Canadian Army General Staff, Historical Section of, ed. [hereafter HSGS]. "The War of the American Revolution: The Province of Quebec under the Administration of Governor Sir Guy Carleton, 1775–1778," in *A History of the Organization, Development and Services of the Military and Naval Forces of Canada from the Peace of Paris in 1763 to the Present Time with Illustrative Documents* (2 vols., Canada), vol. 2, 4; Biography of **Charles-Louis Tarieu de Lanaudière**. *DCB*, vol. 5. b.1743; d.1811, Quebec City. Wife — Geneviève-Elizabeth de la Corne, d/o La Corne Saint-Luc, m.1769. Officer, Regiment de la Sarre. Aide to Carleton, 1775 and 1776. At siege of Quebec City. Led Cdn Volunteers at Valcour Island, 1776. In conjunction with La Corne Saint-Luc, raised 170 Canadien Volunteers and on July 10, 1777, brought them to the army with the western Indians. He led Canadien Volunteers at Bennington. Gavin K. Watt, *The British Campaign of 1777*, vol. 2, *Burgoyne's Native and Loyalist Auxiliaries: The Burgoyne Expedition* (Milton: Global Heritage Press, 2013).

14. The *Quebec Gazette*, February 16, 1775. Governor Wentworth's proclamation dated Salem, NH, January 10, 1775. Also, a report of these events in the *Quebec Gazette*, May 4, 1775, of interest: one of the leaders in these seizures was John Sullivan, who played a role in Quebec in 1776. *http://en.wikipedia. org/wiki/Fort_William_and_Mary*.

15. For a brief look at John Brown's extensive service in the Revolutionary War, see *en.wikipedia.org/wiki/John_Brown_of_Pittsfield*. **Brown's death**: for details of his death in battle at Stone Arabia in the Mohawk Valley in 1780, see Gavin K. Watt, research assistance by James F. Morrison, *The Burning of the Valleys: Daring Raids from Canada Against the New York Frontier in the Fall of 1780* (Toronto: Dundurn, 1997), chapter 5.

16. Brown to the Boston Committee, March 29, 1775, from the *American Archives*, Peter Force, ed., Fourth Series, vol. 2, 243–45, cited in Stevens, chapter 6, 369.

CHAPTER TWO: Loyalism in New York Province

1. Alexander Clarence Flick, *Loyalism in New York During the American Revolution* (New York: The Columbia University Press, 1901), 22.
2. Flick, 9–10.
3. Flick, 11, 24–25.
4. **Committees**: The Albany County Committee was formally known as the "Committee of Safety, Protection and Correspondence," but "Committee of Correspondence" became the most commonly used title. James Sullivan and Alexander C. Flick, eds., *Minutes of the Albany Committee of Correspondence, 1775–1778* (2 vols., Albany: State University of New York, 1923 & 1925), vol. 1, iii; "Narrative of John Peters, Lieutenant-Colonel of the Queen's Loyal Rangers in Canada, written in a letter to a friend in London, Pimlico [England] June 5, 1786" [hereafter *Peters's Narrative*]. Archives of Ontario [hereafter AO], H.H. Robertson Papers, *The Daily Globe*, Toronto July 16, 1877.
5. Lanctot, 23–24.
6. A brief biography of William Williams is found in the *Records of the Council of Safety and Governor and Council of the State of Vermont, to which are prefixed the records of the General Conventions from July 1775 to December 1777*, E.P. Walton, ed., 3 vols. (Montpelier: Steam Press of J. & J.M. Poland, 1873), vol. 2, 111–12fn.
7. For an analysis of the steps taken by Sir William Johnson in the management of the far western fur trade, see Paul L. Stevens, *A King's Colonel at Niagara 1774–1776* (Youngstown: Old Fort Niagara Association, 1987) vol. 1, 7.
8. Biography of **Luc de La Corne / Chapt de La Corne / La Corne Saint-Luc**. *DCB*, vol. 4. b.~1711, Contrecoeur; d.1784, Montreal. Father-in-law of Major John Campbell and Chevalier de Lorimier. Military and Indian Department officer/trader. Fluent in four or five native languages. Wives — 1. Marie-Anne Hervieux, m.1742; 2. Maire-Joseph Buillimin, m.1757; 3. Marie-Marguerite Boucher de Boucherville, sister of René-Amable. Famous partisan of Seven Years' War. Taken at the fall of Fort St. John's and imprisoned by rebels, 1775. De facto second-in-command, Quebec Indian Department, 1777. Biography of **John Campbell**. *DCB*, vol 4. b.1731, Scotland; d.1795, Quebec City. Nicknamed "Handsome Jack." Wife — Marie-Anne, d/o La Corne Saint-Luc, m.1763. Entered 43rd (42nd) Regiment, 1744. Fought at Culloden, 1746. Lieutenant, 42nd Regiment, 1748, and dangerously wounded at Ticonderoga, 1758. Captain, 27th Regiment, at Havana, 1762, and at Trois-Rivières, 1763. Appointed Inspector of Indian Affairs by Governor Murray, 1765, which was reversed by Sir William Johnson. Campbell took half-pay, 1771. Appointed Superintendent of Quebec Indian Affairs by Governor Carleton in 1773 with the nominal rank of major and returned to Quebec, 1775. Led the force that captured Ethan Allen, 1775. Taken at the fall of Fort St. John's. See also Stevens, chapter 2, 86. Campbell had two titles: "Commandant of the Indians, and Superintendent and Inspector of Indian Affairs, within our Province of Quebec in America" and "Commissary for Indians." See Stevens, chapter 6, 366. Returned to Quebec in 1777 and managed Canada and Western Indians during Burgoyne's campaign and surrendered on October 17, was

exchanged and returned to Montreal by November 1777. Received courtesy rank of Lieutenant-Colonel, 1777, and Colonel, 1782. Campbell managed scouts and couriers for the balance of the war. His courtesy rank reverted to Lieutenant-Colonel after the war. He continued to serve as Canada Indians' Superintendent under Sir John Johnson until his death in 1795.

9. "Col. Claus's Remarks on the Management of Northern Indian Nations," March 1, 1777, transcribed in *Documents Relative to the Colonial History of the State of New York*, E.B. O'Callaghan, ed. (Albany, NY, 1857), vol. 8, 700–04.

10. **Autonomous branch**: I have taken this phrase from Stevens, chapter 1, 10.

11. **Interpreters**: For the Algonquins, Jean-Baptiste Rousseau, dit Saint-Jean; and for the Iroquois, Louis Perthius. Stevens, chapter 2, 84.

12. Stevens, "*Savage*" *Allies*, passim.

13. Biography of **Alexander McKee**. *DCB*, vol. 4. b.~1735, Pennsylvania; d.1799, Ontario. Lieutenant, Pennsylvania Provincials, Seven Years' War. Entered Indian Department, 1760. In March 1778 fled Fort Pitt into Ohio Country, then went to Detroit. Captain/Interpreter, Indian Department. Saw extensive service during Revolution. Postwar, drew land opposite Detroit, continued as Deputy Agent at Detroit. Involved in 1790s native campaigns. Deputy Superintendent and Deputy Inspector Indian Affairs, 1794.

14. **Lernoult, Richard Berringer**. Commanded three line companies at Detroit. When Lieutenant-Colonel Caldwell died at Niagara, Lernoult was the regiment's senior Captain in America and immediately left Detroit to take command at Niagara. John Butler credited Lernoult and Lieutenant-Colonel Caldwell in fixing the Confederacy "in the interests of the King." Lernoult saw important service throughout the war, latterly as Haldimand's Adjutant-General. Major, 1783. Stevens, *King's Colonel*, 68 and HSGS, vol. 2, 234, 236. Biography of **Arent Schuyler DePeyster**. *DCB*, vol. 6. b.1736, NY; d.1822, Scotland. Ensign, 50th Regiment, 1755. Lieutenant, 51st Regiment, 1755. New Jersey Provincial Regiment, Seven Years' War. Likely taken prisoner at Oswego, 1756. Exchanged from France, 1757. In England, transferred to 8th Regiment, 1757. Served in Germany, 1760. Captain-Lieutenant, July 1767 and Captain, November 1767. Came to Quebec, 1768. Sat on court trying Major Robert Rogers in Montreal. Recruiting in Albany, 1771. Appointed commandant of Michilimackinac, 1774. Particularly adept in native diplomacy. Major, 8th Regiment, May 1777. Transferred to Detroit, 1779. Appointed Lieutenant-Colonel in the army, November 1782 and Lieutenant-Colonel, 8th Regiment, September 1783. Commanded at Niagara, 1784. Left Quebec 1785. Many postings in Britain. Retired to Scotland, 1794.

15. These conflicts haunted the two Indian departments in the war's early years, but ultimately their efforts blended reasonably harmoniously, particularly after Sir John Johnson was appointed as superintendent; Stevens, chapter 1, 12 and chapter 2, 97, 125, 187, 192–94.

16. **Dunmore's War**. The *Quebec Gazette*, February 2, 1775. An article dated Williamsburg, December 8, 1774, announced that Dunmore had concluded a peace with the Shawnees, Delawares, and other nations, who ceded vast areas of their hunting territories. From the native perspective, it was a thoroughly unhappy conclusion.

17. Lanctot, 24–33. Lanctot provides an excellent discussion of the clever subtleties in Congress's letter to the Quebeckers; Biography of **François Cazeau**. *DCB*, vol. 5.
18. Lanctot, 35.
19. *Quebec Gazette*, April 20, 1775.
20. Stanley, *Invaded*, 11–12; Lanctot, 41; Elinor Kyte Senior, "Montreal in the Loyalist Decade, 1775–1785," in *The Loyalists of Quebec 1774–1825, a Forgotten History* (Montreal: Heritage Branch, United Empire Loyalists Association of Canada, 1989), 15; Governor Carleton's proclamation of May 8, 1775, offered a $200 reward and was printed in the *Quebec Gazette*, May 11, 1775.
21. *Albany Minutes*, vol. 1, 11–33.

CHAPTER THREE: Open Conflict Erupts

1. Gage to Carleton, April 21 and 27, 1775 cited in Stevens, chapter 5, 307.
2. Biography of **Moses Hazen**. *DCB*, vol. 5. b.1733, MA; d.1803, NY. Wife — Charlotte de La Saussaye, m.1770 in Montreal. Hazen's biographer, Allan S. Everest, notes that Hazen served as a company commander under Robert Rogers during the attack on Louisbourg in 1758 and that, when he transferred to the Quebec theatre, he introduced "Rogers's form of brutal partisan warfare." True or not, Governor Murray attributed to Hazen, "so much still Bravery and good Conduct as would Justly Entitle him to Every military Reward he Could ask or Demand."
3. Biography of **Benedict Arnold**. *DCB*, vol. 5. b.~1741, CT; d.1801, England. Apothecary, merchant. Wives — 1. Margaret Mansfield, m.1767; 2. Margaret (Peggy) Shippen, m.1779. Arnold had a complicated, highly accomplished, and controversial career during the Revolution which cannot be done justice here. Further investigation is recommended to the reader.
4. **Preston, Sir Charles**. b.1735, Scotland. Second Lieutenant, 5th Marines, 1747. Half-pay, 1748. From half-pay, Lieutenant, 26th Regiment, 1753. Captain, 26th Regiment, 1759. Major, 26th Regiment, 1768. Retired, 1777. Houlding, John A., "The King's Service: The Officers of the British Army, 1735-1792" (n.d., u.p.) and Library and Archives Canada [hereafter LAC], Charles Preston fonds, Cain No.275000; The *Quebec Gazette*, May 25, 1775, carries a report of the capture of Ticonderoga. It credits Allen with the raid on Fort St. John's that took the sloop *George*.
5. **Bindon's escapade**. Senior, 15–16 and Bradley, 84.
6. Stanley, *Invaded*, 21–26; Stevens, chapter 6, 362; HSGS, vol. 2, 51–52.
7. Braisted research. "The Petition of William Friend, late Commander of one of His Majesty's Sloops on Lake Champlain." Public Records Office [hereafter PRO], AO13/54, ff.411–12. Friend states that his 200-acre property on Lake George at Ticonderoga was looted by Allen at the outbreak of the rebellion.
8. **Skene, Andrew Philip**. b.1753, Scotland; d.1826. Ensign, 27th Regiment, 1762. Lieutenant, 72nd Regiment, 1762. Half-pay, 1763. Lieutenant, 43rd Regiment, 1774. Captured by Green Mountain Boys at Skenesborough, May 9, 1775. Appointed to Fraser's Company of Select Marksmen, September 10, 1777. Captain, 1783. Captain, 4/60th Regiment, 1787. Captain, 5th Dragoons,

1789. Captain, 9th Light Dragoons, 1792. Watt, *Burgoyne's Auxiliaries.*

9. A biography of Philip Skene written by editor Rogers may be found in Lieutenant James M. Hadden, *A Journal Kept in Canada and Upon Burgoyne's Campaign in 1776 and 1777.* Horatio Rogers, ed. (Albany: Joel Munsell's Sons, 1884), Appendix 16, 505–17.

10. **Martial Law.** Carleton's proclamation dated June 9, 1775 was printed in the *Quebec Gazette,* June 15, 1775. It may also be found in HSGS, vol. 2, 53; Biography of **Simon Sanguinet.** *DCB,* vol. 4. b.1733, Varennes; d.1790, Montreal. Notary, lawyer. Wife — Thérèse Réaume, m.1759.

11. Biography of **Etienne Montgolfier.** b.1712, France; d.1791, Quebec. *DCB,* vol. 4.

12. Anonymous letter from Quebec of July 20, 1775 transcribed in HSGS, vol. 2, 61.

13. A letter of Chief Justice William Hey excerpted in HSGS, vol. 2, 10; Biography of **William Hey.** *DCB,* vol. 4. b.~1733, England; d.1797, England. Arrived in Canada in 1766 with Francis Maseres. Both men became submerged in incredibly difficult attempts to reconcile French law with British. He was in England in 1774 to assist in drafting the Quebec Act. Having returned to Quebec, he left in the midst of the 1775 invasion and did not return.

14. Carleton to Dartmouth, June 7, 1775 transcribed in HSGS, vol. 2, 51–53.

15. Senior, 30; Biography of **François-Marie Picoté de Belestre.** b.1716, Lachine; d.1793, Montreal. A Chevalier de Saint-Louis. Chief roads commissioner. Wives — 1. Marie-Anne Nivard Saint-Dizier, m.1738, six children; 2. Marie-Anne Magnan, m.1753, two children. In 1739, at thirteen years of age, he participated in the campaign against the Chickasaws. Second Ensign, 1742. June–October, 1746, fought in Acadia, recruited the Malacite Indians. In 1747, sent with La Corne Saint-Luc to the western Indians to encourage them to visit Montreal. Made post commander at Fort Saint-Joseph (Michigan) in 1748. Lieutenant, 1751. Visited France to describe the colony's failing fortunes in the far west. Maintained a successful fur-trading venture at Detroit, Michilimackinac, and Fort Miamis. In 1756 led a party of Miamis and Shawnees against a Carolina village. In 1757 participated in Montcalm's capture of Fort William Henry in New York Province and in the fall of that year terrorized the German Flatts in the Mohawk Valley. In May 1758 he became commandant at Detroit. In January 1759 he became a Chevalier de Saint Louis and was promoted to Captain. Surrendered to Robert Rogers at Detroit, 1760, and went to France. Returned to Quebec ~1764. In March 1769, after taking an oath of allegiance to King George, he was listed as a potential legislative councillor, which role he occupied in 1775. Picoté de Belestre was the senior of the Canadien officers at the defence of Fort St. John's. When he returned from captivity Carleton appointed him chief commissioner of roads and in 1790 he was awarded the provincial rank of Lieutenant-Colonel in recognition of his services during the revolution.

16. The *Quebec Gazette,* July 27, 1775, contains an article mentioning that on the previous Saturday, two hundred anglo-Canadians paraded in the city to form a militia battalion; Lanctot, 58–59.

17. George M. Wrong, *A Canadian Manor and Its Seigneurs, The Story of a Hundred Years, 1761–1861* (Toronto: The Bryant Press, Limited, 1908), 63–65.

18. **Mackay brothers**. Alexander V. Campbell, *The Royal American Regiment – An Atlantic Microcosm, 1755–1772* (Norman, OK: University of Oklahoma Press, 2010), 202–03.

19. Senior, 37.

20. Biography of **Jean-Baptise-Melchior Hertel de Rouville**. *DCB*, vol. 5. b.1748, Quebec City; d.1817, Quebec City. Seigneur, politician. Wife — Marie-Anne Hervieux. Ensign, Régiment du Languedoc, 1760. To France, 1760. Served in Corsica, 1764. Returned to Quebec, 1772. Taken prisoner at Fort St. John's, 1775. Captain, Independent Company, 1777. His company was retained on strength for the duration of the war. Militia Colonel, Chambly, 1790. Officer Commanding, 2nd Batallion, Chambly militia, 1812. For his activities as commander of a fighting company under St. Leger, see Gavin K. Watt, *Rebellion in the Mohawk Valley: The St. Leger Expedition of 1777* (Toronto: Dundurn Press, 2002), 75, 131, 212, 231, 255.

21. Proceedings of July 8, 1775, *Albany Minutes*, vol. 1, 131–32.

22. **Chevalier**. The title for a man who was a Knight of the Royal and Military Order of Saint Louis, a military Order of Chivalry founded on April 5, 1693. Conditions for the order did not include nobility; however, Catholic faith was mandatory, as well as at least ten years' service as a commissioned officer in the army or the navy. Members of the Order received a pension and were entitled to wear the Croix de Saint-Louis. See Chartrand, vol. 1, 153–54.

23. Lanctot, 48–49.

24. Lanctot, 62.

25. *Albany Minutes*, vol. 1, 33.

26. *Albany Minutes*, vol. 1, 33–36.

27. **Cuyler, Abraham**. The mayor's loyalist sympathies caught up with him later and he was removed from office and sent to Connecticut. In 1779, he was condemned to death under the Act of Attainder. He survived this proscription and sought to return to the city after the war, but was rebuffed. He finished his days in Canada. *http://en.wikipedia.org/wiki/List_of_mayors_of_Albany,_New_York*.

28. *Albany Minutes*, vol. 1, 38–51.

29. **Maclean, Allan**. From Scots-Dutch Brigade to Lieutenant, 4 Company, Royal American Regiment [hereafter RAR], 1756. Captain-Lieutenant, 1 Company, RAR, 1758; Captain New York Independent Company, 1759. Major-Commandant, 114th Regiment, 1761. Half-pay 1763. Brevet Lieutenant-Colonel, 1772. From half-pay at Lieutenant-Colonel Commandant, Royal Highland Emigrants [hereafter RHE], 1775. Brevet Colonel in army, 1780. Retired 1784. Houlding, "King's Service"; Mary Beacock Fryer, *Allan Maclean, Jacobite General: The Life of an Eighteenth Century Career Soldier* (Toronto: Dundurn Press, 1987), Brigadier-General in America, 1777.

30. Lanctot, 52–53.

31. Lanctot, 48–49.

32. **"affable and competent."** A description taken from Senior, 22.

33. Letters of Carleton to Dartmouth and Gage, June 1775. Stevens, chapter 6, 394.

34. Senior, 14. From the petition of James Cusack, Montreal, April 20, 1782. LAC, MG21, B214, 381.

35. *Vermont Records*, vol. 2, 6–10. Footnotes to this source provide details of the Green Mountain Regiment.

36. **Daly, Patrick.** Daly was an Irish immigrant who had been domiciled in Johnstown, NY, and was likely recruited by Maclean's officer when he visited the Mohawk Valley. Daly kept a journal of the siege of Quebec, which was consulted for this work. He chose to transfer to the King's Royal Yorkers when that regiment was established on June 19, 1776. He was 1KRR [1st Battalion, King's Royal Regiment of New York, hereafter (battalion number) KRR] paymaster and, at disbandment, the third-senior captain. Daly drew land in Royal Township No. 2 in 1784. Ernest A. Cruikshank and Gavin K. Watt, *The History and Master Roll of the King's Royal Regiment of New York* [hereafter *KRR NY*] (Milton, ON: Global Heritage Press, 2006).

37. **Watts, Stephen.** b.1754, New York City; d.1810, Jersey. Son of John Watts, a prominent politician in NYC. Brother of Mary (Polly) Watts, wife of Sir John Johnson. Wife — Sarah Nugent, fourteen children. Lieutenant, RHE, June 14, 1775. Captain of Light Infantry Company, 1KRR, June 19, 1776. Grievously wounded in the Battle of Oriskany, August 6, 1777. Lower leg amputated. Captain, 8th Regiment, March 8, 1778. As such, commanded hospital in Montreal. On September 27, 1778, it was recommended that he go to England for hot baths to regain the flexibility of his knee in order to adapt to an artificial leg. Captain, Invalid Company, Island of Jersey, December 12, 1781. Barrack master of Jersey, April 1796. Badly wounded in a duel on Jersey, November 1796. A military census of 1806 showed Watts as a major and barrack master. In December, 1809, Watts was noted as formerly of the 3rd Royal Veterans Battalion and dismissed from the service. Committed suicide in London, 1810. (Research by Les de Belin, Australia, and Cruikshank and Watt, *KRR NY*, 331.)

38. Biography of **Daniel Robertson**. *DCB*, vol. 5. b.1733, Scotland; d.1810, Quebec City. Landowner, magistrate, justice of the peace, school commissioner. Wife — Marie-Louise Réaume, m.~1761, d.1773, six children. Surgeon's Mate, 42nd — Regiment, 1754. Ensign, 42nd Regiment, 1756. Lieutenant, 42nd Regiment, 1762. Major, Montreal militia, 1775. Captain-Lieutenant, RHE, 1775. Commanded Oswegatchie. Led raid on Ellice's Mills, Mohawk Valley, 1782. Commanded Michilimackinac, 1782. Major, army, 1790. Captain, 60th Regiment, 1793. Lieutenant-Colonel, Army, 1794. Colonel, army, 1798.

39. HSDS, vol. 2, 3; **Prescott, Richard**. b.1725; d.1788. Major, 33rd Regiment, 1756. 72nd Foot, 1758. Lieutenant-Colonel, 17th Regiment, 1761. 50th Regiment, 1762, and served in Germany, Seven Years' War. Transferred to 7th Regiment. Colonel in army and captured at Longueuil, 1775. Exchanged 1776. Colonel, 7th Regiment, November 1776. On expedition to Rhode Island, December 1776 and captured there, July 1777. Exchanged for General Charles Lee. Major-General, August 1777; Lieutenant-General, November 1782. *Wikipedia*.

40. Carleton to Dartmouth, August 14, 1775, "The Indians on the St. Lawrence have promised their assistance and with some Mississaugas from north of Lake

Ontario have done duty with the troops at St. John's since the 18th of June."
Transcribed in Percy J. Robinson, *Toronto During the French Régime, A History of the Toronto Region from Brûlé to Simcoe, 1615–1793* (Toronto: University of Toronto Press, 1965), 155.

41. Guy Johnson's Journal. *New York Colonial Documents* (Albany, NY, 1857) vol. 8, 660.

42. **Stopford, Joseph.** b.1742, Ireland. Coronet, 18th Light Dragoons, 1759. Captain, 107th Regiment, 1761. Half-pay, 1763. Exchanged f/half-pay, Captain, 7th Regiment, 1764. Major, 7th Regiment, 1772. Brevet Lieutenant-Colonel, 1777. Lieutenant-Colonel, 15th Regiment, 1778. Brevet Colonel, 1782. Retired, 1786. Houlding, "King's Service."

43. Stanley, *Invaded*, 35–36.

44. A report in the *Quebec Gazette*, August 31, 1775; Stevens, chapter 7, 420; de Lorimier gave Louis Atayataghronghta's name as "Louis Le Nègre," in reference to his mixed-blood extraction. Claude-Nicholas-Guillaume de Lorimier, *At War with the Americans*, Peter Aichinger, ed. and tr. (Victoria, BC: Press Porcepic, n.d.), 28; **Walker, Thomas.** For an excellent profile of Walker, see Senior, 7–8.

45. **Schuyler as Indian Commissioner:** See Barbara Graymont, *The Iroquois in the American Revolution* (Syracuse: Syracuse University Press, 1972), 65–66, and for the Indian Council at Albany, 71–74.

46. Jonathon Gregory Rossie, *The Politics of Command in the American Revolution* (Syracuse: Syracuse University Press, 1975), 36–37.

CHAPTER FOUR: INVADED BY THE KING'S ENEMIES

1. Biography of **Richard Montgomery.** *DCB*, vol 4. b.1736, Ireland; d.1775, Quebec. Professional soldier, farmer. Elected to NY Provincial Congress, 1775. Wife — Janet Livingston, m.1773. Ensign, 17th Regiment, 1756. Lieutenant, 17th Regiment, 1758. Adjutant, 17th Regiment, 1760. Captain, 17th Regiment, 1762. Sold out, 1772. Appointed Continental Brigadier-General, 1775.

2. **James Livingston:** b.1747, Albany; d.~1833, Schuylerville, NY. Lawyer and wheat merchant in Chambly, Quebec. Wife — Elizabeth Simpson, b.1750, m.~1770. Commanded Congress's Own First Canadian Regiment, which was accredited to New York State. James F. Morrison, *Colonel James Livingston: The Forgotten Livingston; Patriot of the War of Independence* (Col. James Livingston Historic Research Committee, 1988), vol. 1, 17.

3. "Memorial of **John Platt**, Quebec June 17, 1781." Braisted research. Haldimand Papers [hereafter HP], AddMss21874, ff.211–12.

4. Rossie, 41; Stevens, chapter 7, 427.

5. Hey to Earl Bathurst, the Lord Chancellor, August 28, 1775, transcribed in Lanctot, 49.

6. **Canada warriors:** Stevens notes warriors representing the Kahnawake and Kanehsatake Mohawks, St. Francis Abenakis, and Lorette Hurons were present. Stevens, chapter 7, 428; Graymont, 76.

7. The *Quebec Gazette*, September 14, 1775, has an account of these operations that is somewhat at variance with Stevens, chapter 7, 428–30; de Lorimier, 29. Note: the accounts of de Lorimier and Stevens conflate several events of the early defence of Fort St. John's, but the substance remains the same. In the early days Canada Indians participated in sizeable numbers, but not always with a strong commitment, and many others supported the invaders.

8. HSDS, vol. 2, 5.

9. Biography of **Joseph-Dominique-Emmanuel Le Moyne de Longueuil**. *DCB*, vol. 5. b.1738, Soulanges; d.1807, Montreal. Wife — Louise Prud'homme, m.1770. Entered the Colonial Marines at twelve. Second Ensign, 1751. At Fort Duquesne, 1754. That year he captured Fort Necessity and revenged the death of his brother, de Villiers de Jumonville. Ensign, 1755, and led the Hurons at Monongahela. At Fort William Henry, 1757. Specialized in reconnaissance and skirmishing operations. At defence of Carillon, 1758. Commanded company of volunteers on Lac du Saint-Sacrement that year. Appointed adjutant to troops at Trois-Rivières, 1759, and promoted to rank of infantry Lieutenant. In 1759 participated at Beauport and on the Plains of Abraham. Wounded at Sainte-Foy, 1760. Went to France after the defeat. Captain, 1766. Returned to Quebec and married, 1770. Led volunteers in defence of Fort St. John's, captured and held in Albany and New Jersey till 1777. Upon return to Quebec, was appointed Inspector of Militia, November 1777. Appointed a legislative councillor, 1778; **Thomas Walker**. Senior, 30.

10. HSGS, vol. 2, 12–13; the *Quebec Gazette*, September 21, 1775, reports this muster of September 17. **Vessels**. The *Quebec Gazette*, October 5, 1775, reports that the snow *Fell*, Commodore Napier, of sixteen 9-pdrs plus swivels had just moored offshore and the ship *Charlotte*, Captain Littlejohn, was nearing completion. Two others were already fitted out under Captains Chabot and Lizet.

11. **Jeremiah Duggan**. In a journal entry of February 16, 1776, a New York regimental commander observes "That Duggan (tho' a Barber) has more influence over the Canadians than either Livingston, Hazen or Antill." Morrison, *Livingston*, 13n7; Patrick Daly, "Journal of the Siege & Blockade of Quebec by the American Rebels in Autumn 1775 & Winter 1776," *Manuscripts Relating to the Early History of Canada, Fourth Series* (Quebec City: Literary and Historical Society of Quebec, 1875), 4; Daly's *Journal* refers to Duggan as Jerry and Jeremiah and gives his rank on December 5, 1775 as major. Other sources refer to him as Jeremy; Morrison, *Livingston*, 4. Morrison gives Duggan's rank as captain; in a letter of the Conspiracy Commissions to Governor Clinton dated September 19, 1781, Duggan was noted as a colonel in the United States service currently in France. *Public Papers of George Clinton* (8 vols, Albany, State of New York, 1904), vol. 7, 339.

12. Morrison, *Livingston*, 2.

13. HSDS, II, 5; Stevens, VII, 432; Stanley, *Invaded*, 41.

14. A Monsieur Hertel and a Monsieur Rouville were taken prisoner at St. John's. The latter's full surname was Hertel de Rouville; however, the Hertel referred to by Kontitie is more likely Chevalier Joseph-Hippolite Hertel de

Saint-François, who later served in the Quebec Indian Department. "List of Prisoners taken at Chambly and St. John's" includes a "Return of the French Officers taken Prisoners at St. John's, November 3, 1775." *American Archives*, Peter Force, ed., Fourth Series, vol. 3, 1426.

15. De Lorimier, 31.
16. Biography of **Moses Hazen**, *DCB*, vol. 5; **Timber Partners**, Senior, 8.
17. *Platt Memorial.*
18. Lanctot, 66–67.
19. Biography of **Louis-Joseph Godefroy de Tonnancour**. Not to be confused with his son, Joseph-Marie, who was captured at the fall of Fort St. John's. *DCB*, vol. 4. b.1712, Quebec; d.1784, Quebec. Keeper of Stores, King's attorney, seigneur, merchant. Wives — 1. Mary Scamen/Scammon, m.1740, four children; 2. Louise Carrerot, m.1749, twelve children.
20. Stanley, *Invaded*, 42.
21. Lanctot, 59–60.
22. Stanley, *Invaded*, 46.
23. Senior, 27.
24. Biography of **Richard Montgomery**. *DCB*, vol. 4.
25. Stanley, *Invaded*, 35, 49–54.
26. Guy Johnson to Lord Dartmouth October 12, 1775. The *Canadian Antiquarian and Numismatic Journal* 4 (1875), 25–28 and *New-York Colonial Documents* 8, 635–36.
27. Johnson to Dartmouth October 12, 1775, *New-York Colonial Documents* 8, 635–36; the *Quebec Gazette*, October 5, 1775, provides a report from Montreal of September 28; the *Quebec Gazette*, Thursday, October 19, 1775; HSDS, vol. 2, 82–83; **Desautels**: Stanley, *Invaded*, 45.
28. **Johnson, Peter**: b.1759, NY; d.1777, PA. Spoke and wrote English, Mohawk, and French. Was to inherit his mother's real property. Lois M. Huey and Bonnie Pulis, *Molly Brant, A Legacy of Her Own* (Youngstown, NY: Old Fort Niagara Association, Inc., 1997), 84–85; Graymont states that Johnson died of disease as a subaltern of the 26th Regiment while under arms at Philadelphia in 1777. Graymont, 79; Houlding's "King's Service" records indicate that Peter was made Ensign, 26th Regiment on February 24, 1776 and died November 14, 1777. Houlding advises that Lieutenant George Inman's list of officers' deaths noted that Johnson "Shot himself on board a transport in the Delaware." Suicide seems very unlikely, unless he was so grievously sick or wounded that he could not face a future life. More likely, his death resulted from an accidental discharge, which seems odd given his extensive experience with firearms, but accidents do happen. The date of his death conforms to the timing of the attacks on Mud Island that occurred on November 16, 1777, when the Delaware River must have been full of transports; Elizabeth Kelsay's biography of Joseph Brant states he died at Mud Island, but offers no source. Isabel Thompson Kelsay, *Joseph Brant 1743–1807: Man of Two Worlds* (Syracuse: Syracuse University Press, 1984), 272.
29. The *Quebec Gazette*, May 25, 1775.
30. Stanley, *Invaded*, 51.

31. Kim Stacy research. From Walker's account of the action transcribed in chapter 2 of Stacy's unpublished history of the 84th Regiment; **McDonell, John (Aberchalder).** b.~1753, Scotland; d.1809, Quebec City. Wife — Helena Yates, b.1766. He had migrated with his father in 1773 and settled at Johnstown, NY. He came off with Guy Johnson in 1775, met with Allan Maclean and joined the RHE as Ensign. Smy states that he served with the first RHE detachment to come under enemy fire, which likely refers to the action against Thomas Walker. He was taken at Fort St. John's and held prisoner for fourteen months before being exchanged. Lieutenant, April 1777. Transferred to Butler's Rangers as Captain, August 1778. Very active officer and very popular with the native allies.

32. The *Quebec Gazette*, November 16, 1775, reports the sailing of the *Adamant* with Johnson's party.

33. Stanley, *Invaded*, 112; An excerpt from a letter submitted by Civis Canadiensis and printed in French only. The *Quebec Gazette*, October 5, 1775.

34. Lanctot, 84–85. This author provides considerable detail about the clergy's support.

35. Biography of **Henry Hamilton**. *DCB*, vol. 4. b.~1734, Ireland; d.1796, Antigua. Wife — Elizabeth Lee, m.1795. Ensign, 15th Regiment, 1755. Lieutenant, 15th Regiment, 1756. Captain, 15th Regiment, 1762, in Cuba. In garrison at Trois-Rivières and commanded at Crown Point, 1766. Brigade Major for Carleton, 1767. Sold out 1775 and appointed Civil Governor of Detroit that year. On October 8, 1778, set out with 60 Natives, 30 Regulars and 145 Canadien militia and recaptured Vincennes, which he lost in 1779. Held captive until 1781, and, because he was blamed by the rebels for the western Indian wars, much of that time was in irons. Returned to Quebec in 1782 as lieutenant governor. Became embroiled in political opposition to Haldimand's regime and was recalled in 1785. He became Governor of Bermuda in 1788 and of Dominica in 1794. He died there two years later.

36. Maseres, "Additional papers concerning the Province of Quebeck" transcribed in HSGS, vol. 2, 107.

37. HSGS, vol. 2, 10–11.

38. Lanctot, 86–88.

39. Stanley, *Invaded*, 53.

40. Stanley, *Invaded*, 54–55. While it is generally stated that Stopford shamefully capitulated without serious cause, de Lormier reported that the rebels' solid shot penetrated the fort's walls with their first discharge. The large number of women and children in the fort must have weighed on the major's conscience. De Lorimier, 15.

41. **Maseres, Francis.** b.1731, England; d.1824, England. For a profile of this very complex man, see *DCB*, vol. 6.

42. Maseres's "Additional papers."

43. HSGS, vol. 2, 13.

44. Lanctot, 89.

45. **Cash payment**: HSGS, vol. 2, 11. This source claims $1,000; Lanctot, 89, reports £400.

46. "Journal of Major Henry Livingston of the Third New York Continental Line, August to December 1775," Gaillard Hunt, ed. *www.iment.com/maida/*

familytree/henry/writing/prose/revdiary.htm#carleton. Another interesting account of the rebel defence of Longueuil is the diary of Lieutenant John Fassett Jr. of Warner's regiment. A transcript can be found at *http://miniawi. blogspot.ca/2011/01/battle-of-longueuil-2.html*.

47. Of the ninety-one Canadian prisoners, forty-one were recorded as officers. Many surnames suffered typical anglophone misspellings and require interpretation. E.g., "Longuellea" for Longueuil, "Borcehervalle" for Boucherville, and "Moquin" for Monin. "Return of the French Officers taken Prisoners at St. John's, November 3, 1775," *American Archives*, Fourth Series, vol. 3, 1426.

48. *Platt memorial.*

CHAPTER FIVE: The Rebels Lay Siege to Quebec City

1. HSGS, vol. 2, 13–14; **RHE recruits and artificers**. The exact numbers are recorded in Daly's *Journal* and repeated in Thomas Ainslie, *Canada Preserved — The Journal of Captain Thomas Ainslie* [hereafter *Ainslie's Journal*], Sheldon S. Cohen, ed. (The Copp Clark Publishing Company, 1968); **Malcolm Fraser**. *DCB*, vol. 5. b.1738, Scotland; d.1815, Quebec City. Wives — 1. Marie Allaire, five children; 2. Marguerite Ducros, three children. Ensign, 78th Regiment, 1757. At Louisbourg and Cape Breton, 1758, and Quebec, 1759. Half-pay, 1763. Major, Quebec militia battalion, 1787. Colonel, Kamouraska militia battalion, 1794. Colonel, Baie-Saint-Paul militia battalion, 1805. Close friend of John Nairne; the *Quebec Gazette*, November 9, 1775.

2. For a wonderful historical-fiction account of Arnold's expedition, see Kenneth Roberts, *Arundel*, and for Arnold's naval contest on Lake Champlain, see his *Rabble in Arms*.

3. **RHE organization**. "Orderly Book of Captain Malcolm Fraser, 1RHE, 1775–76." LAC, Malcolm Fraser and family fonds, MG23-K, R3704-0-3-E, V.20. The orderly book advises that Lieutenant Watts was assigned to Captain Malcolm Fraser's company, November 15, 1775; Biography of **John Nairne**. *DCB*, vol. 5. b.1731, Scotland; d.1802, Quebec. Wife — Christine Emery, 1769, nine children. Enlisted Scots-Dutch Brigade at 14. Lieutenant, 78th Regiment, 1757. At Louisbourg, 1758, and Quebec, 1759. Captain, 78th Regiment Purchased land at La Malbaie, Quebec, at Murray Bay with his friend and comrade-in-arms Malcolm Fraser, who was living at Mount Murray. On half-pay ~1762. By 1775, had built a manor house and was very successful. Called upon by Governor Carleton on July 13, 1775 to organize a regiment of Canadiens from his local area. On September 9, 1775, summoned to Quebec and joined the Highland Emigrants as a captain. Served with distinction during siege. Major in the army, August 29, 1777. In 1781 replaced the deceased Major Daniel McAlpin as the officer commanding the miscellaneous loyalist corps left over from Burgoyne's expedition. Lieutenant-Colonel in the army, February 19, 1783. Postwar held several important civil roles. Lieutenant-Colonel, Quebec militia

battalion, 1794. For Nairne's activities with the loyalist battalions, see Gavin K. Watt, *A Dirty, Trifling Piece of Business* — *Volume 1: The Revolutionary War as Waged from Canada in 1781* (Toronto: Dundurn Press, 2009).

4. Stanley, *Invaded*, 78–79.

5. Lanctot, 98; **Firing on truce party**. Carleton's biographer, A.G. Bradley, claims this report "was a fable for use in the American press," yet, despite Bradley's protestation, the *Quebec Gazette*, March 21, 1776, printed the text of Montgomery's summons of December 7, 1775, in which he states that Arnold's flag of truce had been fired upon. Montgomery first sent his summons in the hands of an elderly woman and, days later, had a copy lofted over the walls attached to an arrow. He wrote, "Firing upon a Flag of Truce, hitherto unprecedented even among Savages, prevents my taking the ordinary mode of communicating my sentiments."

6. HSGS, vol. 2, 14–15; Bradley, 111.

7. Stanley, *Invaded*, 83.

8. Biography of **Joseph (-Claude) Boucher de Niverville**. *DCB*, vol. 5. b.1715, Quebec; d.1804, Quebec. Seigneur. Wife — Marie-Josephte Châtelin, m.1757, eleven children. Niverville is thought to have been the longest-serving Canadien military officer in the eighteenth century. His biography reveals a truly incredible career. In brief, he began as a Cadet of Metropolitan troops in 1734. In subsequent years, he campaigned in Louisiana, Acadia, Massachusetts, New York, and the Ohio Country. He explored Manitoba in 1750. He commanded at Michilimackinac in 1755 until recalled to command the Abenakis under Dieskau. Lieutenant, 1756, and led the Abenakis at Fort William Henry the following year. He took up arms under Carleton in 1775 and served in the Indian Department and as a militia colonel until 1803.

9. Biography of **Jean-Baptiste Bouchette**. *DCB*, vol. 5. b.1736, Quebec; d.1804, Quebec. Schooner owner. Wife — Marie-Angélique Duhamel, m.1773. Commissioned Master and Commander and Captain, the snow *Seneca*, on Lake Ontario, ~1779. Commissioned Captain of militia at Quebec City, 1787.

10. Stanley, *Invaded*, 84.

11. *Fraser's Orderly Book*, November 17, 1775; **Necessaries**. These were such items as shirts, neckstocks, various types of stockings, various types of gaiters, linen drawers, haversacks, knapsacks, oil bottles, musket tools. George Smith, *An Universal Military Dictionary* ... (London: J. Millan, 1779; limited edition, Ottawa: Museum Restoration Service, 1969), 193. As indicated, company commanders were held responsible for these items. On September 11, 1776, the captains commanding the Emigrants' newly formed Grenadier and Light Infantry companies were to complete their men with the "following Necerays[,] three Good Shirts[,] 3 pair Stokings Good, one pair trusers do.[,] 2 Pr. Good Shoes." As further examples, on April 10, 1776, the captain of each company was instructed to order "Everry Nesesery material for the Cleaning the mens Cloaths." And on May 20, 1776, captains were ordered to provide their men with "Bruches and Blackball," the latter for dressing their shoes and leather accoutrements. The captains' responsibility extended

to the condition of the men's firelocks. On April 29, the officer immediately in charge of a soldier whose firelock was out of order was instructed to have it repaired. *Fraser's Orderly Book*.

12. **Carleton's Proclamation.** The *Quebec Gazette*, November 30, 1775; Lanctot, 102–03; **Antill, Edward.** b.1742, NJ; d.1789, Quebec. Lawyer. Wife — Charlotte Riverin, b.1752, m.1767 in Quebec City, d.1785, NY, eleven children. Appointed Chief Engineer of the Continental Army in Canada by Montgomery, 1775, and Adjutant-General of same by Arnold, May, 1776. Captured on Staten Island, August 1777, not exchanged till 1780. Led Congress's Own Canadian Regiment at Yorktown, 1781. *www.iment.com/ maida/familytree/antill/coloneledward.htm#coled*. **Hay, Udney.** Cubbison, Douglas R., "Forgotten Quartermaster of the American Revolution — Udny Hay," *www.stonefortconsulting.com* (accessed September 17, 2011).

13. *Ainslie's Journal*, 4; *Daly's Journal*, 4; Bradley, 114; **Thompson, James.** Gentleman Volunteer, 78th Regiment, 1757. Grenadier Serjeant, 78th Regiment, at Louisbourg, 1758, and Quebec, 1759. Discharged in Quebec and became the clerk of works with the city's Engineers Department. In 1772 he was appointed overseer of works. For a fascinating account of Thompson's life, see *A Bard of Wolfe's Army: James Thompson, Gentleman Volunteer, 1733–1830* [hereafter *Wolfe's Bard*], Earl John Chapman and Ian Macpherson McCulloch, eds. (Montreal: Robin Brass Studio, 2010), 27, 29, 173; **Artificers.** Presumably, Thompson reported to Lieutenant George Lawe, RHE, who had command of all the artificers in the city, according to *Fraser's Orderly Book*.

14. *Daly's Journal*, 4.

15. "William Friend petition." PRO, AO13/54, ff.411–12.

16. **Bellet, François.** For details of this father and his son, see *DCB*, vol. 6; **Destroys powder.** Lanctot, 98–99.

17. Stanley, *Invaded*, 66–67.

18. Biography of **François Cazeau.** *DCB*, vol. 5. Cazeau was also active in 1777, buying three large bateaux and filling them with supplies of clothing and food for the rebel garrison at Ticonderoga. His boats were discovered and destroyed by Burgoyne's army during their investment of the works. In 1779 Cazeau distributed a proclamation to the Canadiens from the French vice-admiral, Comte D'Estaing, urging an uprising against the British. He was imprisoned for treason, but escaped in 1782 and took refuge in the United States. He spent four fruitless years seeking compensation for his losses from Congress, and after a period in France returned to the States to take up his cause again without success. He returned to France and died without recompense in 1815; **Livingston's Commission.** Morrison, *Livingston*, 3.

19. Montgomery to Schuyler, December 5, 1775. *The Spirit of Seventy-Six: The Story of the American Revolution as Told by Participants*, Henry Steele Commager and Richard B. Morris, eds. (Cambridge, MA: Da Capo Press, 1968), 202–03, ex Force, *American Archives*, Fourth Series, vol. 4.

20. *Daly's Journal*, 6; Morrison, *Livingston*, 3; *Fraser's Orderly Book*, November 15, 1775; As noted above, a copy of Montgomery's demands was attached

to an arrow and lofted over the walls a few days later. The complete text was transcribed in the *Quebec Gazette*, March 21, 1776.

21. Lanctot, 104–05.

22. *Ainslie's Journal*, 27.

23. Wrong, 72.

24. *Fraser's Orderly Book*, December 29, 1775.

25. Schuyler to the President of Congress, January 13, 1776, cited in Lanctot, 105.

26. Colonel Henry Caldwell to General James Murray, Jun15, 1776. *Spirit of Seventy-Six*, 204; Wrong, 74.

27. *Daly's Journal*, 8; *Fraser's Orderly Book*. It was ordered on November 18, 1775 that "The Great bell at the Cathedral is not to ring but in Case of an alarm [. W]hen it does ring every man to assemble Imediately."

28. *Wolfe's Bard*, 231. Thompson's account of this action credits Serjeant Hugh McQuarters, RA, for being in charge of the Barrier-Guard at Près-de-Ville and in command of the single gun emplaced there, which he claims was charged with "grape and musket balls." He says that McQuarters gave the order to fire at the appropriate moment. Thompson made no mention of the sea captain and his sailors, nor of Volunteer Coffin; *Ainslie's Journal*, 36. His account states there was a battery commanded by a merchant sea captain named Barnsfair who had his men stand by the guns with lit matches as soon as the alarm bells rang. Barnsfair gave the command to fire. Ainslie made no mention of the Canadien militiamen; *Daly's Journal*, 8. He mentions a guard of about thirty and cannon, i.e., "cannon," plural; Braisted research. John Nairne to his sister Magdalene Nairne, Quebec May 14, 1776. LAC, John and Thomas Nairne fonds, MG23, GIII23, V.3, Entrybook of Correspondence, 275–79. Nairne states the barrier was protected by six pieces of cannon loaded with grapeshot. The battery opened fire at twenty yards, followed by the musketry of the guard; Biography of **Louis-Alexandre Picard**. *DCB*, vol. 4. b.~1728, France; d.1799, Quebec. Silversmith. In French cavalry, ~1750. Arrived Quebec City, 1755. Lieutenant, Quebec Canadien militia, August 1775; Biography of **John Coffin**. *DCB*, vol. 5. b.1729, MA; d.1808, Quebec. Merchant, distiller, ship owner. Wife — Isabella Child, eleven children. Migrated to Quebec City, 1775. He was building a distillery at Près-de-Ville at the time of the siege and volunteered for the militia; Ruch advises that John Coffin served in the Commissary Department in 1782 as the substitute deputy commissary at Chambly. John Ruch, "Loyalists in the Inspectorate and the Commissary," *The Loyalists of Quebec 1774–1825, a Forgotten History* (Montreal: Price-Patterson Ltd., 1989), 183. For a significantly different account of the Près-de-Ville action, see the excerpt from Abner Stocking's journal in *Spirit of Seventy-Six*, 204.

29. Account of John Henry. *Spirit of Seventy-Six*, 206.

30. Colonel Arnold to his wife Hannah, January 6, 1776. *Spirit of Seventy-Six*, 210.

31. Colonel Henry Caldwell to General James Murray, June 15, 1776. *Spirit of Seventy-Six*, 205.

32. Nairne to his sister Magdalene, Quebec, May 14, 1776. Nairne reports that the rebels "forced our advanced post, where we had four pieces of Cannon; afterwards got possession of another Barrier, and forced their way through a narrow Street

to the last Barrier, which if they had gained, they would have been in the low Town." This is the only account that I have consulted that reports that Arnold's and Morgan's men confronted three barriers. **First barrier**. In Arnold's letter to his wife of January 6, 1776, he states "Capt. Oswald is among the Prisoners, he was with me in a selected Party of about 25 who attacked the first battery: He behaved gallantly and gained much Honour." The *Quebec Gazette*, March 14, 1776. I assume that the "first battery" and "first barrier" were synonymous.

33. Stanley, *Invaded*, 91.

34. John Nairne to Captain Francis Boucher, Murray Bay, Quebec, February 25, 1799. Braisted research. LAC, John and Thomas Nairne fonds, MG23, GIII23, V.3, Entrybook of Correspondence, 441–42; For James Thompson's account of Dambourgès's bravery, see *Wolfe's Bard*, 36.

35. Nairne to his sister Magdalene, Quebec May14, 1776.

36. Colonel Henry Caldwell to General James Murray, June 15, 1776. *Spirit of Seventy-Six*, 205.

37. **Lawe, George**. On November 17, 1775, Captain "Laws" is noted as an engineer in *Fraser's Orderly Book* in command of all of the King's artificers. On November 29, 1775, the recently arrived artificers from Halifax and Newfoundland were placed under Lawe's direction. Houlding provides this profile — Second Lieutenant, 61st Regiment, 1756. First Lieutenant, 76th Regiment, 1759. Captain, 76th Regiment, 1762. Half-pay, 1769; Captain-Lieutenant, RHE, 1775: Houlding, "King's Service." In command of Burgoyne's artificers. Built first bridge across Hudson, ~August 14, 1777. Appointed barrack master of Montreal and Fort Chambly, November 20, 1777. Captain Geo Lowe, 84th RHE, April 16, 1781: Watt, *Burgoyne's Auxiliaries*. Biography of **Alexander Fraser**. *DCB*, vol. 4. b.~1729, Scotland; d.1799, Quebec. Wife — Jane McCord, m.~1765, d.1767, two daughters. Ensign and Lieutenant, 78th Regiment, 1757. At Louisbourg, 1758, and Quebec, 1759. Wounded, 1760. Bought seigneuries of La Martinière, 1763; Vitré, 1775; and Saint-Gilles, 1782. Captain, RHE, June 14, 1775. Assigned as Captain of St. John's militia, 1777–April 1778. In May 1779, Nairne recommended that Fraser be allowed to retire and he likely did so that year.

38. **Dearborn, Henry**. b.1751, NH; d.1829. "Dearborn rose from captain to lieutenant-colonel and commanded the provisional light infantry battalion during the Saratoga campaign [serving in a brigade under Colonel Daniel Morgan with a rifle battalion.] After the Revolution he was the U.S. secretary of war (1801–1809) and eventually the senior major-general in the Army (1812–1815.)" Robert K. Wright, Jr., *The Continental Army* (Washington: Army Lineage Series, Center of Military History, United States Army, 1989), 117.

39. Biography of **John Nairne**. *DCB*, vol. 5.

40. **9-pdr**. Colonel Henry Caldwell to General James Murray, June 15, 1776: *Spirit of Seventy-Six*, 206. **Casualties**. Caldwell reports 20 rebel dead, upwards of 40 wounded and 400 taken prisoner. John Henry of Pennsylvania reports three officers and fifty or sixty noncoms and soldiers killed: *Spirit of Seventy-Six*, 209. Carleton reports the rebels had six or seven hundred men and forty or

fifty officers killed, wounded, or captured. The garrison lost one naval lieutenant and four rank and file killed and thirteen rank and file wounded, of which two had died: Carleton to Howe, Quebec, January 12, 1775, printed in the *Quebec Gazette*, September 5, 1776.

41. *Ainslie's Journal*, 36–37.

42. *Wolfe's Bard*, 233–38.

43. Maclean to Coffin, July 1776, transcribed in Biography of **John Coffin**, *DCB*, vol. 5.

44. Lanctot, 108; *Ainslie's Journal* for January 1, 1776, 39.

45. *Ainslie's Journal*, 40–41, 43, 50.

46. *Ainslie's Journal*, 42.

CHAPTER SIX: RELIEF ARRIVES

1. **Closed churches**: Burt, 206–07. Burt treats the church closings as rumours. Stanley, *Invaded*, 111–12, believes that actual closings occurred.

2. Lanctot, 110.

3. Hazen's quotation taken from Curtis Fahey's Biography of **Benedict Arnold**. *DCB*, vol. 5.

4. Arnold's sentiment about Montgomery is in a letter to his wife Hannah, January 6, 1776: *Spirit of Seventy-Six*, 209. This letter also appeared in the *Quebec Gazette*, March 14, 1776.

5. Biography of **Benedict Arnold**. *DCB*, vol. 5. Provides the date of Arnold's promotion; Stanley, *Invaded*, 106–07; Lanctot, 112. Biography of **Moses Hazen**. *DCB*, vol. 5. Biographer Allan Everest states that Hazen accompanied Antill on his trip to Montreal and then to Congress, but I have not been able to confirm this, and the contention conflicts with Arnold's assignment of Hazen to command the Richelieu River posts. Everest adds that Hazen was able to personally set conditions with Congress for his acceptance of their appointment, such as a guarantee of compensation for his loss of British half-pay, and assurances that his Quebec properties would not be confiscated by the British. After the war, Hazen battled with Congress for his loss of British half-pay; the pillaging and physical loss of his properties in Quebec, and the expenses of recruiting his regiment. These issues were not resolved before his death.

6. National Archives Kew, Audit Office, Class 13, vol. 55, folios 195–96.

7. *Albany Minutes*, vol. 1, 351.

8. Willis T. Hanson, *A History of Schenectady During the Revolution to which is appended a Contribution to the Individual Records of the Inhabitants of the Schenectady District During that Period* (self-published, 1916), 57–58.

9. Lanctot, 113, 115; Biography of **Moses Hazen**, *DCB*, vol 5.

10. Biography of **Louis Liénard De Beaujeu de Villemonde**. *DCB*, vol. 5. b.1716, Quebec; d.1802, Ontario. Metropolitan army officer. Seigneur. Wives — 1. Louise-Charlotte Cugnet, m.1747, d.1748 in childbirth, one daughter; 2. Geneviève Le Moyne de Longueuil, m.1753, seven children. Second Ensign, 1732. First Ensign, 1738. Lieutenant, 1744. Captain, 1751. Awarded Cross of Saint Louis, 1759. De Beaujeu had an amazing service career throughout French North America commanding many famous posts.

11. Lanctot, 132.
12. Lanctot, 133.
13. Stanley, *Invaded*, 118.
14. De Lorimier, 43–46; Stanley, *Invaded*, 118; Paul L. Stevens, *King's Colonel at Niagara 1774–1776* (Youngstown: Old Fort Niagara Association, 1987), 50–51.
15. Lanctot, 127–28, 134–35; **Walker's house**: Senior, 8; Biography of **Fleury Mesplet**. *DCB*, vol. 4. b.1734, France; d.1794, Montreal. He founded the *Montreal Gazette*.
16. A prisoner roll published in the *American Archives*, Peter Force, ed. (6 vols, 1837), vol. 1, 167–69, lists two reasonably full and nine part companies accredited to Bedel's New Hampshire Regiment, and one full and two part companies accredited to "Burrell's" [Charles Burrall] Connecticut Regiment. Colonel Patterson's 1st Massachusetts Regiment lists men from eight part-companies, which represents the reinforcement led by Major Sherburne that surrendered to de Montigny and de Lorimier at Quinze Chiens.
17. **Bedel, Timothy**. Peters spells the name "Beadle," as did the *Quebec Gazette*, August 22, 1775, and *Peters's Narrative*. **Bedel's regiment**. Wright, *Continental Army*, 199; Stanley, *Invaded*, 118; **Promote natives' friendship**. Stevens, chapter 10, 618.
18. *Peters's Narrative*. Peters claims that he met with "Forrester" at Cataraqui, but the captain was at Oswegatchie at this time and Cataraqui was unoccupied. For confirmation of Forster's posting, see Steven, *King's Colonel*, 51.
19. Stanley, *Invaded*, 119. Stanley claims that Bedel abandoned his post in the face of a warning about an imminent attack; Wikipedia states that Bedel was sick in hospital at Lachine at the time of the attack. Swain, David, "The Timothy Bedel Papers and Andrew Park Pamphlet." At the court martial, the inconclusive evidence about Bedel's absence from The Cedars led to him being found guilty of "quitting his post" and he was cashiered from the service. Bedel's second-in-command, Isaac Butterfield, was also cashiered and prohibited from future commissions. Bedel was later rehabilitated and saw extensive service. *davidlibraryar. blogspot.ca/2010/11/timothy-bedel-papers-and-andrew-park.html*.
20. Stevens, chapter 9, 587–91.
21. *Albany Minutes*, vol. 1, 20, 28.
22. Cruikshank and Watt, *KRR NY*, 168.
23. **Maxwell, William and Anderson, Adjutant Ephraim**. For a short history of Colonel William "Scotch Willie" Maxwell, see Wikipedia "2nd New Jersey Regiment"; New Jersey's Second Battalion's first establishment lists among the Field and Staff Officers, "Colonel William Maxwell and Adjutant Ephraim Anderson." See *www.archive.org/stream/officialregister00newjuoft/officialregister00newjuoft_djvu.txt*.
24. **Chaucer, Alexander**. He was a conductor in Nathaniel Day's Quebec Province commissary department in 1777–78. *The Parliamentary register: or, History of the proceedings and ...*, vol. 11, 195.
25. "Joseph Anderson's memorials and related papers." Braisted research. National Archives Kew, AO13/11, ff.30–42.

26. *Ainslie's Journal*, 74.

27. This appears to be **Evans, Simon**. Houlding, "King's Service"; Ensign, 28th Regiment, 1762. Lieutenant, 28th Regiment, 1763. Retired, 1768. As the 28th went home to Ireland in 1767, he may have sold out in order to remain in America; B. Bruce-Biggs research. Simon Evans was involved in McDonell's arrest of Thomas Walker in October 1775. He was imprisoned in Reading, PA, 1776.

28. *Ainslie's Journal*, 75–76.

29. *Ainslie's Journal*, 79, 103en57.

30. Stanley, *Invaded*, 107, 126.

31. Biography of **Moses Hazen**. *DCB*, vol. 5.

32. Lanctot, 138–39; Burt, 210. Burt provides a quite different story of the fire ship, suggesting that no forewarning was received of its coming. He advises that Judge Livius wrote an account for the *Quebec Gazette* which stated that the crew was able to pull away in three boats, one of which was sunk by gunfire.

33. *Ainslie's Journal*.

34. *The Naval Chronicle for 1805: Containing a General and Biographical History of the Royal Navy ...*, vol.14 (London: I. Gold, 1806), 443fn; Biography of **Charles Douglas**: *DCB*, vol. 4, and Wikipedia. b.1727, Scotland; d.1789, Scotland. Spoke six languages. **Adjutant** 1. Lydia Schimmelpinck, three children; 2. Sarah Wood, two children; 3. Jane Baillie. Douglas served 1740–89. Entered Royal Navy at 12 and served for some time in the Dutch Navy. British Midshipman at Louisbourg, 1745. Lieutenant, 1753. Commander, 1759. In 1763, took part in recapturing Newfoundland. During 1764–65, served in Russia reorganizing Catherine the Great's navy. Made a Fellow of the Royal Society, May 1770 for experiments in water temperature. Awarded a baronetcy, 1777. At Battle of Ushant, September 1777. In 1781, Captain-of-the-Fleet under Lord Rodney on the flagship *Formidable* in the Battle of the Saintes, April 12, 1782. Often credited with the manoeuvre that broke the French line. Commanded the Halifax station, 1784. Rear-Admiral of the Blue, September 1787.

35. Lanctot, 138–39; *Ainslie's Journal*. The captain reports that eight hundred men marched out at 12 o'clock; Carleton's report to Germain, Quebec May 14, 1776, was carried by Lieutenant-Colonel Caldwell to Whitehall. It was printed in the *Quebec Gazette*, September 5, 1776. Caldwell and Maclean were singled out for their contributions to the defence.

36. Biography of **Jean-Claude Mathevet (Ouakoui)**. *DCB*, vol. 4. b.1717, France; d.1781, Montreal. Entered the Sulpician seminary, 1736. Received orders, 1737. Deacon, 1739. Came to Canada, 1740. Assigned to Lake of Two Mountains mission, 1746. Priest, 1747. Saw widespread service during Seven Years' War. Became a specialist in the Algonquin language, wrote a grammar, sermons, sacred history, and a life of Christ in Algonquin. Also proficient in Iroquois and wrote eleven notebooks in that language. Paralyzed in 1778 and died in the Montreal seminary, 1781; Biography of **François-Auguste Magon de Terlaye**. *DCB*, vol. 4. b.1724, France; d.1777, Oka. Deacon and member of Sulpician seminary, 1754. Came to Canada that year. Priest, 1755. Served the Iroquois and garrison at La Présentation during Seven Years' War. Appointed

to Lake of Two Mountains mission, 1758. Wrote widely in Iroquois — a grammar, Onondaga and Cayuga dictionaries, sermons, and a Jewish history.

37. Stevens, chapter 9, 611–13.
38. *Joseph Anderson's memorials.*
39. *Albany Minutes*, vol. 1, 410–11, 431, 497, 534.

CHAPTER SEVEN: THE CEDARS

1. Stevens, *King's Colonel*, 53.
2. De Lorimier, 47–48. De Lorimier claims that only twenty-two Six and Lakes' Nations men joined his recruits, but Stevens (*King's Colonel*, 53) reports that the Niagara contingent was fifty strong.
3. **William of Canajoharie.** William was as bold as his father and became a notorious Tory in the Mohawk Valley. When he returned from Canada in 1776 he made a famous, challenging declaration. "I am a King's Man, who dare say anything aginst it; I have Killed so many Yankies at Fort St. John's with this Sword of my Father, they are no Soldiers at all, etc...." William joined Joseph Brant's volunteers and saw service at Fort Stanwix, Oriskany, and Cherry Valley. He seems to have disappeared from view in 1779. Penrose, *Mohawk Valley*, 57.
4. De Lorimier, 51–52. De Lorimier consistently reports Bedel's two fieldpieces as 2-pdrs, but U.S. sources state the guns were 4-pdrs, which I have accepted.
5. Stevens, chapter 10, 619.
6. Franklin gained little pleasure from Mrs. Walker's companionship, as she taunted him cruelly about the lack of success of his mission. When the lady and her husband were reunited en route to Albany, the pair was so critical about the rebels' conduct in Canada, Franklin was tempted to quarrel. He later wrote to friends, "I think they both have an excellent Talent at making themselves Enemies, and, I believe, live where they will, they will never be long without them." Writings of Benjamin Franklin, Collected and Edited with a Life and Introduction by Albert Henry Smyth (10 vols, London: MacMillan and Co., Ltd., 1907) vol. 6, 448, and vol. 10, 296fn. *http://archive.org/stream/writingsofbenjam06franuoft/writingsofbenjam06franuoft_djvu.txt* and *http://archive.org/stream/writingsofbenjam10franuoft/writingsofbenjam10franuoft_djvu.txt* (accessed October 9, 2013).
7. Stanley, *Invaded*, 119; Lanctot, 140. During Wilkinson's march north, he told of meeting "Bishop" Carroll at Albany, who gave him "such unfavourable accounts of the situation of affairs, as made it necessary to accelerate my march." James Wilkinson, *Memoirs of My Own Times, 1757–1825* (4 vols., Philadelphia, 1816), vol. 1, 30.
8. Stevens, *King's Colonel*, 53; de Lorimier, 53. De Lorimier spells Bird's name, "Borde"; In the later war, Bird saw extensive service in the far west at Detroit. He settled on the Canadian side of the river; **Bird, Henry.** b.1737, Wales. Ensign, 31st Regiment, 1763. Lieutenant, 80th Regiment, 1764. On half-pay 1764. Exchanged from half-pay to Lieutenant, 8th Regiment on eve of the regiment's embarkation for Quebec, 1768. Captain-Lieutenant, 8th Regiment, 1778; Captain, 8th Regiment, 1781. On half-pay, 1783. Houlding, "King's Service."

9. Biography of Jean-Baptiste-Pierre Testard Louvigny de Montigny. *DCB*, vol. 5. I have accepted the *DCB* as the authority for this man's identity. Biographer François Béland advises that Jean-Baptiste-Jérémie Testard de Montigny "particularly distinguished himself by formulating a strategy ... for capturing Major Henry Sherburne." His brother, Jean-Baptiste-Pierre Testard Louvigny de Montigny, was a veteran of the defence of Fort St. John's and escaped capture when he was sent as a courier to Carleton. Louvigny was with J-B-J on this occasion, but played a minor role. Both men are sometimes confused with their very accomplished father, Jean-Baptiste-Philippe Testard de Montigny.

10. **Maurer, Johann Jacob [de Maurera]**. Stevens, chapter 10, 622, and Cruikshank and Watt, *KRR NY*, 255. Wife — Josette Coyteaux, m.1768, Montreal. Entered 1KRR June 19, 1776, as a Lieutenant in Munro's Company, 1777. Seconded to the quartermaster-general's department as deputy inspector of bateaux, a critical assignment that he held throughout and after the war. Directed Herkimer's Bateaux Company, 1780. Ranked as second-senior captain, 2KRR, on disbandment and managed the transportation of the loyalist families to upper Quebec in 1784.

11. **Quinze Chiens**. The Wikipedia article on the Battle of the Cedars claims this community was known as Quinze-Chênes (Fifteen Oaks) at the time of this action, and later as Quinze Chiens (Fifteen Dogs), and presently as Vaudreuil. De Lorimier uses "Quinze Chiens" and Carleton's orders of August 4, 1776 states "Quinchcin." *http://en.wikipedia.org/wiki/Battle_of_The_Cedars* and the *Quebec Gazette*, September 12, 1776.

12. Stevens, chapter 10, 621–26; de Lorimier, 53–57.

13. James Wilkinson is one of the most controversial military officers and politicians of U.S. early history. His later career is left for the reader to examine. Wilkinson, *Memoirs*, vol. 1, 30–31.

14. **Parke, Andrew**. Stevens, *King's Colonel*, 43, 53. Stevens advises that Parke left Montreal on November 2, 1775, and joined Forster at Oswegatchie. He gave Parke's rank at the time of The Cedars as Lieutenant, but Houlding notes him as a Captain-Lieutenant, i.e., ranked as junior Captain and paid as a Lieutenant; b.1746, Ireland. Ensign, 66th Regiment, 1759. Lieutenant, 107th Regiment, 1761. On half-pay, 1763. Exchanged from half-pay to Lieutenant, 8th Regiment, 1767. Captain-Lieutenant, 8th Regiment, November 22, 1775. Captain, 8th Regiment, 1776. Major, 8th Regiment, 1786. Retired ~1793. Houlding, "King's Service"; as Parke was ranked as Captain-Lieutenant during The Cedars action, why he continued to serve in the Light Infantry Company instead of the Colonel's Company is a mystery, unless his purchase of that rank was later backdated for seniority purposes.

15. I have not been able to determine when Brown was promoted to colonel.

16. Wilkinson, *Memoirs*, vol. 1, 32–33.

17. *Peters's Narrative*.

18. Wilkinson states that Arnold's attempted crossing was very hastily and sloppily executed. He mentions nothing about one of the boats being sunk, nor anything about being sniped at during the withdrawal downriver. Wilkinson, *Memoirs*, vol. 1, 33.

19. Lanctot states that 115 Canadiens were retained by Forster. Lanctot, 142; Wilkinson supplies interesting details of Arnold's actions. See Wilkinson, *Memoirs*, vol. 1, 32–34; the details of the agreement regarding a prisoner exchange made by Forster and Arnold were printed in the *Quebec Gazette*, September 19, 1776, with the editor's commentary on the rebels' subsequent refusal to adhere to the agreed terms.

20. De Lorimier, 58; Despite de Lorimier's criticisms of Forster's performance, the British Army saw the events in a different light. Forster was promoted to Major, 21st Regiment and surrendered with Burgoyne's army in 1777. Stevens, vol. 1, 53; the *Quebec Gazette*, August 22, 1776, printed an account of the several actions known collectively as The Cedars that had appeared in a New Hampshire paper on June 15 and, in turn, was reprinted from a New York City paper of June 8. The three rebel officers who authored the article reported a substantial rebel victory, which the *Quebec Gazette* decried as "the grossest absurdity," which indeed it was.

21. Stevens, chapter 10, 632, 2081n12.

CHAPTER EIGHT: THE HESITANT COUNTERATTACK

1. Burt, 217.

2. **Beloved, etc.** Quoted from Captain Thomas Pringle, RN. Stanley, *Invaded*, 126; The recipient of Maclean's letter is designated only as "My Lord." Stanley, *Invaded*, 125.

3. Stanley, *Invaded*, 125–26.

4. J. [Muriel] Fraser, *Skulking For The King: A Loyalist Plot* (Erin, ON: Boston Mills Press, 1985) 16 ex AO13/11, ff.476–77.

5. **Thompson, William.** b.1736, Ireland; d.1781, U.S. Lived Carlisle, PA. Served in Seven Years' War as Captain. After Bunker Hill, commissioned Colonel, Pennsylvania rifle battalion, which, after several iterations, became the 1st Pennsylvania Continental Line. Brigadier-General, 1775. His brigade at Sorel was composed of the 8th New Hampshire and the 15th, 24th, and 25th Massachusetts. Captured at Trois-Rivières, but not parolled for four years and saw no further service. Wright, 60, and *www.aohcumberland2.Org/about-us/ general-william-thompson*; Wilkinson lists Thompson's brigade as Starke's New Hampshire Regiment, Wayne's and Irvine's Pennsylvania Regiments, and Winde's and Dayton's New Jersey Regiments. Wilkinson, *Memoirs*, vol. 1, 29; it is unlikely that any element of Dayton's New Jersey Regiment was with the brigade, as it had been sent in mid-May into the Mohawk Valley to arrest Sir John Johnson. See Watt, *Rebellion*, 30, and Joseph Bloomfield, *Citizen Soldier: The Revolutionary War Journal of Joseph Bloomfield*, Mark E. Lender and James Kent Martin, eds. (Newark: New Jersey Historical Society, 1982), 50–65.

6. **Sullivan, John.** b.1740, NH; d.1795. Lived Portsmouth, NH. Lawyer. Delegate to First Continental Congress. Appointed Brigadier-General, June 1775. Sent to take command in Canada after death of Thomas. Captured in Battle of Long Island, 1776. Parolled to Congress by the Howe brothers. Released from his parole and joined Washington in time for the battles

of Trenton and Princeton, 1777. In 1779, Sullivan led a major expedition into Indian Territory that destroyed a great many villages and enraged the Natives. Wikipedia. See also *Notes from Collections of Tioga Point Museum on the Sullivan Expedition of 1779 and its Centennial Celebration of 1879 including Order Book of General Sullivan ...*, Murray, Louis Welles, ed. (Athens, PA: Tioga Point Historical Society, 1929; Reissued, Tioga Point Museum, 1975) and *The Sullivan-Clinton Campaign in 1779, Chronology and Selected Documents* (Albany: University of the State of New York, 1929).

7. Lanctot, 143–44.
8. Stanley, *Invaded*, 127.
9. *Peters's Narrative.*
10. Lanctot states that General Simon Fraser was in command at Trois-Rivières, but Stanley and Fryer say otherwise. Lanctot, 144; Stanley, *Invaded*, 126; Mary Beacock Fryer, *Allan Maclean, Jacobite General, The Life of an Eighteenth Century Career Soldier* (Toronto & Oxford: Dundurn Press, 1987), 140. Fryer says that Fraser landed at Trois-Rivières, but Maclean retained overall command as Carleton's Adjutant-General.
11. Stanley, *Invaded*, 127.
12. Biography of **François Guillot, dit Larose.** *DCB*, vol. 4. b.1727, France; d. U.S. soldier, merchant. Joined the rebels in 1775 and subsequently commanded a company in Hazen's 2nd Canadian Regiment. Details of Antoine Gautier's guiding of Thompson's force are from Guillot's biography.
13. Lanctot, 144.
14. Biography of **Joseph (-Claude) Boucher de Niverville.** *DCB*, vol. 5.
15. Stanley, *Invaded*, 128; Biography of **François Guillot.** *DCB*, vol. 4. This source claims the rebels lost five hundred officers and men, killed and wounded.
16. Lanctot, 144.
17. Burt, 217–18. This author explores in considerable depth Carleton's treatment of the rebels that caused his subordinates confusion and distress and earned him the King's and the American Secretary's displeasure. **Captain England.** Wilkinson, *Memoirs*, vol. 1, 39–40.
18. After the confrontation with Forster, Arnold withdrew his troops to Montreal and requested that Wilkinson join his suite as aide-de-camp, to which he assented "being flattered by the preference of an officer, who had at that period acquired great celebrity." Wilkinson rose steadily in rank during and after the war. In the War of 1812 he was discredited over his management of an attack into Canada. As to his account of his reconnaissance on behalf Arnold, see Wilkinson, *Memoirs*, vol. 1, 36–37.
19. *Peters's Narrative*; Wilkinson provides a few details of attempts to pass off Continental scrip. Wilkinson, *Memoirs*, vol. 1, 35–36.
20. Arnold's letter of May 31, 1776, transcribed in the Biography of **Benedict Arnold.** *DCB*, vol. 5.
21. Biography of **Thomas-Ignace Trottier Dufy Desauniers (also signed Dufy Desauniers).** *DCB*, vol. 4. b.1712, Quebec; d.1777, Quebec. Merchant, militia officer. Captain, Montreal Militia, 1745. Distinguished militia career,

serving in virtually every campaign of the Seven Years' War. Appointed colonel of Montreal militia by Carleton in 1775. Member of Legislative Council,
1777, and died that year.

22. De Lorimier, 58.
23. Watt, *Rebellion*, 27–32.
24. Biography of **Moses Hazen**. *DCB*, vol. 5.
25. Wilkinson, *Memoirs*, vol. 1, 37; de Lorimier, 59.
26. Biography of **Moses Hazen**. *DCB*, vol. 5.
27. Stanley, *Invaded*, 130–32; **Colonel Louis Atayataghronghta**: Stevens, chapter
10, 639–40; Wilkinson writes, "we took an affectionate leave of Colonel Louis,
the faithful chief of the Cauchnawaga tribe, and the only Canadian who accompanied the army in its retreat from Canada." Wilkinson, *Memoirs*, vol. 1, 39.
28. *Peters's Narrative*. **Skinner**. Watt, *Burgoyne's Auxiliaries*.
29. Watt, *Rebellion*, 32; Cruikshank and Watt, *KRR NY*, 10–11; Account of mon-
eys issued to the 1st Battalion of the Royal Highland Emigrants in America.
Braisted research. LAC, Malcolm Fraser and family fonds. MG23-K, R3704-
0-3-E, V.11. This document notes that Watts and Daly continued to be paid
by the RHE "by order of the Commander in Chief."

CHAPTER NINE: CARLETON CLEARS THE LAKE

1. Burt, 218; Wilkinson had a great deal to say about Carleton's handling of this
campaign. Here is one of his comments: "By what a slight thread was the issue
of the revolution at this moment suspended! If our Canadian army had been
lost, it is not improbable that the dubious question of independence, not yet
decided at the juncture, would have been negatived, or possibly a negotiation
opened with the British commissioners, and a reconciliation with parent state
might have followed." Wilkinson, *Memoirs*, vol. 1, 41.
2. Russell P. Bellico, *Sails and Steam in the Mountains: A Maritime and Military
History of Lake George and Lake Champlain* (Fleischmanns, NY: Purple
Mountain Press, 1992), 27–29. This author supplies superb details of these
various vessels. See also, Robert Malcomson, *Warships of the Great Lakes
1754–1834* (London: Chatham Publishing, 2001).
3. Stanley, *Invaded*, 134.
4. Carleton to Germain, July 8, 1776, transcribed in Stanley, *Invaded*, 133.
5. Stanley states that Phillips was assigned the task of constructing a fleet
of boats at St. John's, but Phillips's biography mentions nothing of this.
Stanley, *Invaded*, 134, and Robert P. Davis, *Where a Man Can Go, Major
General William Phillips, British Royal Artillery, 1731–1781* (Westport, CT:
Greenwood Press, 1999), 45–47.
6. Biography of **John Schank**. *DCB*, vol. 6. b.~1740, Scotland; d.1823, England.
Schank played a vital role in Canada during the Revolution. In contrast to
several other sources, which state that the naval yard was located at St. John's,
the *DCB* states that a yard was established on Île-aux-Noix, where Schank
took command and "supervised the unprecedentedly speedy construction of a
flotilla which included the 300-ton ship *Inflexible*."

7. Bellico, 27–29; **Douglas, Charles**. Douglas met these many challenges and made several clever improvisations with aplomb and efficiency that reflected his great personal expertise. His leadership in these matters was recognized by the awarding of a baronetcy.

8. Douglas R. Cubbison, *The Artillery Never Gained More Honour: The British Artillery in the 1776 Valcour Island and Saratoga Campaigns* (Fleischmanns, NY: Purple Mountain Press, 2007), 44, 59.

9. Bradley, 150; Watt, *Rebellion*, 43.

10. Stevens, chapter 10, 642.

11. Stevens, chapter 10, 643–48.

12. De Lorimier, 60; Stevens, chapter 10, 651.

13. Stanley, *Invaded*, 134–36.

14. Lanctot, 150–52.

15. Stevens, chapter 10, 675–82.

16. "Memorial of Robert Leake," HP, AddMss21874, ff.38–39.

17. *Albany Minutes*, vol. 1, 481.

18. *Albany Minutes*, vol. 1, 519, passim; Watt, *Flockey*, 29–30, 46–47.

19. Stevens, chapter 10, 683.

20. Stevens, chapter 11, 695–98.

21. The *Quebec Gazette*, August 15, 1776. A letter from an officer dated Boston Harbour, March 25, 1776.

22. Stevens, chapter 12, 789.

23. For the individual assignments of these officers, see the chart regarding the Quebec Indian Department in Watt, *Burgoyne's Auxiliaries*.

24. Braisted research. Nairne to Captain Gardner, Point au Tremble, July 29, 1776. LAC, John and Thomas Nairne fonds, MG23, GIII23, V.3, Entrybook of Correspondence, 162–63. And Gardner to Nairne, Chambly August 9, 1776. *Ibid*, 163.

25. Stevens, chapter 12, 789–91; **Company of Select Marksmen (Fraser's British Rangers)** *www.csmid.com/marksmen.html*.

26. Stevens, chapter 12, 795–97.

27. Carleton to Germain, September 28, 1776, transcribed in Lanctot, 153–54.

28. Braisted research. Foy to Sir John Johnson, Chambly, September 26, 1776. HP, AddMss21699, f.45.

29. Burt, 218.

30. Bellico, 29–33.

31. Quotation taken from the biography of **Benedict Arnold**. *DCB*, vol. 5.

32. **Gates, Horatio**. The posturing between Gates and Schuyler for command of the Continental Northern Army is a complex story in its own right. For an excellent analysis, see Max M. Mintz, *The Generals of Saratoga – John Burgoyne and Horatio Gates* (New Haven, CT: Yale University Press, 1990).

33. Stanley, *Invaded*, 136.

34. Stevens, chapter 12, 789.

35. Stevens, chapter 12, 800.

36. Stevens, chapter 12, 802; de Lorimier, 60–61.

37. De Lorimier, 60–61; **De Bleury, Clement-Christophe de Sabrevois.** De Bleury was a nephew of the de Lorimier brothers. He was stationed at Akwesasne to administer to the Iroquois of that settlement.
38. Stevens, chapter 12, 803.
39. **Adams, Dr. Samuel.** Chris Armstrong research. AO12/53, 79–81. Samuel Adams's claim, Montreal, July 10, 1787: "Served under Major Carleton with the Savages, served on that Campaign…"; Armstrong research. *www.historiclakes.org/Valcour/valcour_battle.htm*: This source states, "With the British ships out gunning him to the south [55 guns versus 123] and receiving small arms fire from Indians and British troops under Captain Christopher Carleton on the New York Shore and another group under Captain Alexander Fraser from Valcour Island." As noted in the text, de Lorimier reported that de Lanaudière led the party on Valcour Island.
40. Bellico, 33–34; Stanley, *Invaded*, 141–42.
41. De Lorimier, 61.
42. Stanley, *Invaded*, 143; **Rebel losses.** As reported in the *Quebec Gazette*, October 31, 1776. Blown up — the schooner *Royal Savage*, the row galley *Congress*, and five gondolas. Sunk — gondola *Boston*. Taken — row galley *Washington*, gondola *Jersey*.
43. Stevens, chapter 12, 804–05.
44. Max Von Eelking, *Memoirs, Letters and Journals of Major General Riedesel During his Residence in America*, William L. Stone, trans. and ed. (2 vols., Albany: J. Munsell, 1868), vol. 1, 69–74. This source provides substantial detail about the movements and posts of the portion of the army left behind during the naval phase of Carleton's campaign.
45. Braisted research. Edward Foy to Sir John Johnson, Crown Point, October 23, 1776. PRO, HP, AddMss21699, f.57.
46. "Deposition of Joseph Egelston," November 1776. Braisted research. New York Public Library [hereafter NYPL], Philip Schuyler Papers, Box 40. The deposition spelled Hewetson as Huston and McDoull as McDowl. Hewetson's story is told in Gavin K. Watt, *The Flockey — 13 August 1777: The Defeat of the Tory Uprising in the Schoharie Valley* (King City, ON: self-published, 2002), 29–30, 46–47. Amos Moore and two other men named Moore, Jonathon Jones, Hezekiah Willis, and John McDoull served in Jessup's King's Loyal Americans in 1777. Watt, *Burgoyne's Auxiliaries*; Egelston served in the 16th ACM (Cambridge); *New York in the Revolution as Colony and State*, Roberts, James A., comptroller (Albany: New York, 1897; reprinted in 2 vols, 1904) vol. 1, 237.R
47. **Edmeston, William.** b.1731, England. Ensign, 59th Regiment/48th Regiment, Flanders, 1747. Lieutenant, 48th Regiment, 1755. Captain, 48th Regiment, 1758. Brevet Major, 1772, Brevet Lieutenant-Colonel, England, 1777. Major, 50th Regiment, England, 1782. Lieutenant-Colonel, 75th Regiment, England, 1782. Brevet Colonel, 1782. On half-pay, 1783. From half-pay to Lieutenant-Colonel, 50th Regiment, 1783. Major-General, 1793. Houlding, "King's Service"; Edmeston was residing at his home of Mount

Edmeston in German Flatts when the Tryon Committee took action against him. On May 28, 1777, they resolved that this "half pay officer of the King of G. Britain" be arrested and taken to Albany where General Schuyler could decide his disposition. See *Mohawk Valley in the Revolution, Committee of Safety Papers & Genealogical Compendium*, Maryly B. Penrose, ed. (Franklin Park, NJ: Liberty Bell Associates, 1978), 78. The general kept him in Albany until mid-October and then ordered him sent to Berkshire County, MA, with a number of other Tories. Although this decision was reversed, Edmeston remained under such close surveillance that he was unable to join McAlpin and instead returned to England in 1777. Albany Minutes, vol. 1, 580–81.

48. **Swords, Thomas.** *Albany Minutes*, vol. 1, 715. See also Todd Braisted's article, *www.royalprovincial.com/genealogy/fems/fams3.shtml*. On April 9, 1777, the Albany Committee's minutes noted that Swords, who like McAlpin was a "principle ringleader in a dangerous conspiracy," had escaped, but he did not join Burgoyne and was likely reconfined and sent to Connecticut.

49. Phillips to Burgoyne, Crown Point, October 23, 1776, transcribed in Cubbison, *Artillery*, 64.

50. Mary Beacock Fryer, *Buckskin Pimpernel: The Exploits of Justus Sherwood, Loyalist Spy* (Toronto: Dundurn Press, 1981), 27.

51. "Memorial of Justus Sherwood," *Loyalist Narratives from Upper Canada*, James J. Talman, ed. (Toronto: Champlain Society, 1946), 398–400.

52. "Petition of Ensign John Wilson to Governor Carleton," n.d.[1778] National Archives Kew, War Office Papers 28/9, f.40.

53. Eula C. Lapp, *To Their Heirs Forever* (Belleville, ON: Mika Publishing, 1977), passim.

54. Loyalist services. **Watt, *Burgoyne's Auxiliaries*;** Sherwood, Justus. **Fryer, *Pimpernel*;** Details of Sherwood's extensive activities. Watt, *Dirty Trifling, Piece of Business: Volume 1: The Revolutionary War as Waged from Canada in 1781* and *I Am Heartily Ashamed: Volume 2: The Revolutionary War's Final Campaign as Waged from Canada in 1782* (Toronto: Dundurn Press, 2010).

55. [Carleton] to Phillips, Quebec, November 29, 1776. HP, AddMss21699, f.68.

56. Ebenezer Jessup to Sir John Johnson, Montreal, November 14, 1776. Sir John Johnson fonds. McCord Museum, McGill University.

57. See Watt, *Burgoyne's Auxiliaries.*

BIBLIOGRAPHY

PRIMARY SOURCES — ARCHIVAL
Library and Archives Canada
Fraser, Malcolm. "Orderly Book of Captain Malcolm Fraser, 1RHE, 1775–76."
   Malcolm Fraser and family fonds, MG23-K, R3704-0-3-E, V.20. Braisted research.
Nairne, John and Thomas fonds, MG23, GIII23. Braisted research.
McCord Museum, McGill University
Jessup, Ebenezer. Ebenezer Jessup to Sir John Johnson, Montreal, November 14,
   1776. Sir John Johnson fonds.
National Archives Kew, Britain
Anderson, Joseph. Joseph Anderson's memorials and related papers. Audit Office
   13/11, ff.30–42. Braisted research.
Willson, John. "Petition of Ensign John Wilson to Governor Carleton," n.d.(1778.)
   Subtitled, "the remains of Twenty Eight Loyal Subjects who joined the King's
   Troops under your Excellency's Command at Crown Point the 27th Octr.
   1776." War Office Papers 28/9, f.40.

PRIMARY SOURCES — PUBLISHED
Newspapers and Periodicals
Peters, John. "Narrative of John Peters, Lieutenant-Colonel of the Queen's Loyal
   Rangers in Canada, drawn by himself in a letter to a friend in London, Pimlico June
   5, 1786." AO, H.H. Robertson Papers, the *Daily Globe*, Toronto, July 16, 1877.
The *Quebec Gazette* for the years 1775 and 1776.

PUBLISHED DOCUMENTS, JOURNALS, MAPS, AND CONTEMPORARY WORKS
Ainslie, Thomas. *Canada Preserved — The Journal of Captain Thomas Ainslie.*
   Sheldon S. Cohen, ed. Toronto: The Copp Clark Publishing Company, 1968.

Allen, Ethan. "Ethan Allen's Description of His Capture by Peter Johnson." Appendix G in Lois M. Huey and Bonnie Pulis, *Molly Brant, A Legacy of Her Own.* Youngstown, NY: Old Fort Niagara Association, Inc., 1997.

Canadian Army General Staff, Historical Section of, ed. "The War of the American Revolution, The Province of Quebec under the Administration of Governor Sir Guy Carleton, 1775–1778." In *A History of the Organization, Development and Services of the Military and Naval Forces of Canada From the Peace of Paris in 1763 to the Present Time with Illustrative Documents.* 2 volumes, Canada.

Claus, Daniel. "Col. Claus's Remarks on the Management of Northern Indian Nations." March 1, 1777, transcribed in *Documents Relative to the Colonial History of the State of New York....,* vol. 8, E.B. O'Callaghan, ed. Albany: NY, 1857.

Daly, Patrick. "Journal of the Siege & Blockade of Quebec by the American Rebels in Autumn 1775 & Winter 1776." *Manuscripts Relating to the Early History of Canada, Fourth Series.* Quebec City: Literary and Historical Society of Quebec, 1875.

De Lorimier, Claude-Nicholas-Guillaume. *At War with the Americans.* Peter Aichinger, ed. and tr. Victoria, B.C: Press Porcepic, n.d.

Egelston, Joseph. "Deposition of Joseph Egelston, November 76." Braisted research. NYPL, Philip Schuyler Papers, Box 40.

Force, Peter, ed. *American Archives, Consisting of a Collection of Authentick Records....* 6 vols. 1837.

Hadden, Lieutenant James M. *A Journal Kept in Canada and Upon Burgoyne's Campaign in 1776 and 1777.* Horatio Rogers, ed. Albany: Joel Munsell's Sons, 1884.

Jessup, Ebenezer. "The Memorial of Ebenezer Jessup." National Archives Kew, Audit Office, Class 13, vol. 55, folios 195–96.

Johnson, Guy. "Guy Johnson's Journal." In *Documents Relative to the Colonial History of the State of New York,* vol. 8, E.B. O'Callaghan, ed. Albany: NY, 1857.

_____. "Guy Johnson to Lord Dartmouth October 12, 1775." *The Canadian Antiquarian and Numismatic Journal* 4 (1875).

Livingston, Henry. "Journal of Major Henry Livingston of the Third New York Continental Line, August to December 1775," Galliard Hunt, ed. *www.iment. com/maida/familytree/henry/writing/prose/revdiary.htm#carleton.*

McAlpin, Daniel. "Memorial of Daniel McAlpin, Quebec November 13, 1778." HP, AddMss21874, 79-80.

Penrose, Maryly B., ed. *Mohawk Valley in the Revolution, Committee of Safety Papers & Genealogical Compendium.* Franklin Park, NJ: Liberty Bell Associates, 1978.

Platt, John. "Memorial of John Platt, Quebec June 17, 1781." HP, AddMss21874, ff.211–12. Braisted research.

Sherwood, Justus. "Memorial of Justus Sherwood." In *Loyalist Narratives from Upper Canada,* James J. Talman, ed. Toronto: Champlain Society, 1946.

Smith, Captain George, Inspector of the Royal Military Academy at Woolwich. *An Universal Military Dictionary, A Copious Explanation of the Technical Terms &c. — Used in the Equipment, Machinery, Movements, and Military Operations of an Army.* London: J. Millan, 1779. Reprint — limited edition, Ottawa: Museum Restoration Service, 1969.

Sullivan, James and Alexander C. Flick, eds., *Minutes of the Albany Committee of Correspondence, 1775–1778*. 2 vols. Albany: State University of New York, 1923 and 1925.

Walton, E.P., ed. *Records of the Council of Safety and Governor and Council of the State of Vermont, to which are prefixed the records of the General Conventions from July 1775 to December 1777*. 3 vols. Montpelier: Steam Press of J. & J.M. Poland, 1873.

Wilkinson, James. *Memoirs of My Own Times, 1757–1825*. 4 vols. Philadelphia, 1816.

SECONDARY SOURCES — BOOKS

Bellico, Russell P. *Sails and Steam in the Mountains: A Maritime and Military History of Lake George and Lake Champlain*. Fleischmanns, NY: Purple Mountain Press, 1992.

Bradley, Arthur Granville. *Lord Dorchester*. The Makers of Canada series. Toronto: Morang & Co., Limited, 1911.

Burt, Alfred Leroy. *The Old Province of Quebec*. 2 vols. Toronto: McClelland & Stewart Limited, 1968.

Campbell, Alexander V. *The Royal American Regiment – An Atlantic Microcosm, 1755–1772*. Norman, OK: University of Oklahoma Press, 2010.

Chartrand, René. *Canadian Military Heritage*. 2 vols. Montreal: Art Global Inc., 1995.

Commager, Henry Steele and Richard B. Morris, eds. *The Spirit of Seventy-Six: The Story of the American Revolution as Told by Participants*. Cambridge, MA: Da Capo Press, 1968.

Cruikshank, Ernest A., and Gavin K. Watt. *The History and Master Roll of the King's Royal Regiment of New York*. Milton, ON: Global Heritage Press, 2006.

Cubbison, Douglas R. *The Artillery Never Gained More Honour: The British Artillery in the 1776 Valcour Island and Saratoga Campaigns*. Fleischmanns, NY: Purple Mountain Press, 2007.

Davis, Robert P. *Where a Man Can Go: Major General William Phillips, British Royal Artillery, 1731–1781*. Westport, CT: Greenwood Press, 1999.

Flick, Alexander Clarence. *Loyalism in New York During the American Revolution*. New York: The Columbia University Press, 1901.

Fraser, J. [Muriel], *Skulking For the King: A Loyalist Plot*. Erin, ON: Boston Mills Press, 1985.

Fryer, Mary Beacock. *Allan Maclean, Jacobite General, The Life of an Eighteenth Century Career Soldier*. Toronto: Dundurn Press, 1987.

_____. *Buckskin Pimpernel: The Exploits of Justus Sherwood, Loyalist Spy*. Toronto: Dundurn Press, 1981.

Graymont, Barbara. *The Iroquois in the American Revolution*. Syracuse: Syracuse University Press, 1972.

Hanson, Willis T. *A History of Schenectady During the Revolution to which is appended a Contribution to the Individual Records of the Inhabitants of the Schenectady District During that Period*. Self-published, 1916.

Huey, Lois M. and Bonnie Pulis. *Molly Brant, A Legacy of Her Own*. Youngstown, NY: Old Fort Niagara Association, Inc., 1997.

Kelsay, Isabel Thompson. *Joseph Brant 1743–1807: Man of Two Worlds*. Syracuse: Syracuse University Press, 1984.

Lanctot, Gustave. *Canada and the American Revolution, 1774–1783*, Margaret M. Cameron, tr. Toronto: George G. Harrap & Co. Ltd, 1967.

Lapp, Eula C. *To Their Heirs Forever*. Belleville, ON: Mika Publishing, 1977.

MacLeod, D. Peter. *Northern Armageddon: The Battle of the Plains of Abraham; Eight Minutes of Gunfire that Shaped a Continent*. Vancouver: Douglas & McIntyre, 2008.

Malcomson, Robert. *Warships of the Great Lakes, 1754–1834*. London: Chatham Publishing, 2001.

Morrison, James F. *Colonel James Livingston: The Forgotten Livingston Patriot of the War of Independence*. Col. James Livingston Historic Research Committee, 1988.

The Naval Chronicle for 1805: Containing a General and Biographical History of the Royal Navy..., vol.14. London: I. Gold, 1806.

New York in the Revolution as Colony and State, James A. Roberts, comptroller. Albany: NY, 1897; reprinted in 2 vols., 1904.

Robinson, Percy J., *Toronto During the French Régime: A History of the Toronto Region from Brûlé to Simcoe, 1615–1793*. Toronto: University of Toronto Press, 1965.

Rossie, Jonathon Gregory. *The Politics of Command in the American Revolution*. Syracuse: Syracuse University Press, 1975.

Ruch, John. "Loyalists in the Inspectorate and the Commissary." In *The Loyalists of Quebec 1774–1825: A Forgotten History*. Montreal: Price-Patterson Ltd., 1989.

Senior, Elinor Kyte. "Montreal in the Loyalist Decade 1775–1785." In *The Loyalists of Quebec 1774–1825: A Forgotten History*. Montreal: Heritage Branch, United Empire Loyalists Association of Canada, 1989.

Stanley, George F.G. *Canada Invaded, 1775–1776*. Toronto: Samuel Stevens Hakkert & Company, 1977.

Stevens, Paul L. *A King's Colonel at Niagara, 1774–1776*. Youngstown: Old Fort Niagara Association, 1987.

Thompson, James. *A Bard of Wolfe's Army: James Thompson, Gentleman Volunteer, 1733–1830*. Earl John Chapman and Ian Macpherson McCulloch, eds. Montreal: Robin Brass Studio, 2010.

Von Eelking, Max. *Memoirs, Letters and Journals of Major General Riedesel During His Residence in America*. William L. Stone, trans. and ed. 2 vols. Albany: J. Munsell, 1868.

Watt, Gavin K., research assistance by James F. Morrison. *The Burning of the Valleys: Daring Raids from Canada Against the New York Frontier in the Fall of 1780*. Toronto: Dundurn, 1997.

_____, research assistance by James F. Morrison. *Rebellion in the Mohawk Valley: The St. Leger Expedition of 1777*. Toronto: Dundurn Press, 2002.

_____. *The Flockey —13 August 1777: The Defeat of the Tory Uprising in the Schoharie Valley*. King City, ON: self-published, 2002.

_____. Research assistance by James F. Morrison and William A. Smy. *A Dirty, Trifling Piece of Business — Volume 1: The Revolutionary War as Waged from Canada in 1781*. Toronto: Dundurn Press, 2009.

_____. Research assistance by James F. Morrison and William A. Smy. *I am Heartily Ashamed — Volume 2: The Revolutionary War's Final Campaign as Waged from Canada in 1782.* Toronto: Dundurn Press, 2010.

_____. Research assistance by Todd W. Braisted. *Burgoyne's Native and Loyalist Auxiliaries: The Burgoyne Expedition.* Vol. 2 of *The British Campaign of 1777.* Milton: Global Heritage Press, 2012.

Wright, Jr., Robert K. *The Continental Army.* Army Lineage Series, Center of Military History, United States Army. Washington, 1989.

Wrong, George M. *A Canadian Manor and Its Seigneurs: The Story of a Hundred Years, 1761–1861.* Toronto: The Bryant Press, Limited, 1908.

SECONDARY SOURCES — UNPUBLISHED MANUSCRIPTS

Houlding, John A. "The King's Service: The Officers of the British Army, 1735–1792."

Stacy, Kim. "No One Harms Me with Impunity: The History, Organization, and Biographies of the 84th Regiment of Foot (Royal Highland Emigrants) and Young Royal Highlanders, During the Revolutionary War 1775–1784." Manuscript in progress, 1994.

Stevens, Paul L. "His Majesty's 'Savage' Allies: British Policy and the Northern Indians During the Revolutionary War: The Carleton Years, 1774–1778." Ph.D. diss., 6 vols. Buffalo: Department of History, State University of New York at Buffalo, 1984.

SECONDARY SOURCES — WEBSITES

"2nd New Jersey Regiment"; "New Jersey's Second Battalion's first establishment. Field and Staff— Colonel William Maxwell and Adjutant Ephraim Anderson." *www.archive.org/stream/officialregister00newjuoft/officialregister00newjuoft_djvu.txt.*

Antill, Edward. *www.iment.com/maida/familytree/antill/coneledward.htm#coled.*

Battle of The Cedars. *http://en.wikipedia.org/wiki/Battle_of_The_Cedars.*

Company of Select Marksmen (Fraser's British Rangers). *www.csmid.com/marksmen.html.*

Cubbison, Douglas R. "Forgotten Quartermaster of the American Revolution — Udny Hay." *www.stonefortconsulting.com* (accessed September 17, 2011).

Swain, David. "The Timothy Bedel Papers and Andrew Park Pamphlet." The David Library of the American Revolution. *http://davidlibraryar.blogspot.ca/2010/11/timothy-bedel-papers-and-andrew-park.html.*

Stewart, Robert B. "The Invasion of Canada and Siege of Quebec." His Majesty's 7th Regiment (The Royal Fuzileers). *www.royalfuzileers.com/index.html.*

The Dictionary of Canadian Biography [DCB]. *www.biographi.ca.*

Valcour Island action. *www.historiclakes.org/Valcour/valcour_battle.htm.*

Index

1. All page entries in bold indicate that the subject appears in an image or on a map.
2. A native's affiliation is designated by a two- or three-letter abbreviation after his/her name, e.g. Abenaki (Ab); Kahnawake (Kah); Kanehsatake (Kan); Stockbridge (St).